Revenge
of the
Tipping Point

ALSO BY MALCOLM GLADWELL

The Bomber Mafia

Talking to Strangers

David and Goliath

What the Dog Saw

Outliers

Blink

The Tipping Point

Revenge of the Tipping Point

OVERSTORIES, SUPERSPREADERS, AND THE RISE OF SOCIAL ENGINEERING

Malcolm Gladwell

Little, Brown and Company

NEW YORK BOSTON LONDON

Little, Brown and Company
Hachette Book Group
1290 Avenue of the Americas, New York, NY 10104
littlebrown.com

First Edition: October 2024

Little, Brown and Company is a division of Hachette Book Group, Inc. The Little, Brown name and logo are trademarks of Hachette Book Group, Inc.

The publisher is not responsible for websites (or their content) that are not owned by the publisher.

The Hachette Speakers Bureau provides a wide range of authors for speaking events. To find out more, go to hachettespeakersbureau.com or email hachettespeakers@hbgusa.com.

Little, Brown and Company books may be purchased in bulk for business, educational, or promotional use. For information, please contact your local bookseller or the Hachette Book Group Special Markets Department at special.markets@hbgusa.com.

ISBN 9780316575805 (hardcover), 9780316584432 (signed edition), 9780316584449 (B&N signed edition), 9780316584456 (B&N Black Friday signed edition)

LCCN 2024911841

Printing 2, 2024

LSC-C

Printed in the United States of America

For Edie, Daisy, and Kate

Contents

CONTENTS

Author's Note

Twenty-five years ago, I published my first book. It was entitled *The Tipping Point: How Little Things Make a Big Difference.*

Back then I had a little apartment in the Chelsea neighborhood of Manhattan, and I would sit at my desk, with a glimpse of the Hudson River off in the distance, and write in the mornings before I headed to work. Because I had never written a book, I had no clear idea how to do it. I wrote with that mix of self-doubt and euphoria common to every first-time author.

"*The Tipping Point* is the biography of an idea," I began, "and the idea is very simple."

It is that the best way to understand the emergence of fashion trends, the ebb and flow of crime waves, or, for that matter, the transformation of unknown books into bestsellers, or the rise of teenage smoking, or the phenomena of word of mouth, or any number of the other mysterious changes that mark everyday life is to think of them as epidemics. Ideas and products and messages and behaviors spread just like viruses do.

The book was published in the spring of 2000, and the first stop on my book tour was a reading at a small independent bookstore in Los Angeles. Two people came, a stranger and the mother of a friend of mine — but not my friend. (I have forgiven her.) I said to myself, *Well, I guess that's it.* But it wasn't! *The Tipping Point* grew like the epidemics it described — at first gradually, then all in a rush. By the time the paperback came out, it had entered the zeitgeist. The book spent several years on the *New York Times* bestseller lists. Bill Clinton referred to it as "that book everyone has been talking about." The phrase *tipping point* became part of the vernacular. I used to joke that those words would be written on my tombstone.

Do I know why *The Tipping Point* touched such a chord? Not really. But if I had to guess, I would say that it was because it was a hopeful book that matched the mood of a hopeful time. The new millennium had arrived. Crime and social problems were in freefall. The Cold War was over. I offered in my book a recipe for how to promote positive change — as the subtitle suggested, to find a way for little things to make a big difference.

Twenty-five years is a long time. Think about how different you are today than you were a quarter-century ago. Our opinions change. Our tastes change. We care more about some things and less about others. Over the years, I would sometimes look back on what I had written in *The Tipping Point* and wonder how I ever came to write the things I did. An entire chapter on the children's television shows *Sesame Street* and *Blue's Clues*? Where did that come from? I didn't even have children back then.

I moved on to write *Blink, Outliers, David and Goliath, Talking to Strangers,* and *The Bomber Mafia.* I started the podcast *Revisionist History.* I settled down with the woman I love. I had two children and buried my father and took up running again and cut my hair. I sold the Chelsea apartment. I moved out of the city. A friend and I started an audio company called Pushkin Industries. I got a cat and named him Biggie Smalls.

You know the feeling of looking at a picture of yourself from long ago? When I do that, I have difficulty recognizing the person in the photograph. And so I thought it might be interesting to revisit *The Tipping Point,* on the occasion of its twenty-fifth birthday, to reexamine what I wrote so long ago through a very different set of eyes: In *The Tipping Point 2.0,* a writer would return to the scene of his first, youthful success.

But then, as I immersed myself once again in the world of social epidemics, I realized that I didn't want to return to the same ground I had covered in *The Tipping Point.* The world seemed too different to my eyes. In *The Tipping Point,* I introduced a series of principles to help us make sense of the kinds of sudden shifts in behavior and belief that make up our world. I still consider those ideas useful. But now I have different questions. And I find that I still do not understand many things about social epidemics.

When I reread *The Tipping Point,* in preparation for this project, I found myself stopping every few pages to ask, *What about this? How could I have left out that?* In some far corner of my mind, I discovered, I had never stopped arguing with myself about how best to explain and understand tipping points and their many mysteries.

And so I began again, with a fresh sheet of paper. And *Revenge of the Tipping Point* is the result: a new set of theories, stories, and arguments about the strange pathways that ideas and behavior follow through our world.

Revenge
of the
Tipping Point

The Passive Voice

"HAS ALSO BEEN ASSOCIATED . . ."

1.

Chairwoman: I'd like to ask you one final question, and I'd like to begin with you, Dr. _____. Will you apologize to the American people…?

A group of politicians has called a hearing to discuss an epidemic. Three witnesses have been subpoenaed. It's the height of the pandemic. The meeting is virtual. Everyone is at home, in front of bookcases and kitchen cabinets. We're an hour into the proceedings. I'm leaving out all the identifying details for the moment because I want to focus exclusively on what was *said:* the words that were used, and the intentions behind them.

Witness #1: I would be happy to apologize to the American people for all of the pain they have suffered and for the tragedies that they've experienced in their families and — and I thought I did that earlier in my opening comments. That was my intention.

Witness #1 is in her seventies. Short, white hair. Dressed in black. At the beginning, she seemed to struggle with how to work the Mute button. She still seems flustered. She isn't used to this. She comes from a world of privilege. Being confronted over her own behavior is clearly not something that has happened in her life with any frequency. Her fashionable glasses look like they might slide off the end of her nose.

Witness #1: I also am very angry. I'm angry that some people working at _____ broke the law. I'm angry about it from 2007, and I'm angry about it now again in 2020. It's — it's — I think that —

Chairwoman: I know you're angry. And I'm sorry, but that's not the apology we were looking for. You've apologized for the pain people have suffered, but you've never apologized for the role that you played in the _____ crisis.

So, I'll ask you again, will you apologize for the role you played in the _____ crisis?

Witness #1: I have struggled with that question. I have asked myself over many years. I have tried to figure out, was — is there anything that I could have done differently, knowing what I knew then, not what I know now. And I have to say, I can't — there's nothing that I can find that I would have done differently, based on what I believed and understood then and what I learned from management in the reports to the board and what I learned from my colleagues on the board. And it is extremely distressing. And it's —

The chairwoman turns to Witness #2. He's the cousin of the woman in black: a young man, well-manicured, in a suit and tie.

Chairwoman: Mr. _____, will you apologize for the role that you played...?
Witness #2: I echo much of what my cousin said.

Does anyone expect the witnesses to admit that they started an epidemic? Probably not. A squadron of lawyers has clearly coached them beforehand in the art of self-preservation. The righteousness with which they deny responsibility, however, suggests another possibility: that they have not yet accepted their own culpability, or that they started something that spiraled out of control in a way they could not understand.

An hour later comes the crucial moment. Another member of the investigating committee — let's call him the politician — turns to Witness #3:

Politician: Dr. _____, has any executive in the _____ company ever spent a day in jail for the actions of the corporation?
Witness #3: I believe not.

None of the witnesses hold themselves responsible. But apparently no one else does either.

Politician: Madam Chair, it's easy to feel outrage about the misdeeds of this corporation, but what about our government that gives license to this kind of corporate irresponsibility and criminality and impunity?

The politician turns to Witness #2, the young man. His family's company has just reached an agreement with the government to settle a series of criminal charges. He had once sat on the board of directors and is the heir apparent to the empire.

> **Politician #1:** Mr. _____, as part of the DOJ settlement, did you have to admit any wrongdoing or liability or responsibility for causing America's crisis of _____?
>
> **Witness #2:** No, we did not.
>
> **Politician #1:** Were you interviewed by the Department of Justice, as part of this investigation, about your role in these events?
>
> **Witness #2:** No.
>
> **Politician #1:** Do you take any responsibility for causing America's nightmarish experience with the _____ crisis?
>
> **Witness #2:** Well, though I believe the full record, which has not been publicly released yet, will show that the family and the board acted legally and ethically, I take a deep moral responsibility for it, because I believe our product, _____, despite our best intentions and best efforts, has been associated with abuse and addiction, and —

Has been associated.

> **Politician #2:** You're using the passive voice there when you say it's "been associated with abuse," which implies somehow you and your family were not aware of exactly what was taking place...

If you listen to all 3 hours and 39 minutes of the hearing, that single phrase stays in your head: "the passive voice."

2.

Twenty-five years ago, in *The Tipping Point*, I was fascinated by the idea that in social epidemics little things could make a big difference. I came up with rules to describe the internal workings of social contagions: the Law of the Few, the Power of Context, the Stickiness Factor. The laws of epidemics, I argued, could be used to promote positive change: lower crime rates, teach kids how to read, curb cigarette smoking.

"Look at the world around you," I wrote. "It may seem like an immovable, implacable place. It is not. With the slightest push — in just the right place — it can be tipped."

In *Revenge of the Tipping Point*, I want to look at the underside of the possibilities I explored so long ago. If the world can be moved by just the slightest push, then the person who knows where and when to push has real power. So who are those people? What are their intentions? What techniques are they using? In the world of law enforcement, the word *forensic* refers to an investigation of the origins and scope of a criminal act: "reasons, culprits, and consequences." *Revenge of the Tipping Point* is an attempt to do a forensic investigation of social epidemics.

In the pages that follow, I'm going to take you to a mysterious office building in Miami with a very strange group of tenants, to a Marriott Hotel in Boston for an executive retreat that went badly awry, to a seemingly perfect town called Poplar Grove, to a cul-de-sac in Palo Alto, and on from there to places you've heard of and places you haven't. We're going to investigate what's weird about Waldorf schools, meet a long-overlooked drug warrior named Paul E. Madden, learn about a 1970s television miniseries that changed the world, and raise an eyebrow at Harvard University's women's rugby team. All of these are cases where people — either deliberately or inadvertently, virtuously or maliciously — made choices that altered the course and shape of a contagious phenomenon. And in every case those interventions raised questions we have to answer and problems we have to solve. That's the *revenge* of the Tipping Point: The very same tools we use to build a better world can also be used against us.

And at the end of the book I want to use the lessons gleaned from all of these examples to tell the *real* story of Witness #1, Witness #2, and Witness #3.

> **Politician #1:** We have a letter from a mother in North
> Carolina...who lost her child, twenty years old, and
> hasn't recovered yet. She said, "The pain is too intense.
> It's more than I can bear. I have trouble finding the will to
> live and carrying on every single day...."
>
> Mr. ____, I wanted to lay out these stories we've been
> receiving, and I'd like your personal response to these
> stories.

Witness #2 starts to talk. But there's no sound.

> **Politician #1:** I can't hear. He's muted.

The witness fumbles with his computer.

> **Witness #2:** I'm sorry...

His first true apology of the day, for not unmuting his microphone. He goes on:

I feel tremendous empathy, sorrow, and remorse that a product like _____ that was produced to help people and, I believe, has helped millions of people has also been associated with stories like you're telling. I feel incredibly sorry for that. And I know our entire family does as well.

Has also been associated.

It's time for a hard conversation about epidemics. We need to acknowledge our own role in creating them. We need to be honest about all the subtle and sometimes hidden ways we try to manipulate them. We need a guide to the fevers and contagions that surround us.

Part One

Three Puzzles

CHAPTER ONE

Casper and C-Dog

"IT WAS JUST LIKE WILDFIRE. EVERYONE
WAS JUMPING INTO THE GAME."

1.

In the early afternoon of November 29, 1983, the Los Angeles field office of the Federal Bureau of Investigation received a call from a Bank of America branch in the Melrose District. The call was taken by an FBI agent named Linda Webster. She was the person in the office who fielded what were known as *2-11s:* reports of bank robberies. There had just been a holdup, she was told. The suspect was a young white male wearing a New York Yankees baseball cap. Slender. Polite. Southern accent. Well dressed. He said *please* and *thank you.*

Webster turned to her colleague, William Rehder, who ran the FBI's local bank-robbery division.

"Bill, it's the Yankee."

The Yankee Bandit had been active in Los Angeles since July of that year. He had hit one bank after another, slipping away each time with thousands of dollars in a leather suitcase. Rehder was growing frustrated. Who was this man? All the Bureau had to go on was that telltale baseball cap. Hence the nickname: the Yankee Bandit.

13

Half an hour passed. Webster got another 2-11. This one was from a City National Bank sixteen blocks west, in the Fairfax District. They had been taken for $2,349. The caller gave Webster the details. She looked at Rehder.

"Bill, it's the Yankee again."

Forty-five minutes after that, the Yankee hit a Security Pacific National Bank in Century City, then immediately walked one block down the street and held up a First Interstate Bank for $2,505.

"Bill, it's the Yankee. Twice. Back to back."

Less than an hour passed. The phone rang again. The Yankee had just hit an Imperial Bank on Wilshire Boulevard. If you drive from Century City to the Imperial Bank on Wilshire, you pass right by the FBI's office.

"He probably waved at us," Rehder told Webster.

They were now on notice. History was being made. They waited. Could the Yankee possibly strike yet again? At 5:30, the phone rang. An unknown white male — slender, Southern accent, Yankee cap — had just robbed the First Interstate Bank in Encino, fifteen minutes north on the 405 freeway, for $2,413.

"Bill, it's the Yankee."

One man. Four hours. Six banks.

"It was a new world's record," Rehder would write later in his memoirs, "still unbroken."

2.

No criminal has ever held as exalted a position in American culture as the bank robber. In the years after the Civil War, the country was riveted by the exploits of bands such as the

James-Younger gang, who terrorized the Wild West with bank holdups and train robberies. In the Depression, bank robbers became celebrities: Bonnie and Clyde, John Dillinger, "Pretty Boy" Floyd. But in the years after the Second World War, the crime seemed to be fading.

In 1965, a total of 847 banks were robbed across the entire United States — a modest number, given the size of the country. There was speculation that bank robberies were headed toward extinction. Few major crimes had higher arrest-and-conviction rates. Banks felt that they had learned how to protect themselves. A definitive 1968 study of bank robbery was entitled "Nothing to Lose," meaning the act seemed so irrational that its perpetrators must have run out of other options. It seemed like the twentieth-century equivalent of cattle rustling. Who does that anymore?

But then came an epidemic. In a single year, from 1969 to 1970, the number of bank robberies nearly doubled, then rose again in 1971 and once more in 1972. In 1974, 3,517 banks were robbed. In 1976 the number was 4,565. By the beginning of the 1980s, there were five times more bank robberies than there had been at the end of the 1960s. It was a crime wave without precedent. And it was just getting started. In 1991, the FBI fielded a 2-11 call from a bank somewhere in the United States 9,388 times.

And the center of this astonishing surge was the city of Los Angeles.

A *quarter* of all bank robberies in the United States in those years happened in Los Angeles. There were years when the local FBI office handled as many as 2,600 bank robberies — so many robbers, robbing so many banks, that Rehder and the Bureau were forced to give them nicknames to keep them straight: The man who disguised himself with surgical gauze became the Mummy Bandit. The man who wore a single glove became (naturally) the Michael Jackson Bandit. A two-man team who wore fake mustaches were the Marx Brothers. A short, obese robber was Miss Piggy. A beautiful robber was the Miss America Bandit. A guy who waved a knife was the Benihana Bandit. On and on it went: There were robbers named after Johnny Cash and Robert DeNiro. One group robbed in threes — one dressed as a biker, another as a cop, and the third as a construction worker. Do you need to ask what they were called? This was the 1980s. They were known as the Village People.

"It was just like wildfire," remembers Peter Houlahan, one of the unofficial historians of the L.A. bank-robbery surge. "Everybody was jumping into the game."

Ten years into the surge, incredibly, things got much worse. The trigger was the emergence of a two-man group called the West Hills Bandits. The first generation of L.A. robbers were like the Yankee Bandit: They walked up to a teller, said they had a gun, scooped up whatever cash was on hand, and fled. People called them, a bit dismissively, *notepassers*. But the West Hills gang went back to the grand tradition of Jesse James and Bonnie and Clyde. They came in *hot,* in wigs and masks, waving assault weapons. They would force their way into the teller's cage and clean out the entire bank — empty the vault if they could — before executing a meticulously planned escape. The bandits had a bunker in the San Fernando Valley filled with military-grade weapons and 27,000 rounds of ammunition, to prepare for what their leader believed was an imminent Armageddon. Even by the standards of 1990s Los Angeles, the West Hills gang was a little crazy.

On their fifth robbery, the West Hills crew broke into the vault of a Wells Fargo Bank in Tarzana and made off with $437,000 — more than $1 million in today's dollars. And then Wells Fargo made a crucial mistake: The bank told the press exactly how much the West Hills gang had stolen. It was like putting a match to kindling. *$437,000? Are you kidding me?*

One of the first to take notice was an enterprising twenty-three-year-old named Robert Sheldon Brown. His street name was Casper. Casper did the math. "I've robbed, I've done burglaries, I've done a little bit of everything," he would explain later. "But the money couldn't compare to the banks. You could go into a bank and in two minutes get what on the streets would take you six or seven weeks to get."

John Wiley, one of the prosecutors who eventually brought Casper to justice, remembers him as a "standout." "Casper was really ripped and he was really smart." Wiley said:

> He figured out the problem with robbing banks is going into the bank. So he got somebody else to do that. You would think, *How could you possibly get someone to rob a bank for you?* And that was his particular talent…recruiting people to rob banks for him. And he recruited an unbelievable number of folks….He was kind of a producer, in Hollywood terms.

Casper had a partner in crime, Donzell Thompson, also known as C-Dog. They would pick a bank they thought was ripe for a hit. Then they'd find a getaway car — known, in gang-speak, as *the G-ride*. In the early 1990s, Los Angeles experienced an astonishing surge in carjackings — which were treated in the press as another separate indication of the random mayhem sweeping the streets. But a good chunk of it was actually Casper and C-Dog. They had a guy they paid to acquire their G-rides. If you were doing as many bank robberies as Casper was, you needed a lot of cars. Then he would pick the crew. Prosecutor Wiley again:

A lot of his robbers were just kids. I think he probably paid some of them nothing. He just coerced them into robbing. He's a big, threatening guy. And, you know, he was a member of the Rolling Sixties, which was a very notorious Crips gang.

Wiley recalled a particular recruit who was "very young" — as young as thirteen or fourteen:

I remember he took the kid out of school and said, "When can you rob this bank for me?" And the guy said, "During a nutrition break." So during nutrition break, they picked him up, and Brown and [C-Dog] explained how to do it. You go in, scare everybody to death, get the money, get out.

Casper taught his recruits a technique he called "goin' kamikaze." His kids would come busting in, waving their machine pistols and assault rifles, firing rounds at the ceiling and screaming obscenities: "On the floor, mother—er!" They would stuff all the cash they could find into pillowcases, grab wallets, and rip rings off women's fingers if they wanted a little extra treasure for the road.

On at least two jobs, Casper "borrowed" a school bus to ferry his young charges to safety; another time, he borrowed a postal service truck. Casper had *imagination*. He would exercise managerial oversight of his operations from a position of safety, parked in a car somewhere far down the block, then follow his handpicked team as they raced through the streets.

"These guys knew if they tried to get away with all the money, then they would have these two Crips after them," Wiley said, "and that would not improve their life."

The G-ride would be abandoned. The whole crew would retreat to Casper's hideout, usually in a motel, where he would pay them a pittance and let them go. They were kids — chances are they would get caught. But Casper didn't care. His attitude, Wiley said, was:

> I mean, okay, so that wasn't great. My guys got caught. Now we have to get new guys. But we do that all the time.

In just four years, Casper "produced" *175 robberies,* which remains the lifetime bank-robbery world record, crushing the Yankee Bandit's previous mark of 72. Casper and C-Dog even came close to the Yankee Bandit's one-day mark of six heists. On a single day in August of 1991, they produced five: a First Interstate Bank on La Cienega Boulevard, then banks in Eagle Rock, Pasadena, Monterey Park, and Montebello. And remember, the Yankee Bandit was a one-man show. Casper was doing something infinitely more difficult: organizing and supervising teams of robbers.

Once Casper showed the world how easy it was to take over a bank, other gangs jumped in. The Eight Trey Gangster Crips started putting together crews. A duo called the Nasty Boys did almost thirty takeovers in under a year — just the two of them. The Nasty Boys were...*nasty*: They liked to herd everyone into the bank vault, talk loudly about executions, and fire their guns next to people's ears just for the fun of it.

"In retrospect, 1992 turned out to be the peak year for bank robberies. 2,641 robberies in one year," Wiley said.

So that averages one bank robbery every forty-five minutes for each banking day. And the worst day was twenty-eight bank robberies in one day. This drove the FBI completely crazy. I mean, they were completely exhausted.

Robbing a bank takes minutes. Investigating a bank robbery takes hours. As the robberies piled up, the FBI would fall further and further behind.

If you're having twenty-seven robberies a day, if one team is committing five robberies in one day, I mean, just think physically how you investigate that. These guys are driving all over town as fast as they can, robbing. So just keeping up with them in L.A. traffic is a problem. You get to the bank and how many people have witnessed the robbery? Well, how many people were in the bank? You know, twenty people. So you need to get witness statements from twenty witnesses. This is a big project.

Then, just as you start, what happens?

You're on the scene for five or ten minutes and there's another bank-robbery emergency somewhere across town. The FBI was being run ragged.

The city of Los Angeles was the bank-robbery capital of the world. "There was no reason to think it would crest," Wiley went on. He held up a chart of bank robberies in Los Angeles from the 1970s through the 1990s. "If you look at the trend line it just seems like it's heading for the moon."

The FBI put fifty agents on the case. Over the course of many months, they gathered what they could from Casper and C-Dog's terrified recruits, sorted through the layers of deception the two used to hide their assets, and tracked them from one address to another across South Los Angeles. It took forever to get a grand jury to indict Caspar and C-Dog, because what had they done? Nothing. They didn't rob any banks. They were just sitting in a car down the street. All the FBI had was the testimony of terrified teenagers who skipped school between lunch and recess.

Finally, prosecutors thought they had enough evidence. They found C-Dog at his grandmother's house in Carson and arrested Casper as he stepped out of a cab. With the two of them behind bars, the bank-robbery fever that had seized Los Angeles finally broke: Within roughly a year the number of robberies in the city dropped 30 percent, then drifted even lower. Bank robberies didn't head for the moon. The fever passed.

When Casper and C-Dog got out of federal prison in the summer of 2023, they shopped their story around Hollywood and took meetings with film producers. Movie executives who heard their story were incredulous: That happened *here*?

Yes, it did.

3.

I want to begin *Revenge of the Tipping Point* with a series of puzzles — three interconnected stories that seem, at first glance, to defy explanation. The third involves a little town called Poplar Grove. The second involves the story of a man named Philip Esformes. And this first chapter involves the exploits of the Yankee Bandit and Casper and C-Dog.

The Los Angeles bank-robbery crisis of the early 1990s was an epidemic. It fit all the rules. This was not an outbreak generated inside each robber, like a toothache. It was contagious. A low-grade fever surfaced across the United States at the end of the 1960s. In the 1980s, the Yankee Bandit caught that bug in Los Angeles. The West Hills Bandits later picked up the virus, and in their hands it mutated into something darker and more violent. They passed the new strain on to Casper and C-Dog, who reinvented the process, outsourcing the labor and scaling up dramatically, like the late-twentieth-century capitalists they were. And from there the infection went clear across the city — to the Eight Trey Gangsters and the Nasty Boys and on and on, sweeping up hundreds of young men, until by the time the bank-takeover boom peaked in Los Angeles, the small-time note-passing of the Yankee Bandit era seemed like a dim memory.

Social epidemics are propelled by the efforts of an exceptional few — people who play outsize social roles — and that was exactly how the L.A. outbreak unfolded. This was never a mass-participation event, like one of those big-city marathons where tens of thousands of people sign up. It was a reign of mayhem driven by a small number of people who robbed over and over and over again. The Yankee Bandit robbed sixty-four banks in nine months before the FBI finally grabbed him. He went to prison for ten years, got out, *then robbed eight more banks.* The Nasty Boys did twenty-seven banks. Casper and C-Dog masterminded 175. If you focused only on the Yankee Bandit, Casper, and the Nasty Boys, you would have a pretty complete picture of what happened in Los Angeles in the 1980s and early 1990s: a contagious phenomenon that rose and tipped, fueled by the extraordinary actions of a few. "Casper," Wiley said, "is the superspreader, if you want to talk about epidemics."

Was the context in the 1980s and early 1990s ripe for a bank-robbery explosion? Yes, it was. Between the 1970s and the end of the 1990s, the number of bank branches in the United States tripled. Casper and C-Dog were shooting fish in a barrel.

The fever that swept Los Angeles in the late 1980s and early 1990s makes perfect sense — except for one thing.

There's a puzzle.

4.

In the early morning of March 9, 1950, Willie Sutton rose and applied a heavy coat of makeup to his face. The previous evening he had dyed his hair several shades lighter, so that he was almost blond, and now he wanted to pair that with an olive complexion. He applied mascara to his eyebrows to give them some substance. He stuffed bits of cork inside his nostrils to broaden his nose. Then he put on a gray suit, tailored and padded in such a way as to alter his silhouette. Satisfied that he no longer looked like Willie Sutton, Willie Sutton left his house in Staten Island for Sunnyside, Queens, heading to a Manufacturers Trust Company branch at 44th Street and Queens Boulevard in New York City.

Sutton had spent the previous three weeks standing across the street every morning, learning the routines of the bank's employees. He liked what he saw. There was an elevated subway stop across the street, a bus stop, and a taxi stand. The street was busy, and Sutton liked crowds. The bank's guard, a slow-moving man named Weston who lived nearby, arrived every morning at 8:30, engrossed in his newspaper. Between 8:30 and 9:00, he would let in the bank's other employees, culminating with the bank's manager, Mr. Hoffman, who arrived, like clockwork, at 9:01. The Manufacturers Trust opened to the public at 10:00 — much later than most bank branches. This too made Sutton happy: He regarded the time between the arrival of the first employee and the arrival of the first customer as "his time," and "his time" in this case would be an hour and a half.

At 8:20, Sutton mingled with the crowd waiting at the bus stop. A few minutes later, the custodian Weston turned the corner, lost in his newspaper. As Weston took out his keys to open the door, Sutton slipped in behind him. Weston turned in shock. Sutton looked him in the eye and said, quietly, "Come inside. I want to talk to you."

Sutton wasn't a fan of guns. Guns for him were props. His real weapon was a quiet authority that compelled the attention of others. He explained to the guard what would happen next. First they would let in one of his accomplices. Then the remaining employees would be admitted exactly as they were each morning. As each one entered, Sutton's accomplice would emerge and lead them by the elbow to a row of chairs he set up in preparation.

"Once you've taken control of the bank," Sutton would

write years later in his memoirs — Sutton was sufficiently famous by that point that he wrote not one but two sets of memoirs, like a statesman who feels the need to respond to the turns of history —

It doesn't really matter who comes to the door. A trio of painters once arrived unexpectedly while I was taking a bank in Pennsylvania, and I simply told them to spread out their drop cloths and go to work. "The pay you guys get, the bank can't afford to have you hanging around doing nothing. They're insured against bank robbers but nobody would insure them against you robbers." All during the robbery I was able to keep up a line of chatter about how I could have retired by now if we bank robbers had as strong a union as they did. Everybody had a good time, and by the time we walked out the door with the money they had one of the walls completely painted.

Sutton was terrifyingly charming. Did the employees of the Manufacturers Trust Company realize that the famous Willie Sutton was robbing them that morning? Undoubtedly. They filed into the conference room, one by one. "Don't worry, folks," he told them. "It's only money. And it isn't your money." At 9:05, four minutes late, Mr. Hoffman, the manager, arrived. Sutton sat him down.

"If you give me any trouble, I want you to know that some of these here employees of yours will be shot. I don't want you to have any false illusions about that. Now perhaps you don't care about your own safety, but the health of these here employees of yours are your responsibility. If anything happens to them, the blame will be yours, not mine."

It was a bluff, of course, but it worked every time. He scooped up the money from the vault, ambled out the door to a waiting getaway car, and vanished into the New York City traffic.

Willie Sutton was the New York version of Casper—although that doesn't quite do Willie Sutton justice. Nobody knew much about Casper at the time he was orchestrating his bank-robbery spree. Even his trial barely made a dent in the news. Not so Willie Sutton. Sutton was famous. He dated starlets. He was a master of disguise. He made not one but two daring escapes from prison. He was once asked: "Why do you rob banks?" And he replied: "Because that's where the money is." Later he would deny having said that, but it didn't matter. To this day his quip is known as "Sutton's Law," and it is used to instruct medical students on the importance of considering the likeliest diagnosis first. Hollywood made a movie about his life. A writer turned his story into a biographical novel. In today's dollars he claimed to have stolen more than $20 million over the course of his career. Casper wasn't even in the same tax bracket as Willie Sutton (assuming, of course, that they paid taxes, which neither of them did).

The point is that if anyone were to start a bank-robbery epidemic, you'd think it would be Willie Sutton. You would think that the impressionable criminal classes of New York City would look at "Slick Willie" effortlessly slipping into bank branches without firing a shot and making off with a king's ransom, and say to themselves, *I can do that.* In epidemiology there is a term called the "index case," which refers to the person who kicks off an epidemic. (We're going to talk about one of the most fascinating index cases in recent history later in this book.) Willie Sutton should have been the index case, right? He turned the grubby job of holding up a bank into a work of art.

But Willie Sutton did not start a bank-robbery epidemic in New York City — not in the 1940s and '50s, in his heyday, nor in the years afterward, as he wrote one memoir after another. After talking his way out of prison in 1969, claiming ill health (he would live another eleven years), Sutton re-created himself as an expert on prison reform, giving lectures across the country. He consulted with banks on how to prevent bank robberies. He even did a TV commercial for a credit-card company, pioneering a card with a photo on it: "They call it the *face card*. Now when I say *I'm Willie Sutton*, people believe me." Did that make the world want to be Willie Sutton? Apparently not. In the days of Casper, New York City suffered only a fraction of the bank robberies that Los Angeles did.

An epidemic, by definition, is a contagious phenomenon that does not respect borders. When COVID first emerged in China in late 2019, epidemiologists worried that it would spread everywhere. And they were absolutely right. Yet in the bank case, the fever engulfed Los Angeles but skipped other cities altogether. Why?

This is the first of the three puzzles. And the answer involves a famous observation made by a physician named John Wennberg.

5.

In 1967, fresh out of his medical training, Wennberg got a job in Vermont as part of an operation called the Regional

Medical Program (RMP). These were the years of the Great Society, when the US government was making a concerted effort to expand the American social safety net, and the RMP was a federally funded effort to improve medical care around the country. Wennberg's job was to map the quality of care across the state, to make sure everyone was getting access to the same standard of medicine.

He was young and idealistic. He had studied under some of the best minds in medicine at Johns Hopkins University. Wennberg arrived in Vermont, he said later, still believing "in the general paradigm that science was advancing and that it was being translated rationally into effective care."

Vermont had 251 towns. Wennberg began by dividing up those communities according to where the local residents got their medical care. That left him with thirteen "hospital districts" across the state. He then calculated the amount of money that was spent on medical care in each of those districts.

Wennberg assumed that what he would see was that in some faraway corner of Vermont where there wasn't much money, spending would be low. And by the same logic, in wealthier communities such as Burlington — the biggest city in the state, home to the University of Vermont and Champlain College, where the hospitals were the newest and most sophisticated, and the doctors more likely to have trained at prestigious medical schools — spending would be a bit higher.

He was completely wrong. Yes, there were differences in spending from one hospital district to the next. But the differences weren't small. They were enormous. And they didn't follow any apparent logic. They were, as Wennberg put it, without "rhyme or reason." Surgery for removing hemorrhoids, for example, was five times more common in some districts than in others. Your chances of getting an enlarged prostate surgically removed, or your uterus removed in a hysterectomy, or your appendix removed after an attack of appendicitis were three times higher in some districts than in others.

"Variation, as it turned out, was everywhere," Wennberg said. "For instance, we lived between Stowe and Waterbury. My kids went to the Waterbury school system ten miles down the road. But if we had lived about a hundred yards north, they would have gone to the Stowe school system. In Stowe 70 percent of the kids had their tonsils out by the time they were fifteen years old, as opposed to only 20 percent in Waterbury."

It made no sense. Stowe and Waterbury were both idyllic small towns full of weathered nineteenth-century buildings. Nobody seriously thought that one was more worldly or was in the grip of a different medical ideology than the other. It wasn't that Stowe attracted one kind of person and Waterbury attracted another, very different kind of person. The people were basically the same — except, that is, that the children of Waterbury tended to keep their tonsils and the children of Stowe did not.

Wennberg was now deeply confused. Had he stumbled upon some strange quirk of the small towns of Vermont? He decided to expand his analysis to other parts of New England. Here is a comparison he did of Middlebury, Vermont, versus Randolph, New Hampshire. Take a look at the first ten rows: These two cities are twins. Now look at the last three rows of data. Oh, my. In Randolph, the doctors conducted themselves in a kind of over-caffeinated frenzy: spending freely, hospitalizing and operating on everyone in sight. But Middlebury? Middlebury was a different world.

	Middlebury, Vermont	Randolph, New Hampshire
Socioeconomic characteristics		
White	98%	97%
Born in Vermont or New Hampshire	59	61
Lived in area 20 or more years	47	47
Income level below poverty	20	23
Have health insurance	84	84
Regular place of physician care	97	99
Chronic illness level		
Prevalence	23%	23%
Restricted activity last 2 weeks	5	4
More than 2 weeks in bed last year	4	5
Access to physician		
Contact with physician within year	73%	73%
Post-access utilization of health care		
Hospital discharges per 1,000	132	220
Surgery discharges per 1,000	49	80
Medicare Part B spending per Enrollee	92	142

Wennberg called what he had discovered "small-area variation," and he found evidence of it across the entire United States. And what started as an idiosyncratic observation about the small towns of Vermont has turned into an iron law that — half a century after Wennberg made his startling discovery — shows no signs of going away: How your doctor treats you, in many cases, has less to do with where your doctor was trained, or how well he or she did in medical school, or what kind of personality your doctor has, than with *where your doctor lives.*

Why does place matter so much? The easiest explanation for small-area variation is that doctors are simply doing what patients want. So, for example, let's pick a relatively simple medical event: How many times a doctor visits a patient in the last two years of their life. The national average in 2019 is around fifty-four visits. In Minneapolis, by contrast, the average is much lower: thirty-six. But do you know what it is in Los Angeles? It's 105! *You get three times more doctor visits in your dying days in L.A. than you do in Minneapolis.*

That's a huge difference. Is it because dying Minnesotans behave like stoic Scandinavians, whereas the very old of Los Angeles are needy and demanding? The answer seems to be no. Wennberg and other researchers have found that small-area variation does not result from what patients want their doctors to do. It stems from what *doctors want to do to their patients.*

So, why do doctors behave so differently from place to place? Is this just about money? Maybe more people in Los Angeles have the kind of insurance that rewards doctors for treating their patients aggressively. No, that doesn't seem to explain it either.*

What if this is just random? After all, doctors are people.

---

* The technical term for this is *payer mix.* A city with 100 percent of its citizens covered by fee-for-service insurance, where a doctor gets paid for everything they do, is going to have a very different pattern of care than a city where 100 percent of its citizens are enrolled in "managed care," where payments to hospitals and doctors are fixed. But Los Angeles does not have a radically different payer mix than any other big city.

And people are all over the map in what they believe. Maybe Los Angeles is a place where, by chance, many aggressive doctors happen to practice, while Minneapolis is a place where, by chance, there are very few.

No!

Random would mean that aggressive doctors would be scattered across the country, in patterns that ebb and flow with each passing year. *Random* would mean that every hospital would have a different combination of physicians, representing a sampling of ideas about how to practice medicine. There would be a Dr. Smith, who always took out tonsils; and a Dr. Jones, who never did; and then a Dr. McDonald, who was somewhere in between. But that's not what Wennberg identified years ago. What he found instead were medical *clusters*, where the doctors in one hospital district took on a common identity, as if they had all been infected by the same contagious idea.

"It's a birds-of-a-feather-flock-together puzzle," said Jonathan Skinner, an economist at Dartmouth University who is one of the heirs to Wennberg's work. "Like, okay, doctors have different opinions.…People develop opinions about what works.…But the question is, what is it about an area that causes some people to practice in one way, on average?

"Is it something that's in the water?"

6.

Small-area variation has subsequently become something of an obsession for medical researchers. Books are written about it. Scholars spend their days studying it. But what's fascinating is how the same inexplicable patterns of variation turn up *outside* the world of medical care. Let me give you an example.

The state of California keeps a public database of what percentage of seventh graders at any middle school in the state are up to date with their recommended vaccines: chicken pox, measles, mumps, rubella, polio, and so on. If you give the list — and it's a long list — a cursory glance, it seems pretty straightforward. The overwhelming number of public-school kids in California have received all their shots. What about private-school kids? Private schools tend to be smaller and quirkier. Could there be more variation there? Let's take a look.*

Here are the vaccination rates, chosen at random, from a selection of private elementary schools in Contra Costa County, east of San Francisco.

St. John the Baptist — 100 percent
El Sobrante Christian School — 100 percent
Contra Costa Jewish Day School — 100 percent

The list goes on. There are a lot of private elementary schools in Contra Costa County, and the parents who live there seem pretty intent on protecting their children from infectious diseases.

---

* These statistics are from the 2012–2013 school year. In 2015, California passed a law prohibiting "nonmedical" exemptions for childhood vaccinations. In other words, if you want a sense of what Waldorf parents want for their children — absent government intervention — you have to look at pre-2015 data.

St. Perpetua — 100 percent
St. Catherine of Siena — 100 percent

But wait. There's one school that's very different.

East Bay Waldorf — 42 percent

42 percent? Is this a fluke — a chance deviation from a consistent pattern?

Let's take a look at private schools in El Dorado County, just down the list alphabetically from Contra Costa.

G. H. S. Academy — 94 percent
Holy Trinity School — 100 percent

And then, wait for it:

Cedar Springs Waldorf — 36 percent

Let's try Los Angeles. Most middle schools, like their counterparts around the state, are up in the 90s or at 100 percent. But once again there is an exception, far on the west side of the city in the exclusive neighborhood of Pacific Palisades.

Westside Waldorf — 22 percent

If you've never heard of Waldorf schools, they are a movement started by the Austrian educator Rudolf Steiner in the early twentieth century. Waldorf schools are small and expensive and focus on "holistic" learning — seeking to develop the creativity and imagination of their students. There are several thousand Waldorf schools around the world — mostly kindergartens and elementary schools — and about two dozen in California. And almost without exception, the lowest vaccination rates in any California town that has a Waldorf school are…at the Waldorf school.*

Here is Sonoma County:

St. Vincent de Paul Elementary School — 100 percent
Rincon Valley Christian — 100 percent
Sonoma Country Day School — 94 percent
St. Eugene Cathedral School — 97 percent
St. Rose — 100 percent
Summerfield Waldorf School — 24 percent[†]

California had two measles outbreaks in the mid-2010s — including one that started at Disneyland. The outbreaks led many to say that California was suffering from a problem with vaccine skepticism. But that's wrong. Look again at those elementary schools with 100 percent vaccination rates. It's actually small pockets of people within the state — such as the parents who sent their children to a very specific brand of elementary school — who have a vaccine problem. John

---

* There are other schools with unvaccinated rates as high as Waldorf. But they are rare.
† If you're curious, here are some other Waldorf numbers from California.
    Waldorf School of Orange County — 44 percent
    Sacramento Waldorf — 46 percent
    Waldorf School of San Diego — 20 percent
    San Francisco Waldorf School — 53 percent
    Santa Cruz Waldorf — 60 percent
    Sierra Waldorf — 58 percent

Wennberg would recognize the pattern in an instant. Vaccine skepticism is small-area variation.

This is the first lesson of social epidemics. When we look at a contagious event, we assume that there is something fundamentally wild and unruly about the path it takes. But there is nothing wild and unruly about the L.A. bank-robbery epidemic or the patterns of medical practice in Waterbury versus Stowe or the ideas of Waldorf parents. Whatever contagious belief unites the people in those instances has the discipline to stop at the borders of their community. There must be a set of rules, buried somewhere below the surface.

Which brings us to puzzle number two.

CHAPTER TWO

The Trouble with Miami

"HE WOULD SMOKE A BLUNT, AND THEN BETWEEN EIGHT AND, SAY, NOON HE WOULD LAUNDER UPWARDS OF A MILLION DOLLARS."

1.

Your honor, I stand before you a humbled and broken man....I have lost everything I loved and cared about....I destroyed my marriage. I scarred my children, my three beautiful children. I have caused my aging parents inconsolable suffering. There's no one to blame but myself.

September 12, 2019. Federal Court. The jury has found Philip Esformes guilty in one of the biggest Medicare fraud cases in American history. And now the defendant is pleading with the judge for mercy.

I have lost over fifty pounds since I was incarcerated [on] July 22, 2016. My body is a shell of what it was. My feet have lost circulation. My knees are swollen. I have developed a skin condition. For more than thirty-seven months, I haven't felt the sun.

The government investigation into Esformes's network of nursing homes took years. The trial lasted almost eight weeks. The jury heard about bribery, sham invoices, kickbacks, money laundering, 256 separate bank accounts, and shady doctors. His closest associates wore a wire and collected hours of tapes of Esformes directing his massive empire.

The tapes depict me as a man willing to cut corners without fear of consequences, unappreciative of all the good that surrounded me, a man who acted as if the rules do not apply. I accept responsibility for what I have done.

And then he wept.

2.

Someone, someday, will make a great movie out of the Esformes case. It had everything Hollywood would ever want. First there is Esformes himself — tanned and moviestar handsome, a dead ringer for Paul Newman. He drove a $1.6 million Ferrari Aperta, wore a $360,000 Swiss watch, and flew from coast to coast in a private jet. The jury was told about the many beautiful women he met in luxury hotel rooms, his screaming fits, his predawn phone calls, his insistence on referring to cash as "fettuccine." He was described as "obsessive" and "probably bipolar," a man "who calls all day and all night, and you have to drive around, who drives people crazy, who pushes them as hard as he can, who complains about everything that happens."

That's one of his *own* lawyers talking.

Philip Esformes would keep the Sabbath and then, at midnight, when the religious prohibition on working was lifted, go and visit his nursing homes to double-check that things were working to his satisfaction. He had two sons, the elder of whom he decided, against all athletic expectations, ought to be a college basketball star. If you search YouTube, you can find videos of his diminutive son dutifully doing his drills under the watchful eye of any number of professional coaches and trainers.

"He drove his kids like you can't believe," said Esformes's attorney Roy Black. "Like it was a full-time team." Black went on:

I mean, he was obsessed with that. And he would go on the road with them. And then he would find hotels that were near a synagogue so they could walk to the synagogue on Saturdays. Every little detail he would run in their lives because that's what he was like. He was just like…

Black paused for the right word: "A helicopter parent doesn't even get near. This guy was an entire fucking Air Force."

Black, who has represented every manner of accused drug dealer, fraudster, money-launderer, and con man in the course of his long career, did not seem to enjoy his experience with Philip Esformes.

"I mean, [Philip], he wanted to run the defense, which of course we didn't let him do. He was just very intense," Black said.

I would talk to him, you know, for hours at a time and I'd leave the federal lockup and I'd be soaking wet and have to go home and take a shower. I'd need a Valium or something.

Sitting in the courtroom was Philip's father, the legendary Morris Esformes — brilliant, handsome, witty, in the words of a former classmate, the "coolest guy" in the yeshiva. Morris was an Orthodox Jewish rabbi who built a nursing-home empire in Chicago and donated more than $100 million to charity. Morris programmed the horn on his car to play the theme music from *The Godfather*. He once appeared for an interview with two reporters wearing a purple-and-gold Los Angeles Lakers uniform with matching yarmulke. Should any harm come to the reporters as a result of their investigations into his business, the elder Esformes told them, a council of rabbis in Israel had already agreed to absolve him of the "spiritual consequences."

"I think what motivated Philip is he wanted to prove to his father, living in the shadow of his father, that he could be successful," one of Esformes's lawyers said in a candid moment. Sigmund Freud could have been called as a character witness in the Esformes case.

The trial had stories of orgies and trips to Las Vegas. It had a brief starring role for a wannabe Victoria's Secret model. It had a strange subplot in which Philip bribed the basketball coach at the University of Pennsylvania with bags of cash to recruit his son Moe for the university's basketball team. It had two all-star witnesses, the Delgado brothers. One of them weighed 540 pounds, had a baby with his girlfriend, and then, for the sake of convenience, housed her in an apartment owned by his wife. (The Delgado brothers knew their way around a delicate situation.) If you read through the 9,757 pages of trial transcripts, there are so many moments like this that it starts to feel routine:

Q: And when did it start?

The prosecutor is asking one of the government's many witnesses about a related health-care fraud involving a company called ATC.

A: 2002, when I got my provider number.
Q: And how much did ATC bill to Medicare?
A: $205 million.
Q: And...total amount of kickbacks you were paying per month to different providers, how much was it?
A: It went up all the way to between 300- to $400,000 a month.

A bit later, the lawyer circles back to the kickbacks.

Q: Can you just describe to the jury, paint them a picture of how, on any given month, you would lay out the different amounts of money to be paid?
A: Like I mentioned before, I already had money collected from the money laundering that I was doing. And I would have to have hundred-dollar bills, 50s, 20s, 10s, 5s, stacks of money. And then I have envelopes.

Yes. To hand out $400,000 a month in cash in kickbacks, you need a lot of envelopes. And by the way, if you spend enough time with the case, you may come to the conclusion that maybe — just maybe — Philip Esformes was not all bad.

> He would come to the facilities on Saturday night. He would check the facilities. He would be there day in and day out, running around town doing rounds.

This is one of Philip's lawyers, Howard Srebnick, in a final defense of his client that, at times, reached the level of poetry.

> He brought [basketball star] Dwyane Wade to the facility so the patients could meet him....Mr. Esformes would come to the facilities and give people hugs. He would come to the facilities and dance with his patients. He would come to the facilities and show love to the people that work for him, so much love that those people were willing to come to court and show their love for Mr. Esformes.

What happened to Philip Esformes? Why would a man capable of such love throw his life away so recklessly?

At the sentencing hearing, the most powerful testimony came from the rabbi Sholom Lipskar, who had known the family for years. Lipskar visited Esformes fifty times in the long years he spent in prison, awaiting trial. Lipskar knew Esformes's state of mind as well as anyone.

"His soul has been shattered. His heart has been broken. His personality is changed," Lipskar told the judge. And then:

> I understand Your Honor himself has said in the past that there are bad people who do bad things and then there are

good people who make mistakes.... Philip is one of those people. He started out as Philip Esformes from an extraordinary family of great pedigree. I knew his grandparents. They prayed in our synagogue. His grandfather would come in his wheelchair with his whole heart and soul and pray.... He became then a successful man in Chicago, was Philip of Chicago supporting all the institutions in Chicago. And then he came to Miami, where it's easy to become Philip of Miami, a ruined individual, got stuck in an environment where it wasn't just money that he wanted to make.

Miami. Lipskar thought the problems for Esformes began when he left his hometown for south Florida.

This was, let's remember, a sentencing hearing — an occasion where, by design, a felon arranges for his friends to come and say nice things on his behalf. *It wasn't really his fault* is the standard line of defense for everyone in this position, going back to two little boys sent to the principal's office.

But at the same time, Lipskar's argument sounds awfully familiar. The lesson of bank robberies and Waldorf schools is that patterns of behavior attach themselves to places in ways that can sometimes surprise us. The rabbi was making a small-area-variation argument.

He lost himself. You can ask his family.... Philip will tell you himself: "I lost myself. I went down a wrong path. I dropped to the bottom of the abyss."

He was Philip of Chicago, an honorable businessman from a pedigreed family. Until he became Philip of Miami, and lost himself.* It was as if he had moved from Waterbury to Stowe.

3.

Let us go back for a moment to the story of the Waldorf schools. The most obvious explanation for what is so unusual about Waldorf is that the schools simply attract parents who are already hostile to vaccinations. But when the anthropologist Elisa Sobo studied Waldorf culture, she found that wasn't true. "People didn't necessarily come to the school because they want an oasis where nobody vaccinates," she says. Of course, she went on, *some* people clearly did. But the pattern was in the other direction. "It seems to have been a behavior or an attitude, a belief that people picked up, when they go there," she said. She noticed something interesting about families with multiple children at a Waldorf school. "If you came with a three-year-old in the preschool and then you're building your family and you decide to stay there, your next children would have fewer vaccinations and then your next children would have [even] fewer vaccinations." The Waldorf school casts a spell over its members, and the longer you stay at a Waldorf, the deeper the hold the spell has on you.

So how does the spell work? Consider the following testimony of Waldorf alumni, taken from a promotional video made for a Waldorf school in Chicago. (I chose it at random; there are countless promos like it on YouTube.) The video

---

* Just to be clear, the Esformes were not *absolutely* honorable. They had a few, relatively minor, run-ins with state regulations in Illinois. But nothing on the scale of what happened in Miami.

consists of a number of young, attractive professionals talking about what they learned from their years at Waldorf. Here, for example, is Sarah:

What Waldorf does for you is, it definitely gives you this total curiosity about the world. There's kind of this Waldorf effect of being so eager to learn and curious about everything, instead of it being mashed down and packed into boxes.

Next up is Aurora:

The thing with Waldorf is that they teach you how to learn. And not only do they teach you how to learn, they teach you how to want to learn, creating this desire and ability to find the answers that need to be found and to seek out the information that you need.

There is something wonderful about the way Waldorf fosters in its students a sense of curiosity about the world. But you can see how this idea can give people permission to wander off in some strange directions.

Parents who vaccinate their children are people who agree to defer to the expertise of the medical community. Can I tell you precisely how a vaccine works and what happens to my children's immune systems when they are given a shot? No. But I realize that there are lots of people who know more about this subject than me, and I trust their judgment. There is something about being part of the Waldorf community, by contrast, that encourages people not to default to the judgment of experts: It gives them the confidence to sort through these kinds of difficult subjects for themselves. In the video, a filmmaker named Erik says:

> I could land anywhere and hit the ground running without really skipping a beat.... Having that confidence that I have permission to do that is something that Waldorf really instills.

The final word in the video comes from Sarah. Going to Waldorf, she says, "gives you a little bit of a superhero complex." Then she winks. "That's the only danger of sending your kid there."

Keep in mind that Waldorf parents don't socialize only with other Waldorf parents. They live in a world filled with coworkers and friends and relatives and neighbors who feel strongly that childhood vaccinations are a good idea. No doubt, the Waldorf parents hear those contrary voices all the time. Every time they take their child to the doctor, the pediatrician must look at them like they have lost their minds. But for most of them, none of that outside pressure matters.

"Did they get sick? Yes," writes a blogger who calls herself The Waldorf Mom. She's talking about what happened after she chose to opt out of the recommended vaccination schedule for her kids.

> One Christmas found us under self-quarantine with the chicken pox. (It was quite a treat to skip all the socials that season!) For the younger one, it was very well expressed and he still has a few craters to show for it.

For my older son, it was so mild that it seemed to just pass through him. Years later when other kids in school came down with it, he developed shingles. Indeed, it is a help to have a fully expressed version of the illness. You have it, work through it, and are done.

Of course, there is an easy way to protect your child from shingles — which, on a pain scale of 1 to 10, usually registers a 9 or 10 — and that's to have them vaccinated against chicken pox.

Waldorf Mom continues. She also opted out of the whooping-cough vaccines. And guess what? Her kids got whooping cough.

The worst illness we ever had was whooping cough. The children caught it from another child with whom we had spent an afternoon at the beach. We were in California then and it remains one of the toughest and most grueling experiences of my life. My son had never been more sick. My older one who had two rounds of DPT didn't suffer quite as much, though he still had it. Would I have vaccinated against it if I had known what it would be like? Perhaps. But now that it's behind me, I feel more confident that my sons have the best protection from this illness.

Throughout this grueling round of skin craters, bouts of shingles, and debilitating whooping cough, one thing kept her going.

My children also had Waldorf Education on our side, so there was lots of everyday art and creativity, indoor and outdoor play, and a stress-free, enlivening education that supported their development. I chose not to vaccinate, but I made sure to give them support as best I could.

The Waldorf spell, wherever it comes from, is really powerful.

Let me give you another example, this time directly from the small-area-variation research. If you have a heart problem, one of the tools available to your cardiologist is a cardiac catheter. A catheter is a plastic tube — just over three feet long and about two millimeters wide. The tube is inserted through an artery or vein and carefully threaded up into the heart, where it is used to diagnose heart and blood-vessel problems. But as with all useful medical tools, there's a big difference, from one city to another, in how frequently doctors use it. If you look at the United States, for example, in the period 1998 to 2012, the leader in cardiac catheterization was Boulder, Colorado. If you had a heart attack in Boulder, you got "cardiac cath" 75.3 percent of the time. At the bottom of the list was Buffalo, New York, where catheters were used only 23.6 percent of the time. At this point, I suspect, examples of small-area variation have lost their power to shock. But it's worth pointing out that this difference is *huge*. What it meant to be treated for a heart attack in Boulder in this period was very different from what it meant to be treated in Buffalo.*

---

* It should also be pointed out that this does not necessarily mean that you are better off getting a heart attack in Boulder than in Buffalo. On the contrary, cardiac catheterization is very expensive. It carries risks of its own. There's little evidence that you are more likely to die of a heart attack in Buffalo than in Boulder. If anything, a case could be made that the notoriously wasteful and expensive American medical system would be much improved if everyone who had a heart attack got shipped to western New York State for treatment,

There's an obvious explanation for this. "I can see from my window Fort Erie, Canada, which is right across the lake," says Vijay Iyer, who heads the cardiology department at the University of Buffalo. Buffalo, Iyer argues, is inevitably influenced by its much larger northern neighbor. In those years, he said, Buffalo's cardiac-catheter rates were much closer to, say, Toronto's, than they were to New York City's. Another example of this, he said, was a technique called "radial insertion." For the longest time cardiologists chose the femoral artery as the point of entry for the catheter: That's the artery that runs down your thigh. But then in the late 1980s a Canadian cardiologist named Lucien Campeau started using a different point of entry: the "radial" artery, which runs up from your wrist. Radial entry is more difficult to master, but it turns out to have far fewer side effects, be much easier on the patient, reduce mortality rates, and get people out of the hospital sooner. Buffalo adopted the innovation well before other American cities. "There were two physicians who came from Toronto and brought the skill with them. Another went to Montreal to learn the skill because he felt it was valuable," Iyer said. "I trained [in Buffalo] in 2004 and 2005, when the number of radial cases being done in the United States was probably in the 10 percent range," Iyer goes on. "When the rest of the country was doing 10 percent radial, we were doing 70 percent radial."

Canadian medicine is, in many ways, very different from American medicine. Canada has national health insurance, not a bewildering network of private insurers. In 2022, the

---

and we spent the money saved on encouraging people with high blood pressure to eat better and get more exercise.

United States spent 17.3 percent of its Gross Domestic Product on health care. In Canada, the equivalent number was 12.2 percent — about a *third* lower. In Canada, there is much more of an emphasis on asking whether expensive interventions are worth it. (That's another of the reasons why Canadian doctors were so quick to adopt radial insertion: It's *cheaper* than inserting the tube through the thigh.) Buffalo is Buffalo, in other words, because some of that Canadianness inevitably drifts across the Niagara River and envelops the hospitals of the Buffalo region. When it comes to health care, Buffalo is the eleventh Canadian province. But Boulder? Boulder is hundreds of miles from the Canadian border. Boulder's going to be different.

Now here's where things get interesting. A few years ago, the economist David Molitor wondered: What happens if a cardiologist moves from a place like Boulder to a place like Buffalo?

Molitor's answer is that the Boulder cardiologist turns into a Buffalo cardiologist. The transformation isn't 100 percent (that would be creepy). But basically the cardiologist who changes places moves about two-thirds of the way toward the practice pattern of his or her new home.

"It all happens right away, which tells you something about what's going on. It's something that's happening very, very fast within the first year," Molitor said. "If you thought it was purely some kind of learning — you know, you're gathering new information from your new colleagues and you're updating your beliefs — the pattern of learning would be more gradual," he went on. "There might be an immediate impact, but then you would continue to evolve to look more like your destination region over time."

But that's not what happens. You show up in Buffalo, and *boom*. Think about how strange this is. You are a cardiologist. You've been treating heart attacks for fifteen years at the big teaching hospital in Boulder. You are so good at what you do that you get a tempting offer to work in Buffalo. They don't offer you the job contingent on your undergoing a special Buffalo reorientation. Your new colleagues don't sit you down when you arrive, read you the riot act, and say, *This is the way we do things here.* No, they hired you because they like you just the way you are. So you show up, and your new office looks a lot like your old office, and the technology and drugs you have access to are identical to the ones back in Boulder. The patients you are seeing display exactly the same problems and symptoms as the patients in your former practice. Everything is basically the same! Except that now when you look out the window you don't see the Rocky Mountains anymore, you see Canada. And voilà! Overnight you turn into something very close to the archetypal Buffalo cardiologist. "This isn't really about learning about what works," Molitor says. "It's more about the influences of your environment."

When the rabbi said that something happened to Philip Esformes when he moved to Miami, this is what he was talking about. He was saying, in effect, that his friend was the equivalent of the cardiologist who showed up in Buffalo or the parent who enrolled their child in a Waldorf school. Communities have their own stories, and those stories are contagious.

Actually, the word *story* isn't quite right. A better word is *overstory*. An overstory is the upper layer of foliage in a forest, and the size and density and height of the overstory affect the behavior and development of every species far below on the forest floor. I think that small-area variation — such as what distinguishes Waldorf schools from other schools and what sets Boulder apart from Buffalo — is more like an over-story than a story. It's not something explicit that's drilled into every inhabitant. The overstory is made up of things way up in the air, in many cases outside our awareness. We tend to forget about the overstory because we're so focused on the life going on in front of and around us. But overstories turn out to be really, *really* powerful.

So, puzzle number two: What's the Miami overstory that cast its spell over Philip Esformes? And where did it come from?

4.

Medicare — the health-insurance system the US government runs for America's elderly — covers 67 million people and spends over $900 billion a year. It was created in 1965, and it did not take long for people with criminal intentions to real-ize that a program that large, with that much money, repre-sented a golden opportunity.

Becoming a Medicare provider is, first of all, not that hard. You apply online for a National Provider Identifier (NPI) — a ten-digit number that you use to bill the government for ser-vices and enroll as a provider.

"It's a trust-based system," says Allan Medina. Medina was the lead prosecutor in the Esformes case. He spent just over a decade high up in the Department of Justice, tracking down Medicare fraud cases, and he probably knows as much as anyone can about the ins and outs of how the system is gamed.

"You fill out these forms, and on the back you certify that 'I will follow the rules of Medicare,'" he said. "You made a promise. That's where the trust begins."

Someone has to be identified as the "nominee owner" of the new enterprise. But who is that person? It's hard for a program covering 67 million people to check everyone's identity. The enterprise also has to have an address — a physical place of business — so it can be inspected. But there's a limit to what can be learned from an inspection. "If you know they're coming in on a particular day," Medina said, "you might set it up to look a certain way — and then you're off to the races.

"There are three basic things you need to commit health-care fraud," Medina went on. "You need patients, right? If you have the patients, then you need medical professionals. You need nurses. You need doctors who are willing to sign an order that Medicare will trust and verify. You have the doctor and you have the patients, [but] you still can't do it because you need the third step. You need the files. You need falsified records."

The world of Medicare fraud is essentially a series of endlessly creative variations on the fake patients/doctors/files combination. Sometimes the doctors are in on the scam. Sometimes you just steal the doctor's NPI off the internet. Sometimes you legitimately provide a service, but bill for something far more extravagant. Sometimes you don't even bother at all. You start, say, a physical rehabilitation agency. You recruit patients to say they've been injured when they actually haven't, send them to a doctor who agrees to write a prescription for your rehab facility in exchange for a kickback, and fake a medical record to say that you put the patient through a rigorous routine when in fact you did nothing at all.

But what if someone back at Medicare headquarters gets suspicious? Aren't your name and address on the NPI enrollment form? Not if you put someone else's name on the Medicare enrollment form, and that person is now conveniently out of the country. Medicare pays your fly-by-night company and you immediately withdraw the money, laundering it carefully so the banks don't get suspicious. A good partner for this is a drug dealer. The drug dealer has lots of cash that he wants to get out of the country. You *need* cash for the kickbacks you're giving doctors or hospitals. So maybe you give the drug dealer a piece of your "legitimate" business in exchange for infusions of cash that you can use for bribes.

And then there's the emerging field of telemedicine, where the rules now say that you don't actually have to meet a patient to get paid for treating them. *Are you kidding me?* During COVID, when the telemedicine regulations started loosening, the Medicare fraud world took to the streets to sing hallelujahs. The number and variety of these schemes keep growing more byzantine and creative — to the point where the total amount of Medicare fraud in any given year is estimated to be somewhere around $100 billion. And ground zero for this extraordinary epidemic of criminality is — and always has been — Miami.

Medina grew up in Miami Beach. Growing up in Miami if you are in the business of chasing Medicare fraud is like growing up in the Alps if you want to be a downhill skier. It gives you a leg up on those raised in the flatland. "I didn't notice it until looking back, but you saw pharmacies popping up," he said. "It's pretty brazen. I mean, my grandmother — who passed away recently — she would be approached at bus stops by patient recruiters."

When the federal government started to get serious about cracking down on Medicare fraud, it formed special regional "strike forces," combining the FBI, the US Attorney's Office, and agents from the Office of Inspector General at the Department of Health and Human Services. Where was the first strike force located? Miami. And maybe the simplest way to describe why they chose Miami is with the following chart, which shows how much Medicare spent, per enrollee, on durable medical equipment in 2003. *Durable medical equipment* refers to things such as crutches and braces and orthotics and wheelchairs and walkers. The fraud world has since branched out to more lucrative and exotic schemes. But wheelchairs and walkers were where it all began.

Let's just look at the numbers for the state of Florida.

$211.07	Bradenton, FL	$241.93	Orlando, FL
$233.56	Clearwater, FL	$190.36	Ormond Beach, FL
$198.24	Fort Lauderdale, FL	$321.42	Panama City, FL
$190.90	Fort Myers, FL	$260.36	Pensacola, FL
$283.25	Gainesville, FL	$189.87	Sarasota, FL
$228.26	Hudson, FL	$228.42	St. Petersburg, FL
$249.44	Jacksonville, FL	$294.91	Tallahassee, FL
$287.20	Lakeland, FL	$222.25	Tampa, FL
$238.54	Ocala, FL		

Panama City is the highest on this list, at $321.42 per Medicare patient. The lowest is Sarasota, at $189.87. That's a big difference, and if you were a fraud investigator you might ask, *Why is Medicare being billed 70 percent more for things like wheelchairs in Panama City than in Sarasota?* But otherwise everywhere else looks pretty normal: Fort Lauderdale, Jacksonville, Clearwater, Orlando, and most other cities are all in the $200 per year range.

But wait. I haven't given you the number for Miami. Ready? $1,234.73.

5.

Where does the Miami overstory come from? If you talk to one hundred people from Miami, you'll get one hundred different answers. But perhaps the most persuasive explanation is what might be termed "The 1980 Theory." It comes from a fascinating book called *The Year of Dangerous Days* by Nicholas Griffin.

Griffin's argument goes something like this: Up through the 1970s, Miami was a small, sleepy, struggling Southern city. It had started out as a winter-vacation haven, but jet travel drained away many of the tourists. Orlando had become the state's biggest attraction. Miami was dangerous. Miami Beach was a strip of dilapidated hotels. When business leaders in Miami thought about reviving their community, their models were always conventionally successful American cities. They aspired to be a regional business center like Atlanta, to have the banking industry of Charlotte, to have an inland port like Jacksonville.

But, Griffin argues, three separate things happened in 1980 to turn Miami into something *very* different. The first was drug money. The drug trade in south Florida used to be a mom-and-pop business, with small-time operators moving marijuana up from the Caribbean by boat into the Florida

Keys. But then the market shifted suddenly and dramatically to Latin American cocaine. By the late 1970s, the size of the underground economy in Dade County — where Miami is situated — was estimated at $11 billion. Twenty percent of real-estate deals were all-cash, meaning that the buyer was showing up for the closing with gym bags full of bills. In one three-year stretch in the 1980s, the total amount spent on cars was nearly ten times the amount spent in Jacksonville and Tampa, the state's two other biggest cities. In 1980 alone, one IRS agent estimated that twelve people deposited between $250 and $500 million *each* in Miami banks.

"I think the key thing that year is, first of all, how quickly American institutions are undermined by foreign — or let's call it drug — money, because that's pretty much what it is," Griffin said. The cocaine trade turned the city's banking system into an accomplice of international drug cartels.

That corruption then started to seep into the criminal-justice system. "The homicide department gets totally corrupted by cocaine," Griffin said. A bank that dealt with smugglers put a former city administrator on its payroll. Vice cops started knocking over drug dealers and stealing their product. All of this happened, Griffin went on, at "the very same time when the murder rate spikes up 300 percent." The city was out of control. In the winter of 1979, a young black man was beaten by police after leading them on a high-speed chase, and died a few days later in hospital. A group of officers was brought to trial. When they were acquitted, black Miami erupted in anger, sparking one of the worst race riots in American history. White Miami headed for the exits by the thousands, moving across the county line to Fort Lauderdale, Boca Raton, and other points north.

That same spring — in April of 1980 — Fidel Castro decided to open his country's borders. Griffin calls this the "craziest" of the things that happened that year. "The demographics of Miami change almost overnight. I don't think it's ever happened in another city in America that you can enter a year thinking that it's pretty much still what they call an Anglo city down here, certainly Anglo controlled. And by the end of the year, you've literally got a majority Latin city that's come out of nowhere. And that's because of the Mariel Boatlift: Castro dumps 125,000 people on top of a city that's barely got over 300,000 people in it at the time. And just like that, there's this extraordinary shift, but it's that shift into a city that has just had all those key institutions undermined."

Any single one of those events would be enough to leave a city shaken. Miami had *multiple* traumatic events, and they all had the same effect: They took the institutions and practices that had anchored the city for generations and shook them to their foundations.

"There's this point where it all meets," Griffin said. "And that was the spring of 1980. You can take a six-week period and all of these things hit the city like three hurricanes in the same month."

In the spring of 1980, a columnist for the city's newspaper, the *Miami Herald*, asked Miami's mayor how the city would cope.

Is there a saturation point? How does a community come to grips? I put the question to Miami Mayor Maurice Ferre.

"In the same way that Boston came to grips with the huge Irish influx of the 1870s," he replied.

And how was that?

"They didn't."

They didn't. Miami didn't absorb those three seismic events and continue on as before. Miami became a different place.

So what happens if you are someone who moves down to Miami? If you come before 1980, not much. You're just moving to another relatively generic Southern city, like Jacksonville or Tampa or somewhere in southern Georgia. But if you move in 1980? Now you're moving to a place where institutional authority — the steadying influence of patterns and practices built up over time — has been shattered.

1980 was the peak year for an infamous Colombian money launderer named Isaac Kattan Kassin. He used to pull up in front of a bank on Biscayne Boulevard in downtown Miami, call over the security guard, and have him carry two massive suitcases full of hundreds of thousands of dollars in cash into the bank. Kassin did that every day.

"I think the record was $328 million in the year, all carried in. I mean...[the] bank has to hire five people to work through the night to count the money," Griffin said. "And of course, pretend that there's nothing wrong going on around here. It's just fantastic."

If your morning routine took you down Biscayne Boulevard on any working day in 1980, that's what you would see: A crook in a red Chevy Citation double-parked in front of a bank, unloading the millions he is laundering, *with the help of the bank*. Don't you think that would change the way you see the world?

"Does that parlay directly into Medicare fraud, you know, thirty years later? I don't know, but it seems like having institutions that aren't very well built seems to be part of the game," Griffin said. "You know, it's everywhere down here. When you get a speeding ticket down here, the police officer will tell you not to pay it. He will say, 'Oh, it's much cheaper…if you call my cousin's ticket clinic and pay sixty bucks, he'll come. You don't have any points on your license'…. That's the way it works down here."

6.

One sunny Florida day, I went to the Medicare Fraud Strike Force headquarters in North Miami and sat in a conference room with Omar Pérez Aybar, who runs the Miami office, and one of his colleagues, Fernando Porras. They are both young and speak Spanish and English, switching seamlessly between languages. They seemed to regard the criminals with whom they interacted with a mixture of amusement and moral incredulity. I told them I wanted to hear Miami stories.

"So, Alfredo Ruiz is this money launderer," Pérez began.

Money laundering is a big deal in the fraud world, for obvious reasons. Once Medicare pays you, you need to move that money out of your bank account as fast as possible, before the Strike Force gets on to you and seizes it.

And he would wake up in the morning — these were his words to us. He would smoke a blunt, and then between eight and, say, noon he would launder upwards of a million dollars. And then he was done for the day.

Pérez pointed to the ceiling.

One of the shell companies that was supposed to be laundering money? That literally was upstairs on the fourth floor.

Ruiz had rented office space for one of his fronts upstairs from the very Strike Force whose job it was to shut down his fronts. Pérez and Porras seemed to have a grudging admiration for that kind of audacity. Ruiz drove a $250,000 Lamborghini Urus and kept changing the car's color, which made it difficult to track him down. (The Urus looks like a prop from a Marvel movie. It's the kind of car people drive in Miami and not anywhere else.)

"We got him at the Biltmore Hotel in the Al Capone suite," Pérez said.

Of course they did.

Pérez said there were other parts of the country — notably Los Angeles — that would occasionally beat Miami in some category of suspicious Medicare activity. But there was a certain characteristic shamelessness, a particular kind of brazenness and flamboyance that set Miami apart. Pérez once found a "nominee owner" in a 12-by-10-foot room with a steel gate on the door, locked from the outside. His job was to sign checks. Apparently he had signed enough, so he'd been left to die. Another time, when HIV-infusion scams were the rage, scammers were rounding up homeless people, busing them to clinics, and injecting them with vitamin B_{12}, telling Medicare that it was expensive antiviral medicine. A big part of the Miami overstory was, apparently, *Use your imagination.*

Porras and Pérez then offered to show me some of their favorite hot spots. We jumped into a government-issue Chevrolet and headed south down the Palmetto Expressway to an unassuming neighborhood near the airport called Sweetwater.

We pulled into the parking lot of a small two-story office building called the Fontainebleau Park Office Plaza. It looked completely ordinary from the outside: built in the 1970s but well-kept, lots of windows, freshly painted, lawns neatly manicured. The lobby looked like any other office-building lobby — until, that is, you examined the floor plan on the wall. You've seen them before, those black and white posters outlining every office, corridor, elevator, and fire exit. The Fontainebleau map looks like a *maze,* a rat's warren of small spaces, carved and sublet into even smaller spaces, totaling so many different offices that the numbering system for the building is like something you would see in one of those Chinese mega-apartment complexes: number, letter, number, in seemingly random order. 1-R-2 or 2-F-3 and on, and on.

Keep in mind that this is the plan of a relatively modest-sized building.

"I got here in 2007. And I've visited this building probably

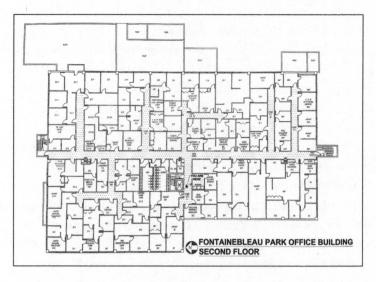

FONTAINEBLEAU PARK OFFICE BUILDING
SECOND FLOOR

thirty times," Pérez said as we walked in. Each door along the long central corridor had a small, standardized sign out front.

Porras pointed at one of the doors. "Okay. So this is a home health agency." As he said that, he rolled his eyes a little. It wasn't really a home health-care agency. How could it be? It was the size of a child's bedroom. A little farther down the corridor was a "medical center" the size of a large closet, then a doctor's office, a rehab facility, and so on.

In a building with dozens of medical offices, you would expect to see patients. Every sign announced office hours, Monday to Friday, and we were there late morning on a Monday. Where was everyone?

We stopped in front of a door. "It's open. It's supposed to be a business," Pérez said. "Just kind of pop your head in there to see what you see." I opened the door a crack. An elderly man was sitting behind a desk, and he looked up, startled, as if he could not imagine why anyone was bothering him. "In each of these offices, it's just one person," Pérez said. "And they wouldn't necessarily be hoping for business."

On the walls of the building, the management had put up posters of beautiful photographs, with inspirational lines underneath such as, "Believe and succeed. Courage does not always roar. Sometimes it's the quiet voice at the end of the day saying, I will try again tomorrow."

The two agents burst out laughing.

"And they do!" Pérez shouted out.

"When your claim is approved!" Porras said.

It was an office full of fronts. Medicare requires all providers to have a physical place of business, and the attitude of the Fontainebleau seemed to be that it wasn't worth trying too hard to make things look kosher.

We got back in the car and headed five minutes away to a "merchandise mart" attached to a hotel. It was a two-story indoor mall, with long corridors lined with small storefronts. The first floor, geared to the garment industry, sold buttons and zippers and cloth samples. But the second floor had been repurposed as a health-care mall. We stopped in front of an empty office with a big window. Large posters taped to the windows advertised medical-rehab services. The door was open. Inside were a desk, a table, a printer, and an unplugged telephone. On the walls was a series of cheap reproduction nineteenth-century prints. On a bulletin board was the firm's paperwork: the patient's bill of rights, the firm's Medicare authorization, and a company organizational chart listing the firm's board of directors, administrator, corporate compliance officer, and office manager. It *seemed* legitimate. Until I looked a little closer at the org chart and realized that under every box — directors, administrator, corporate compliance officer, office manager — *was the same name.* They were every bit as brazen at the merchandise mart as they were at the Fontainebleau.

"What we know is that there are some turnkey operations," Pérez said. "You tell me what type of industry you're interested in or what type of provider you want to be and I'll come in and set it up for you." It was exactly like the real-estate stagers who prepare a home to be put on the market. "We've been to offices that have a monitor, a desktop, a mouse, and a keyboard. But nothing's connected. It's just all the cables are hanging or there's no cables present."*

---

* They once found a firm that would stage a pharmacy for $5,000. "They could get you four bars of soap. You know, pairs of glasses…the minimum amount of stuff that you need on your shelves to show that you're a functioning pharmacy."

This office looked *very* staged, down to the neat rack of business cards on the desk. Pérez wandered next door to talk to a woman manning the reception desk in what advertised itself as a medical-services company. *She will have no idea why she's there,* he predicted. Sure enough, when he asked her what she was doing there, the woman said she had no idea.

Pérez had been to the merchandise mart almost as many times as he had been to the Fontainebleau Park Office Plaza. "I'm surprised they don't have our picture up somewhere: 'If you see these guys coming, don't let them in.'"

Porras, meanwhile, was on his phone, asking someone back at the Strike Force to look up the Medicare billing numbers of the firm with the nineteenth-century prints on the wall.

"Oh, here we go," he said, reading from his texts. "Just to give you a picture. Here it is. Billed $5 million and was paid $1.2 million for Quarter 1 and 2 of 2022. No billing since. They left. They pulled up their stakes and went down to the next one." And they couldn't be bothered to pack up their office.

"You know, I run the state, right?" Pérez said. "So I have offices in Tampa, in West Palm, in Orlando, in Jacksonville. We recognize that the schemes there are different than they are here. It's *much* more blatant. It's much more in your face here in south Florida."

When I was driving around Miami with Pérez and Porras, I asked them about a man named Rick Scott. I didn't expect them to answer the question — the matter is too sensitive for people employed by the federal government. But I could guess what they were thinking, because you can't work in Miami, under the Miami overstory, and not wonder about the impact that people like Rick Scott had on people like Philip Esformes.

Scott used to be the CEO of the large national for-profit hospital chain Columbia/HCA. In 1997, federal agents raided Columbia/HCA. In the first wave of the investigation, five senior company officers were ordered to appear before a grand jury. What division of the company were they all from? You can guess: Florida. Scott was not charged in the case, nor implicated in any wrongdoing. But he was forced to resign in disgrace. And a few years later, Columbia/HCA pleaded guilty to fourteen felonies — involving kickbacks to doctors, false billing, making illegal deals with other providers, and on and on — and ultimately paid what was then a record $1.7 billion in civil settlements.

Where did Scott end up moving after leaving HCA? You can guess that too: Florida. A few years after that, he decided to run for governor of…you guessed it: Florida, where he served two terms before moving on to represent…yes, Florida, in the United States Senate. For a portion of the years that Philip Esformes ran a billion-dollar scheme of kickbacks, false billing, and illegal deals, the governor of his state was someone who had presided over a hospital system that ran a billion-dollar scheme of kickbacks, false billing, and illegal deals.

When Philip Esformes went home at night and saw Rick Scott holding forth on television from the most powerful position in the state, do you think it changed the way he thought about his own behavior? The canopy high over the forest floor casts a shadow on everything beneath it.

The overstory is specific. It is tied to a place. It is powerful. It shapes behavior. And it does not emerge out of nowhere. It happens for a reason.

7.

The Medicare Fraud Strike Force stumbled upon Philip Esformes by accident. "My first-ever case was a pharmacy owner," prosecutor Allan Medina remembers. "He gets detained. He cooperates." The pharmacist told Medina that he had been paying kickbacks to two brothers, Gaby and Willy Delgado, in exchange for their steering patients his way. "That's all I thought it was," Medina says.

But slowly something larger emerged. The Delgado brothers were in the business of arranging "ancillary" services — medical equipment, vision care, mental-health counseling, and the like. Willy, the older brother, was the ringleader. He had gotten into the game just out of nursing school, when he took a job as a field nurse for a company run by a woman named Aida Salazar.

"Well, after a while working with her and she got comfortable," Willy testified at the Esformes trial, "she told me that I could make some extra money by signing some of the visits that really weren't done..."

The portion of the Esformes trial dedicated to Willy Delgado's testimony is a case study in how the Miami overstory is passed down from one generation to the next.

Q: So you wrote fake notes, is that fair?
A: Well, she had somebody transcribe them. I just signed off on them.
Q: So did you always see the patients for the notes that you wrote for her?
A: Did I what?

Willy Delgado seems genuinely incredulous that the prosecutor would ask a question with such an obvious answer.

Q: Always see the patients for the notes that you were writing for her.

A: No, I never saw those patients.

From there, Willy didn't look back.

"After I had learned the business, I wanted to open up my own," he went on. He did the durable-medical-equipment scam for a while, specializing in "oxygen concentrators." He found a very compliant physician — Dr. M — who was the medical director of a number of assisted-living facilities.

A: I would take him the prescriptions, he would sign them off for me, and with that, I can then, in turn, turn and bill Medicare for it.

Q: Have you heard the phrase *loose with the pen*?

A: He never even looked at the prescriptions. He would just sign them. His signature, I know — I mean, just a scribble, take it to him and he would get it done.

Willy Delgado got bigger and bigger. He opened restaurants, cigar stores. He developed a nice sideline repurposing leftover oxycodone pills. Then he and his brother reunited with Aida Salazar, who was now running an outfit called Nursing Unlimited with her son Nelson.

"I was a salesperson," Nelson said at the trial. He took doctors out to basketball games and strip clubs and did a lot of cocaine along the way. When Nelson got home at 3 a.m., he popped a handful of sleeping pills before starting again the next day.

The Delgado brothers were the connection that Medina discovered in his first case with the corrupt pharmacist. The pharmacist told him about the Delgados, whom he gathered evidence on with help from Salazar. And when the Delgado brothers started talking, they mentioned the name of a man they had been working with since the 2000s, just after the man and his father had moved down from Chicago: Philip Esformes.

By that point, Philip Esformes had assembled a massive portfolio of nursing homes and assisted-living facilities in south Florida. According to the Delgados, the three of them hatched a clever scheme to keep Esformes's nursing homes at capacity.

Under the rules of Medicare, if a patient has been hospitalized for at least three days, they are eligible for 100 days in a skilled nursing facility. So they found a hospital partner: the Larkin Community Hospital in South Miami.

Q: Just tell us what was attractive about Larkin Hospital.

Willy Delgado: Well, they are easy to work with. Their mission criteria is very loose.

Q: What do you mean, *easy to work with*?

A: Okay. If you are going to admit a patient in a hospital, when you go to an emergency room you see how hard it is to get a bed…if the patient can walk or is stable or can even get certain care at home — they send you home. But the idea at Larkin is…

I think you can figure out what "the idea at Larkin was": a *loose* mission criteria.

The people at Larkin would get kickbacks. In return, they

would send patients to an Esformes nursing home, where they would stay until they were discharged to an Esformes assisted-living facility. When they were discharged from there, the Delgado brothers would pick them up for ancillary services. And then, if the stars were perfectly in alignment, the patients would be funneled *back* to Larkin: a perpetual-motion Medicare-fraud machine that would end up billing over $1 billion to Medicare, fueled by thousands of bundles of cash in grocery bags, weekend trips to Las Vegas, and doctors with "loose pens."

Esformes was obsessive and demanding. He was a screamer. Gaby Delgado served as his driver and assistant. Esformes would call Gaby at 5 a.m. to give him his daily marching orders. He carried two phones minimum at all times, and would call his father from the car, giving him the daily census counts at every one of their facilities. In the end, as the Strike Force closed in on him, the younger Esformes grew paranoid. He had Gaby Delgado strip naked to meet with him in his pool, and started giving lectures on the merits of the "empty chair defense."

> **Gaby Delgado:** The first time I heard the term was from Phil. He told me, "Gaby, you could use something called the empty chair." And I said, "What's that, Phil? I don't know what that is." He said, "That means with your brother gone, you know, you could say whatever you want or anything. He's not, you know, going to be there. So that's the empty chair."
>
> **Q:** Did the defendant suggest any places that your brother should go?
>
> **A:** And he would also — he said, you got to redo your face, plastic surgery and everything. But one of the places that he said was, he goes, you could leave to Israel. And my

brother, like, you know, flipped out on him, like Israel, you know you are going to have me whacked over there when I get to Israel. [Philip] had ties there...

As I said, it would make a great movie. The handsome villain, charging around Miami Beach in his Ferrari, moving from girlfriend to girlfriend, barking orders at 5 a.m., trying to keep his perpetual-motion machine going. But then again, maybe not, because the story makes sense only in Miami.

Even the trial itself — the point in the story where order and reason are supposed to take over — quickly fell into an abyss of Miami-ness. The prosecution and the defense got into a heated side battle over attorney-client privilege, sprouting a sub-case, which somehow wound its way up to the Supreme Court. Kim Kardashian tweeted about the whole mess. (Of course she did.) And Morris Esformes wound up being thrown out of the trial for shouting things from the public gallery like "He's a liar!" while his son sat in the dock, twisted into a thousand knots.

Through his trial, Philip Esformes insisted that he was innocent. He refused to consider a plea bargain, which might have spared him jail. He didn't say a word to defend himself until the sentencing hearing. He just sat there, while Willy and Gaby Delgado dug a grave for him.

A: Philip had always told us that he had an ace up his sleeve...and he told me one day that he had connections to make things go away. Which he did, by the way. We saw things go away...

Q: Let me stop you right there. So what did he mean — or what did you understand him to mean by *he had aces up his sleeve*...?

A: Well, he said he had some government connections. There was a guy, Jeremy, [who] was connected to the government. I found out — my brother told me he gave a huge donation to a presidential campaign. So he was always throwing it around.

Willy Delgado said that under oath in federal court in February 2019. In December 2020, Philip Esformes had his sentence commuted by Donald Trump.*

And where did Donald Trump move after leaving the White House? South Florida. Of course.

---

* In a final Miami twist, after Esformes was granted clemency by Trump, the prosecution took the unusual step of trying to *re*try him on a variation of the charges they used initially. This time around, Esformes pleaded guilty to avoid a second trial. Under the agreement, he was spared jail time in exchange for a multimillion-dollar fine.

CHAPTER THREE

Poplar Grove

"THE PARENTS ARE OUTTA THEIR F—ING MIND."

1.

One sunny fall day, a real-estate agent named Richard took me around his hometown.

Richard was tall and friendly. As we drove down the winding streets, he would wave at people walking by, or point to a house and tell me who bought it, how many kids they have, and what they do for a living. He had grown up in the area and seemed to know everybody. What did his town have? Everything you'd want, he said: "A feeling of safety and security. A feeling of good neighbors. A feeling of — *I can count on others around me.*"

The downtown had a pleasing, 1950s feel. There were churches everywhere, in respectable red brick. We drove past the community center and the town library, then up into one of the town's many charming neighborhoods.

"We are on the water here." Richard pointed through the trees at a beautiful bay. "So, waterfront is the premium real estate and, and then, and I'll show you, it goes waterfront and then water-privileged neighborhoods."

The streets were narrow and lined with tall oaks. They followed a series of gently sloping hills. The houses were close together, giving the streets an intimate feel.

You are going to know your neighbors here. Somebody that comes here calls me and says, "Hey, I want a waterfront with three or four acres. I want privacy. I don't want to see my neighbors." I'm like, it's just, that's just not what we have to offer. It's like calling a BMW dealership and saying you want a minivan.

The town has a massive park, with dozens of soccer fields and baseball diamonds and tennis courts. It has jogging trails, a petting zoo, a family-friendly golf club, and little beaches with places for boats and kayaks. A generation ago, it was a rather ordinary bedroom community for the surrounding cities. But in recent years it has become desirable. Prices have soared.

"Working-class affluent. That's my client," Richard went on, relishing the oxymoron. "People that have jobs and make a lot of money. So, doctors, lawyers, professional people who are not blue blood." Poplar Grove, he said, wasn't "like fourth generation, you know, sold a company and made $200 million and can't even figure out what to do with their day. We're not Palm Beach.... Everyone here goes to work."

And everyone had a family. "100 percent" of the people Richard sold houses to, who were moving to the community for the first time, had kids. This was a *family* town.

"He's IT, works from home," Richard said, remembering a house he'd sold just that week. "She's a music teacher at a high school. The deplorable [city] public-school system drove him out and they're seeking a safe area where they can raise a family and send their kids to public school. Purchase price: $750,000."

Did the sellers leave the community? No. They stayed. They just wanted a bigger house nearby. Why would they leave the perfect community?

There's no attached housing here. It's all single-family homes. And I don't know the number, but I guess well over 90 percent of homeowners reside in their home. So we don't have condos. We don't have rentals. We don't have lower-end dwellings that attract any type of diversity. So, it has become a very homogeneous place to live, which is probably why there's a "shared value system" of good grades, good sports, go to the best college you possibly can. This very sort of…

He paused, searching for the nicest way to put it, because despite his enormous affection for his town, something about it clearly made him a little uneasy… "*collegial* feeling."

2.

I'm not going to tell you the name of Richard's town. You can guess, but you'll almost certainly be wrong. And Richard's name, by the way, isn't Richard. Neither of those facts matters. The two researchers who investigated what has been happening in the town call it "Poplar Grove," which is as good a name as any. "I hadn't heard of the community at all," says one of them, the sociologist Seth Abrutyn. "It was not on my radar."

It wouldn't be. Poplar Grove is not the kind of place that makes headlines. If you drove by on the highway, you wouldn't stop — which is the way the people of Poplar Grove want it. But you almost certainly know of a town like Poplar Grove. It is a perfect example of a particularly American species of tight-knit, affluent community.

"It just reminded me of the myth of small-town America, where everything is focused on the school and sporting events at the school," Abrutyn said. "A lot of the youth and the adults that we talked to would tell us how they knew all their neighbors and they could go to anybody. I mean, it really kind of just sounded idyllic....It seemed like a great place to raise kids."

Abrutyn studied Poplar Grove with his colleague, Anna Mueller. When they first went there, they were both assistant professors of sociology at the University of Memphis, just starting their careers. They heard about the town by accident. Mueller got into a discussion with someone on Facebook. "After talking with me, she was like, *Can you talk to my mom?*" Mueller said. "So then I had a conversation with her mom."

The mother lived in the town that Mueller and Abrutyn would come to call Poplar Grove. Mueller was so taken aback by the conversation that she got on a plane and went there as fast as she could. Then she went back, this time with Abrutyn, and the two of them returned again and again as they became more and more caught up in the drama unfolding there.

"I mean, it's just beautiful," Mueller said. "Like a scenic community that has a really, really strong sense of itself. People are really proud to be from Poplar Grove." The high school is one of the best in the state. Name the sport, they've won championships. "The theater productions that the kids put on were just spectacular," Mueller said.

A few miles from Poplar Grove is a town that Mueller and Abrutyn call Annesdale. Annesdale is beautiful as well. But there are lots of apartment buildings. The houses are cheaper, and the Annesdale high school isn't top-ranked like Poplar Grove's is. "I wasn't going to send my kid there," one parent told Mueller and Abrutyn. "There wasn't anything wrong with it, but Poplar Grove...is *Poplar Grove.*" If your kids grew up in Poplar Grove, there was little chance they would wander off the path that every upper-middle-class parent wants for their children: to be active, and popular, and work hard at school, and make the kinds of choices that lead to a better life — and then, of course, come home to Poplar Grove. Mueller and Abrutyn would eventually write a book on their time in Poplar Grove called *Life Under Pressure,* a riveting and disturbing work of scholarship, in which they write:

> The clarity and consistency with which Poplar Grovians could name their shared values was sometimes uncanny. "We" was a constant refrain. "When we think of Poplar Grove," Elizabeth, the mother of a teen, shared, "We think of achievement, we speak of scholastic achievement, and we speak of sports achievement."

Here's a teenager named Shannon:

> Our neighborhood is very intimate....Every time I walk down the street, I say hi to everybody I know, even the adults, just 'cause I've known them my entire life. It's a big network of support...

77

It had always been that way. A young woman named Isabel told Mueller and Abrutyn:

> If I got hurt, I knew I could go to any street…and get what I needed. It didn't have to be my parents. I could just walk in [to any house], crying with a busted knee, and they would help.…I love that sense of community that we feel.

We have, so far, explored the idea that social epidemics are not wild and out of control. They attach themselves to places. And the saga of Philip Esformes and Miami tells us that the power of places comes from the stories that communities tell themselves. In this chapter, I want to take those two ideas and add a third question: If epidemics are influenced by the overstories created by the inhabitants of a community, then in what sense are communities *responsible* for the fevers and contagions that plague them?

Puzzle number three.

3.

A generation before the crisis in Poplar Grove, there was another, strangely analogous crisis in the world of zoos. It is asking too much to say that the zoo crisis should have served as a warning to the parents of Poplar Grove, because the two worlds are impossibly distant. It was only in retrospect that the parallels became clear.

This crisis began in the 1970s. Zookeepers around the world began to invest more and more resources in breeding their animal populations in captivity. The logic was clear. Why go to all the trouble of capturing animals in the wild? The growing conservation movement also favored breeding programs. The new strategy was a big success — with one big outlier: the cheetah.

"They seldom had offspring that survived, and many of them when put together couldn't breed," remembers the geneticist Stephen O'Brien, who was then working at the National Cancer Institute.

It didn't make sense. The cheetah seemed a perfect example of evolutionary fitness: a massive nuclear reactor for a heart, the legs of a greyhound, a skull shaped like a professional cyclist's aerodynamic helmet, and semi-retractable claws that, as O'Brien puts it, "grip the earth like football cleats as they race after their prey at sixty miles per hour."

"It's the fastest animal on earth," O'Brien said. "The second-fastest animal on earth is the American pronghorn. And the reason that it's the second-fastest is that it was running from the cheetahs."

The zookeepers wondered if they were doing something wrong, or whether there was something about the make-up of the cheetah that they didn't understand. They came up with theories and tried experiments — all to no avail. In the end, they shrugged and said that the animals must be "skittish."

Things came to a head at a meeting in 1980 in Front Royal, Virginia. Zoo directors from around the world were there, among them the head of a big wildlife-conservation program in South Africa.

"And he says, 'Do you have anybody that knows what they're doing scientifically?'" O'Brien remembers. " '[To] basically explain to us why our breeding program of cheetahs in South Africa has something like 15 percent success while the rest of these animals — elephants and horses and giraffes — they breed like rats?'"

Two scientists raised their hands — both colleagues of O'Brien's. They flew to South Africa, to a big wildlife sanctuary near Pretoria. They took blood and sperm samples from dozens of cheetahs. What they found astonished them. The sperm counts of the cheetahs were low. And the spermatozoa themselves were badly malformed. That was clearly why the animals had such trouble breeding. It wasn't that they were "skittish."

But why? O'Brien's laboratory then began testing the blood samples that had been sent to them. They had done similar studies in the past on birds, humans, horses, and domestic cats, and in all those cases the animals showed a healthy degree of genetic diversity: In most species, around 30 percent of sampled genes will show some degree of variation. The cheetah's genes looked nothing like that. *They were all the same.* "I never saw a species that was so genetically uniform," O'Brien said.

O'Brien's findings were greeted with skepticism by his colleagues. So he and his team kept going.

"I went down to Children's Hospital in Washington and I learned how to do skin grafts at a burn unit," he said. "They taught me how to keep it sterile and how to take the...slices and how to suture it up and everything. And then we did [skin grafts on] about eight cheetahs in South Africa, and then we did another six or eight in Oregon."

Winston, Oregon, was home to the Wildlife Safari, the largest collection of cheetahs in the United States at the time.

The idea was simple. If you graft a piece of skin from one animal onto another, the recipient's body will reject it. It will recognize the genes of the donor as foreign. "It would blacken and slough off in two weeks," O'Brien said. But if you take a patch of skin from, say, one identical twin and graft it onto another, it will work. The donor's immune system thinks the skin is its own. This was the ultimate test of his hypothesis.

The grafts were small — one inch by one inch, sewn onto the side of the animal's chest, protected by an elastic bandage wrapped around the cat's body. First, the team gave some of the cheetahs a skin graft from a domestic cat, just to make sure the animals *had* an immune system. Sure enough, the cheetahs rejected the cat graft: It got inflamed, then necrotic. Their bodies knew what *different* was — and a domestic cat was different. Then the team grafted skin from other chee-tahs. What happened? Nothing! They were accepted, O'Brien said, "as if they were identical twins. The only place you see that is in inbred mice that have been brother-sister mated for twenty generations. And that convinced me."

O'Brien realized that the world's cheetah population must have at some point been devastated. His best guess was that it happened during the great mammal die-off 12,000 years ago — when saber-toothed cats, mastodons, mammoths, giant ground sloths, and over thirty other species were wiped out by an ice age. Somehow the cheetah survived. But just barely.

"The numbers that fit all the data are less than one hundred, maybe less than fifty," O'Brien said. It's possible, in fact, that the cheetah population was reduced to a *single* pregnant female. And the only way for those lonely few cheetahs to survive was to overcome the inhibition that most mammals have against incest: Sisters had to mate with brothers, first cousins with first cousins. The species eventually rebounded, but only through the endless replication of the same narrow set of genes. The cheetah was still magnificent. But now every cheetah represented the exact same kind of magnificence.

O'Brien wrote a memoir of his career as a geneticist called *Tears of the Cheetah,* a reference to the distinctive markings on the cheetah's face that make it look as if it's crying:

> Imagine a young pregnant female somewhere in southern Europe who climbed into a warm cave to slumber through a harsh winter. When she and her cubs crept out in the springtime, they met a different world, one in which the cheetahs and the great predators of the region were gone, victims of a global holocaust....My reverie conjures a vision of the tears on that cheetah-mom that would render an indelible tear-stripe below the eyes of every cheetah from that moment onward.

The word used by biologists to describe an environment where individual differences have been sanded down and every organism follows the same path of development is *monoculture.*

Monocultures are rare; the default state for most natural systems is diversity. A monoculture typically emerges only when something happens, deliberate or otherwise, to upset the natural order — for instance, when a group of affluent parents comes together to create a community that perfectly reflects their commitment to achievement and excellence. The parents of Poplar Grove wanted a monoculture, at least until it dawned on them that a monoculture, even an apparently perfect one, comes with a cost.

Epidemics *love* monocultures.

4.

One of the first things that struck Abrutyn and Mueller was how all the students at Poplar Grove High School sounded the same. Listen to Natalie, a girl they interviewed:

Like, I had 4 Bs on my report card, and I was *mortified*. And I did not want to tell my friends about my grades, because everyone is a straight-A student.

Poplar Grove was so small and insular that it seemed like there was only one kind of conversation. The gossip in the hallways was all about *achievement*. Another student, Samantha, told them:

"Oh, it's classroom registration time — how many APs are you taking next semester? Oh, it's sports transition time — what team are you joining next semester? Oh, your team went to the championships — did you place first? What position did you play?"....[T]hose are all very normal conversations.

Abrutyn and Mueller were perfectly familiar with high-pressure upper-middle-class culture. They are college professors. People like them practically invented high-pressure upper-middle-class culture. But in their experience, there was usually a gap between what the parents wanted for their kids, and what the kids — or at least some of the kids — wanted for themselves. In Poplar Grove, there was no gap. Abrutyn said:

There's a very, very clear ideal type of kid and there aren't very many alternatives for kids to be different....And the pressure was coming from everywhere. It was coming from the school, which wanted to keep its high ranking. It was coming from parents, who were concerned that their kid wouldn't get into the school that they wanted them to go to. And it was coming from the kids, who, you know, needed to take four or five AP classes all the time.*

This idea — that there aren't many alternatives for kids to be different — is strange because, of course, high school has traditionally been a place where young people discover all the ways they *can* be different. Take a look at the following chart. It's the results of a survey done at a large Midwestern high school in 1990. (If you went to high school in that era, the data will be deeply familiar.) Several hundred students were asked to list the different "crowds" that made up their school, and to describe the personality of each crowd. The numbers represent the percentage of each group that fit the descriptions in the far-left column.

If you went to school before the 1990s, or after it, the names of the various groups might be different, but the pattern would be the same. This is what a typical high school looks like. There are groups of kids who really like school and groups who hate school. There are groups who are loud and disruptive, and groups who are studious and quiet. And that diversity is really

---

* There is a lot of this kind of thing in *Life Under Pressure*. One mother says: [They're] little shrunken adults. They need to be in all AP classes and you better be doing sports…and you need to have it all figured out so that you can get into the right college and you better get into the right college so that you'll get the right job, and I often hear friends say, "Oh, my kids are in this sport, we're scheduled to the [hilt], we don't have dinner until nine or ten, and we're always eating out." Or, "My kids are up until 1 or 2 o'clock doing homework."

Percentage of students in high school social groups who fit specific descriptions							
Dress and Grooming	Jock	Druggie	Nobody	Normal	Popular	Tough	Misc.
Neat and clean	16	7	8	32	10	3	21
Casual, athletic	52	24	8	51	21	18	29
Stylish	31	6	1	16	59	4	15
Tough-messy	1	57	30	1	8	66	18
Poor taste	0	5	51	1	1	5	11
Sociability							
Disruptive	2	68	5	1	13	75	1
Not with it	2	4	78	16	6	4	25
Friendly	50	13	6	74	25	9	43
Cliquish	45	11	8	7	54	10	17
Academic Attitude							
Enjoy, try hard	49	1	14	41	50	2	27
Positive	45	10	30	53	31	10	35
Take it or leave it	4	22	38	5	9	23	22
Hate school	0	65	14	1	9	62	13
Extracurricular Participation							
High	53	1	3	33	49	1	23
Moderate	45	10	21	61	34	11	39
Low	1	89	76	6	16	88	38

useful: Teenagers are trying to figure out who they are, and having a school with a wide range of crowds gives them the best possible chance to find peers with whom they feel comfortable. (There is some fascinating research, for example, to show that kids who join crowds like the Goths or Punks — where they dress and groom themselves in a startling, even off-putting manner — are shy. They dress in a way that makes others scared to talk to them because they are scared to talk to others. The Goth look is a suit of armor.)

One of the authors of the high-school survey, Bradford Brown, has a chart he uses to socially "locate" the key groups in the school he studied, which I include below only because it is such a simple (and hilarious) depiction of normal high-school life.

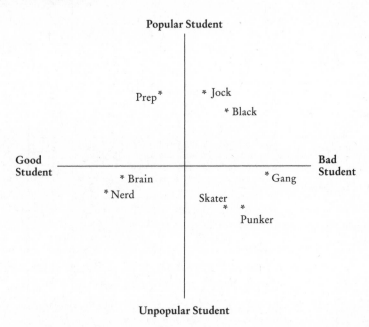

Remember this from high school?

Poplar Grove had crowds as well, of course. But Mueller and Abrutyn's point was that there was no space between the crowds. If you were to do a version of that chart for Poplar Grove, it would look like this:

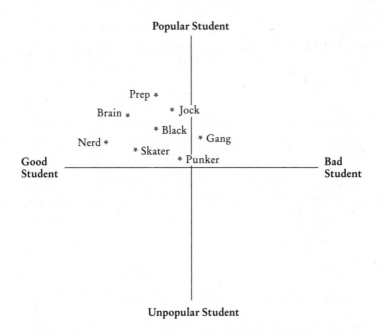

If you're a Skater, you have to be a high-achieving Skater. If you're a Nerd, you have to be a socially popular Nerd. If you're a Punk, you have to be the Punk who gets into your first choice of college.

In one of the most fascinating parts of their research, Abrutyn and Mueller tried to find kids who had rejected Poplar Grove's norms. It wasn't easy. Here is one of their discoveries, Scott:

> I know that high school is important and I do get those feelings, like "Oh, if I don't pass this test then I'm going to wind up homeless."...I don't like that I have to go to that mindset. I wish I could change it. I can't.

Abrutyn and Mueller say that Scott identifies himself as a rebel. But even then he can't shake off the very Poplar Grovian idea that if he fails a test, he'll end up homeless. Abrutyn and Mueller write:

> At times, he was confident in his moral conscience and sense that something was amiss in Poplar Grove, but, at other times, he presented more timidly, as a youth uncertain whether his read on the situation was right. What if? What if the culture in Poplar Grove was not local and limited, but the way the whole world worked? Ultimately, this understandable uncertainty undermined Scott's protective rejection of the culture and affirmation of his own self-worth.

And then there is Molly, another self-described rebel:

> Kind, compassionate, and somewhat quiet and serious, Molly was as well-versed in the intricacies of being an "ideal kid" as any Poplar Grove teen. Heck, she embodied many of those ideals. She told us academics were "very important" and she was determined to work hard and get good grades. She played high school sports (though she wasn't on the coveted lacrosse team) and became close with girls in the popular crowd. After graduation, she headed off to a great university.

This is what rebellion looks like in a monoculture: a deviation from the general path so slight that you would need an MRI to detect it. That lack of "crowd diversity" is what allowed Poplar Grove to score so highly in the state high-school rankings. It's also what reassured parents. Your child might be an outsider, but at least they will be a high-achieving outsider.*

But what you give up in a world of uniformity is resilience. If something went awry in one of the many subcultures that made up the high school described in the two charts, the infection would have difficulty spreading to any other subculture. The groups in the school are too far apart: Each has its own set of cultural antibodies that make it hard for a contagious agent to move, unmolested, through the population of the entire school.

A monoculture, on the other hand, offers no internal defenses against an outside threat. Once the infection is inside the walls, there is nothing to stop it.

Richard, the real-estate agent who knew Poplar Grove as well as anyone, understood this. He chose to live and send his daughters to school in neighboring Annesdale, the town that so many Poplar Grovians disdained. "It was a parenting decision," he said.

---

* I went to a small-town public school in southwestern Ontario, Canada. Only about 20 percent of the students went on to a four-year university. Most of those who continued their education after high school attended the local community college. There were hockey players who dreamed of playing professionally, whose entire world was wrapped up in the local youth leagues. There was a basketball team that, in my vague memory, lost a lot of games, and then a group of people who stood huddled in a little courtyard smoking cigarettes, even in the dead of winter, and seemed to have no interest in doing much of anything. The most prominent club in the school yearbook the year I graduated was the "Apathetic Procrastinators," a group of five of the more popular boys who photographed themselves lying around in various stages of extreme ennui: "The Apathetic Procrastinators experienced a very successful year. Activities included none…" (Somehow I suspect there was no equivalent student group at Poplar Grove.) Since the late 1970s, Poplar Grove's sports teams have won a total of 121 state championships. The equivalent number at my high school, when I was there, was three. To me, Poplar Grove sounds terrifying.

I felt like it was more "real world." And there wasn't as much pressure. [Poplar Grove] is notorious for this high pressure to be extraordinary. Be the best in the band. Be the best basketball player.... You've got to go to MIT. You've got, you know, I mean, this real intensity around being the best. That's part of their reputation. My mom is a middle-school teacher [in Poplar Grove] and would talk about parents coming in and she'd given the kid a B and they were apoplectic that this is going to ruin their Ivy League chances.

He talked about the same thing that Abrutyn and Mueller had settled on: the pressure.

It's palpable, like you can feel it. And we were not willing to put our children in that. I hear it. I mean, when I go out on listing appointments: "Why are you moving?" "It's just a little bit too much pressure. My kid's not fitting in. It's this social grinder." I mean, it's well-known. You could ask anyone.

Richard said he knew the principal of Poplar Grove High School. I asked him what the principal thought of the pressure. "She says, 'The parents are outta their f—ing mind.'"

5.

In 1982, a few months before Stephen O'Brien began conducting his skin-graft experiments at the Wildlife Safari in Oregon, the Safari decided to add to its cheetah collection.

"I had driven down to Sacramento and picked up a couple

of cheetahs from the Sacramento Zoo," Melody Roelke-Parker remembers. Roelke-Parker was the veterinarian who took care of the Wildlife Safari's cheetahs. "Their names were Toma and Sabu. They seemed healthy enough. There was nothing overtly wrong with them. We brought them back and, probably within a week, they were added to our main cheetah-breeding colony."

Roelke-Parker loved cheetahs. She actually raised two cheetah cubs herself, after their mother abandoned them.

> So I had two cheetahs in my house, which was wonderful because they purr and they snuggle and they push you out of bed. It's not anything you'd think of looking at these guys, but living with them was a dream. I was their family.... I would ride back and forth, back and forth to work. They would sit in the seat and they would sit really tall and snuggle, you know, and their heads are tall and it was really fun to watch people on the freeway kind of panicking or freaking out.

The cheetah colony at the Wildlife Safari was like her extended family, which was why what happened to one of the new cheetahs from Sacramento was so distressing.

"Two months later, one of them, the male, collapsed. And we went, 'What in the hell is this?' And so we rushed him up to our clinic and did a big workup." The diagnosis was renal failure. The cheetah died.

> Okay, so that was kind of bizarre because he seemed pretty healthy, but obviously there's a lot of stress when animals are moved to a new social structure, new feeding

regime, what have you. So I thought it was kind of a one-off.

But then Roelke-Parker noticed that other cheetahs in their colony were getting sick.

"[They] started having all kinds of nonspecific issues with diarrhea and weird gum disease. Like if they hiss at you, you'd see the gums were all irritated and bleeding." The cats became lethargic. "They started to lose enormous amounts of weight....We were culturing mouths and finding weird bacteria, having to put them on erythromycin to try to treat the mouth infection. But I didn't know what it was. I didn't have a clue."

One cheetah got so sick that Roelke-Parker had to euthanize him. She did an autopsy.

When I opened the belly and I found these yellow, viscous, stringy...classic symptoms of this disease called Feline Infectious Peritonitis, which was well-known in the domestic cat, but no one had ever reported it in cheetahs.

FIP, as it is known, is a coronavirus — a cousin of the COVID strain that would decades later do so much damage in humans. It's rarely fatal in domestic cats. But for the cheetahs, it was devastating. Roelke-Parker regularly did blood work on all the cheetahs at the Safari, and she went back and started checking the samples for antibodies to FIP. Before Toma and Sabu arrived, none of her cheetahs showed any signs of FIP. But after they arrived, virtually everyone did. The two California cats had started a mini-epidemic.

It took about eight months post-infection when animals started dying, and then they just started, you know, kicking off, and it was, it...was really horrible. Eighty percent of the cats under sixteen months [old] died.

It was a bloodbath. The animals would fall sick. But for some reason they could not get rid of the virus.

Their immune system is trying and trying and trying to thwart it by creating antibodies and their antibody levels end up just rising to super-high level so that the blood proteins are ridiculous. And you get this immunological crisis.

They were walking skeletons. The disease manifestation in domestic cats — say, [FIP] has ten symptoms, but in total any one cat might only present with a few of them. The cheetahs had all of them. They had the diarrhea, the mouth lesions, the wasting...

She tried everything: stomach tubing, immune boosters, fluids. Nothing worked. "We didn't save any of the ones... Once the disease presents — it's over. It's done."

What Roelke-Parker was seeing was the inevitable result of what Stephen O'Brien had discovered. The cheetahs were all the same. That lone pregnant female back at the end of the Pleistocene who emerged from her cave to find herself all alone happened — by sheer genetic chance — to be a cheetah susceptible to feline coronavirus. And because every cheetah descended from her, now every one of the animals was susceptible. In the centuries when cheetahs roamed free, that fact hadn't mattered much. They are solitary animals: Each cheetah occupies a vast area, as far as possible from their peers. An epidemic can't wipe out an entire cheetah population in the wild, because cheetahs practice the animal equivalent of social distancing. But human beings changed that. They brought together large numbers of cheetahs to live cheek by jowl in enclosed spaces. The cheetah epidemic was the zookeepers' fault. "If one animal gets sick, they're all going to get sick," Roelke-Parker said. "And that's exactly what happened."

Then she realized she was seeing only the tip of the iceberg.

"I discovered that there had been an outbreak in Canada somewhere, and that the zoo completely put a lid on it," she said. "They didn't tell anybody, nobody knew it existed, but they wiped out all their cheetahs. The same thing happened in a zoo in Ireland. Nobody was talking about this at all."

She and O'Brien went to a zoo meeting in Florida, and she decided to speak up. She gave a talk about the epidemic going on back at her zoo in Oregon. Afterward, a veterinarian from a zoo in California came up to Roelke-Parker and said, "My boss is in Oregon right now picking up a cheetah."

And I went, "Oh my God." They had not been told anything. The director had told them nothing about this disease outbreak, and I said, "Well, you do not want this. *You do not want it.*" So [she] immediately called her director and said, "You are not bringing home a cheetah from Wildlife Safari." And suffice to say, when I got home, I was told I needed to find another job. Because I had gone public with this and discussed it — and worse, I had stopped a sale by my actions.

My staff quit. They were just outraged by how I was being treated. It was bad.

6.

In Poplar Grove, the epidemic started when a young woman named Alice jumped off a bridge. It was during the day, and there were people around, so Alice survived. She was taken to the hospital.

"By all accounts, Alice was the ideal Poplar Grove teen: bright, outgoing, achievement-driven, and pretty, in others' estimation," Mueller and Abrutyn write.

Her suicide attempt was shocking, and like all shocking events in tight-knit communities, it was much discussed. Why would a girl who seemed to have it all, who showed few signs of struggle, try to end her life?

Six months later, a classmate and teammate of Alice's, a girl named Zoe, jumped from the same bridge. She did not survive. Four months later, Zoe and Alice's classmate Steven ended his life with a gun. The community now had three attempts and two deaths. Seven years passed. It was possible to think it had all been a blip. But then came two more suicides — both boys — within a space of three weeks. Then a "popular" girl named Kate, who had been close to those two boys, jumped off the same bridge as Alice and Zoe. It's perhaps best to let Mueller and Abrutyn describe what happened next:

> Less than a year after Kate's death, another larger cluster emerged: Charlotte and three of her close male friends died by suicide in a six-week period. From that point on, at least one Poplar Grove youth or young adult died by suicide every year. Some years, the community weathered multiple suicide deaths. Numerous kids attempted suicide. In the decade between 2005 and 2016, Poplar Grove High School, a school of just about 2,000 students, lost four adolescent girls to suicide (five if we count a girl who had recently transferred out of PGHS), two middle school students, and at least twelve recent graduates.

Statistically, a "normal" suicide rate at a school of 2,000 students would be one or two deaths every ten years. Poplar Grove was miles beyond that. Kids in middle school would hear about the suicides going on at the high school. Then they would get to the high school and live through another round. People moved to Poplar Grove because they thought it was safe — a refuge from the kind of violence and uncertainty that hangs over so many American communities. That's why the suicide epidemic was so surprising. How could this have happened here? But it shouldn't be surprising. Poplar Grove was a monoculture — a long, straight highway with no off-ramp.

When the first death came, it was an anomaly. When it happened again, it became a concern. But when it happened again and again and again, it became — in the most devastating way possible — normalized.

"In at least three of the four clusters, there was a high-status student that was very visible, who very much embodied the ideal of Poplar Grove's youth," Abrutyn said. "You know, like a three[-season] sports star, probably a captain in one of those sports, you know, a 4.0 GPA, bubbly persona. A lot of the youth who had died by suicide seemed like they were perfect, and then were just gone. So it was sort of like, 'Well, if they can't survive in this context, how can I?'"

7.

In 1983, Melody Roelke-Parker left Oregon to take up the cause of the Florida panther. Barely any panthers were left in Florida, and the state wanted to find a way to rebuild the population. She joined a panther-hunting team. They used foxhounds to track the cats through the swampland of south Florida and chase them up trees, and then they shot them with a tranquilizer gun.

"The first year I think we ended up capturing four cats," Roelke-Parker remembers.

It was really hard. What I didn't understand was the stress of trying to capture these panthers was just through the roof because they were so precious. And they're forty feet up a tree, and you have to evaluate their age, their health status, their physical condition.

One of the team would climb up the tree, where the cat was nervously lurking.

I had to figure out how much drug to give this cat so she wouldn't fall out of the tree, but she [had to be] groggy enough that she wouldn't kill the climber.

The goal was to throw a net over the panther and lower it slowly to the ground, then give the animal a full physical, take blood and skin samples, put an electronic collar on it, and release it back into the wild. "What became obvious really early on is, these animals were ancient," Roelke-Parker said. "There were no young. There were no cubs. The females were on the verge of reproductive senescence. We would collect sperm from males: Ninety-five percent of their spermatozoa was malformed."

The panther, the team soon realized, had gone through not one bottleneck, like the cheetah, but multiple bottlenecks. First was the great mammal die-off at the end of the Pleistocene Era. Then, in the twentieth century, South American panthers trying to move north were blocked by territorial panthers as they tried to cross the narrow Panamanian isthmus. There were no longer any newcomers adding to the Florida gene pool. It got worse. The panthers' principal prey had once been deer, but Florida's deer population was decimated by hunters. Panthers were reduced to eating armadillos. They were malnourished. Those few who remained were forced to inbreed, with the result that one genetic defect after another began to accumulate. The panther had no genetic diversity whatsoever.

"There was one capture where kittens were brought in," Roelke-Parker remembers.

When I went to evaluate them, like a month after they were captured, they knock out this male. I go to palpate his scrotum. He has no testicles, and I just start raving that we've lost it. We have males with no testicles and we had heart defects, heart murmurs now showing up all over the place. Biologically, we've just sort of hit the wall. These cats are hanging on by the skin of their teeth. It was the extinction happening in front of my eyes.

In 1992, everyone involved in the fight to save the Florida panther gathered at an old plantation house on the Georgia border. Roelke-Parker and O'Brien were there, along with thirty others. O'Brien remembers it as an intense few days of listening, posturing, criticizing, struggling, and compromising. The faction led by O'Brien argued for bringing in fresh blood. The Texas cougar was a close cousin of the panther, with twenty times the genetic diversity. Why not bring cougars to Florida?

The private breeders were apoplectic. They said, *Let's just mate wild panthers with the animals we have in captivity.* The idea that there might be something intrinsically wrong with the Florida panther as it was seemed ridiculous to them. The Florida panther was the state mascot!*

"We feel we have pure panthers," one of the private breeders said. "Cross-breeding Texas cougars and Florida panthers is like cross-breeding bald eagles and golden eagles. Eventually, you have nothing."†

---

* As it turns out, the panthers being bred privately were far from "pure." Roelke-Parker did a DNA analysis of some of the animals in captivity. They were mutts — mixes of panthers from all over.

† Meanwhile, the state's leading conservation advocate, Marjory Stoneman Douglas, denounced the panther-tracking project that Roelke-Parker was a part of as "nuts." Why were they tracking panthers with dogs, chasing them up trees, shooting them with tranquilizers, and putting tracking collars on them? "I think that anybody who knows about panthers, knows that a panther with a collar on it is not the same thing as a panther without a collar on

In the end, the meeting reached an agreement. Eight female cougars would be shipped in from Texas and let loose in the Big Cypress Swamp. Texas met Florida, and the transformation began. The two groups began to interbreed. They grew stronger. On one memorable occasion, the offspring of a Texas mother and a Florida father moved into an area occupied by only one other panther. "So guess what?" Roelke-Parker said. "He was outrageously fertile. We know of at least, like, 108 kittens that were sired by him. He became known as Don Juan because he was just so prolific."

"The guy who trained the dogs was named Roy McBride," O'Brien said. "He would always say, 'You know, Steve, I think this genetics is a bunch of horseshit,' but he says, 'I'll do it because they're telling me to do it.' But then when he saw the offspring of the restoration program, what he noticed was that the panthers that were intercrosses or hybrids were bigger. They were stronger. He said they looked like Arnold Schwarzenegger compared to the Florida panthers before."

The panther was saved. Where once the Florida-panther population had numbered in the dozens, now it numbers more than one hundred. But in order to be saved, it had to become something else — a hybrid of Texas and Florida. The best solution to a monoculture epidemic is to break up the monoculture.

Should Poplar Grove do the same thing? Of course it should. But how? The monoculture of Poplar Grove was the creation of the parents of Poplar Grove. They could have sent

---

it," she argued. "It's a wild animal, and it's a cat and a sensitive cat, and we believe that the collar is bad for it, and I don't see why it isn't." She said, "Just leave the animals be, and stay out of the Everglades. Everything will be fine." Of course, it wasn't fine: If you left the panther alone and kept it pure, it was doomed to extinction.

their children to school in Annesdale, as Richard the realtor did. They didn't want to. They wanted a school where every student was in perfect alignment. If the Poplar Grove monoculture were broken up — its students dispersed, the teachers redeployed — the new version of Poplar Grove High would almost certainly not measure up to the old version. The new school might not be nationally ranked. It might not offer as many AP courses. It might not win dozens of state athletic championships. The very thing that attracted the people of Poplar Grove to Poplar Grove would be gone.

Epidemics love monocultures. *But so do we.* Sometimes, in fact, we go out of our way to create them — even though in doing so we put our own children at risk.

In medicine there is a term for the kind of illness that is caused by the intervention of doctors: *iatrogenesis.* You treat someone with a drug, and the side effects turn out to be worse than the disease. You do a minor operation, and the patient dies of complications. Iatrogenic illness is well-intentioned. No one is *trying* to harm the patient. But a doctor has no right to use the passive voice and speak of the patient who *has been* harmed. Iatrogenic epidemics have a cause and a culprit. Poplar Grove was iatrogenesis.

In the time that Abrutyn and Mueller were in Poplar Grove, there were more suicides. Mueller said:

I'm not gonna lie, that was really hard. I still have strong feelings about, you know, about some of the kids that died during our fieldwork.

They believed they had figured out why the epidemic was happening, but they couldn't stop it.

It's just heartbreaking to see the pattern repeat itself.... You know, there's always sort of this irony. Whenever we go to schools, we see this where parents are [saying], you know, "Increasingly, mental health is important. We need to promote it, we need to take care of it. But whatever resources the school has, we want this for AP tests or more extracurriculars, or more...," you know what I mean?

The school continued to emphasize achievement above all else. Here is the principal's message — the first thing you see on the Poplar Grove High School website. The italics are mine.

Learning is our school's central mission and we at [Poplar Grove] believe that all students *can and will learn*. We have created an environment that provides *excellence in teaching and learning* so that all students will participate responsibly in our diverse and changing world. It is [our] mission...to provide a positive and *challenging environment* where *all students will achieve academic, social, emotional and physical success....* Together we achieve and maintain an atmosphere of respect, support, and *high expectations.*

The school's teachers, the principal says, are "talented and hardworking." They strive to create "challenging and relevant" curricula.

All of this reflects our belief that learning is a life-long process and [Poplar Grove] is a place where we *"Reach to Teach and Teach to Reach."*

By the way, I tricked you. That's not the principal's message from Poplar Grove High School. It's the principal's message from one of Poplar Grove's *elementary* schools. The monoculture starts early in Poplar Grove.

Mueller and Abrutyn, incidentally, have now moved on to Colorado, where they are working with a high school whose epidemic may be even worse.

Part Two

The Social Engineers

The Magic Third

"I WOULD SAY, ABSOLUTELY, THERE IS SOME TIPPING POINT IN MY EXPERIENCE."

1.

Palo Alto is the heart of Silicon Valley, home to Stanford University and Sand Hill Road, where many of the venture-capital firms that launched the computer age have their headquarters. There are parts of the city — and the surrounding towns of Menlo Park and Atherton — where the streets and homes are as beautiful as any place in America. To the east and north of the city, however, is the *other* Palo Alto. In parts, the neighborhoods look all but unchanged from the 1950s. And if you take a right off Embarcadero onto Greer, then continue past the Oregon Expressway and Amarillo Avenue, you will arrive at a little bit of forgotten history: Lawrence Lane. Or, as it was known during the brief years of its celebrity, the Lawrence Tract.

Lawrence Lane is a cul-de-sac. There are twenty-five lots in total along the lane and surrounding streets. Some of the original homes remain to this day: single-story two- or three-bedroom bungalows, roughly 1,000 to 1,500 square feet each, with carports and modest lawns — the kind of affordable housing that was built en masse in Northern California in the postwar years.

But from the beginning, Lawrence Lane was different from all the other bungalow subdivisions of that era. It had rules.

2.

In the 1950s, many major cities of the United States faced a problem. African Americans were moving out of the South in greater and greater numbers, trying to escape economic frustration and the heavy hand of Jim Crow. But time and again, in the supposedly liberal cities they were moving to, white people wanted nothing to do with them. In some cases, that meant the newcomers faced intimidation and violence. In other cases, it meant that the minute black families moved into a neighborhood, white families just moved out. The term everyone used was *white flight.*

Every city had its own story. In 1955, in the Germantown district of Philadelphia, a woman living on an all-white street bought a home in another neighborhood, thinking she could easily sell her Germantown home for over $8,000. She couldn't. The highest offer came from a black family. "Her choice, she said, was either to lose her friends or her money, and she was afraid it would have to be her friends," an account of the incident related. She signed the sales agreement, and the next day a local realtor found a crowd of her neighbors at his front door.

The realtor wrote down everything one of the women said.

"I don't know where we'll go, but we're going."
"Jack and I could stand it, but we're not going to expose our kids to it."

"It's not the best class of colored moving in, you know."

"It wouldn't be so bad, but the houses are too darn close together."

"We may not be able to escape forever, but we'll try for a while."

"Prices won't go back up; they'll keep going down."

The report concluded: "In less than twenty-four hours, their whole life had been changed radically because of an innocent purchase by a single nonwhite family."

In Detroit, the first black family moved to the all-white neighborhood of Russell Woods in 1955. Three years later, the neighborhood was 60 percent black. Ten years after that, it hit 90 percent black. In three years, almost two-thirds of the houses on every street changed hands and two-thirds of the white kids in the local public school were no longer there. Ashburton in Baltimore was a well-to-do white neighborhood; then, briefly, a mixed neighborhood; and then, all of a sudden, a black neighborhood. In the 1960s, 60,000 white people fled Atlanta, which at the time had a population of 300,000. That's 20 percent — gone. Then, in the 1970s, another 100,000 white people fled. For years Atlanta had given itself the self-satisfied slogan THE CITY TOO BUSY TO HATE. The joke became that it was THE CITY TOO BUSY MOVING TO HATE.

Exactly the same thing happened in parts of St. Louis and New York and Cleveland and Denver and Kansas City and nearly every other city, big and small, that had a sizable black population. When the US Civil Rights Commission traveled to Chicago to try to figure out what was happening, a community leader told them: "Let there be no mistake about it: No white Chicago community wants Negroes."*

Never in American history had there been this kind of sudden urban upheaval. Public officials were alarmed. Academics began to study the phenomenon: interviewing homeowners, keeping track of housing sales, making maps of shifts in population. And what they discovered was that every major city seemed to have the same pattern. "As the Negro population grows, the black belt tends to expand from the center block by block and neighborhood by neighborhood, sometimes radially and sometimes in concentric circles," the political scientist Morton Grodzins wrote in 1957, in one of the first of what would soon become an avalanche of scholarly analyses of white flight. "Once a neighborhood begins to swing from white to colored occupancy, the change is rarely arrested or reversed."

According to Grodzins, the changeover happened slowly at first, then gathered steam, and then — at a critical juncture — exploded. As he wrote, using a phrase that would thereafter enter the American vernacular:

This "tip point" varies from city to city and from neighborhood to neighborhood. But for the vast majority of white Americans, a tip point exists. Once it is exceeded, they will no longer stay among Negro neighbors.

A *tip point*. Grodzins said that he heard the phrase from realtors, who wanted to move white homeowners out of urban

---

* Then he continued: "In Chicago, *integrated* is usually a term used to describe the period of time that elapses between the appearance of the first Negro and the community's ultimate and total incorporation into the Negro ghetto."

neighborhoods: "Real estate operators, seeking the higher revenues that come with Negro overcrowding, talk freely among themselves about 'tipping a building' or 'tipping a neighborhood.'" For a time in the late 1950s and early 1960s, if you used that phrase, people knew exactly what you meant. (And I liked it so much I borrowed it as the title for my first book.) The *tipping point* was a threshold: the moment when something that had seemed immovable — that had been one way for generations — transformed overnight into something else.

Tipping points can be reached inadvertently. We can happen upon them by accident. Epidemics reach tipping points through their own relentless, contagious energy. But in the next few chapters I want to explore the ways in which tipping points can be *deliberately engineered*. People, it is clear, behave very differently in a group above some mysterious point of critical mass than they do in a group just a little below that point. So, what if you knew exactly where that magical point was? Or — better yet — what if you had a way to manipulate the size of a group so that it was either just below the tipping point or just above it? Miami and Poplar Grove are places that unintentionally opened the door to an epidemic. I'm talking here about taking things one step further: *intentionally* orchestrating the course of contagious behavior. I know that sounds dramatic. But the truth is that all kinds of people engage in this kind of social engineering — and they aren't always honest about what they are doing.

3.

The pioneer in thinking about the implications of tipping points was a sociologist named Rosabeth Moss Kanter. In the

1970s, Kanter began consulting for a big industrial firm head-quartered in New York City. The company had a sales force of 300 people, all men. But for the first time they had hired some women to join the sales teams, and to their surprise, the women weren't doing well. They wanted to understand why.

Kanter showed up with her notebook and began carefully interviewing the women. The problem, she slowly realized, wasn't one of ability. Nor was the problem that the company had some kind of dysfunctional organizational culture. The more she talked to people, the more she realized that the women simply had a problem with the firm's group proportions.

The company's sales force was spread across the country. A typical field office had ten to twelve salespeople, meaning that, with just around twenty women in the whole company, the typical sales team had ten men and one woman. And Kanter's conclusion was that it's really, really hard to be the lone woman in an office with ten men. The women told Kanter that even as they felt under scrutiny, because of their otherness they also didn't feel *seen*. They felt they were being caricatured by the men around them. They could only be Women with a capital *W* — representatives of every stereotype their male coworkers held about the other sex.

"They didn't have a peer group," Kanter remembers. "They were being made into symbols. They had to stand for their whole category rather than just be themselves." When you are part of a small minority, you're a token. And being a token isn't easy.

Kanter reported her findings in a now-famous essay with a misleadingly dull title: "Some Effects of Proportions on

Group Life: Skewed Sex Ratios and Responses to Token Women."* "No token in the study had to work hard to have her presence noticed," Kanter wrote:

> But she did have to work hard to have her achievement noticed. In the sales force, the women found that their technical abilities were likely to be eclipsed by their physical appearance, and thus an additional performance pressure was created.

What really mattered, Kanter realized, wasn't whether or not a group was integrated. It was *how much* it was integrated. "I thought that's really the issue," she says. "Are you alone or are there many like you?"

If the sales teams were all women, nobody would be questioning the performance of women as a category. Nor would it be an issue if the teams were balanced: half men, half women. But Kanter became convinced that there is something uniquely toxic about groups with "skewed proportions," featuring lots of one kind of person and very few of another kind.

Kanter was struck by how often men drew conclusions about women without taking this crucial question of skewed proportions into account. She pointed, for example, to a well-known study of juries, showing that men tend to play "initiating, task-oriented roles...whereas women tend to play reactive, socioemotional roles." The men dominated and

---

* If you have never read a work of sociology, Kanter's essay is a great place to start. It's brilliant.

made the decisions. The women hung back. But wait a minute, Kanter said. There were twice as many men as women on the juries studied. How do we know *that* wasn't the key factor?

"Perhaps," she wrote, "it was women's scarcity in skewed groups that pushed them into classical positions and men's numerical superiority that gave them an edge in task performance."

Kanter was also struck by an observation that had been made about kibbutzim in Israel. Many Israelis had tried to establish gender equality on the kibbutz, sharing responsibilities equally, but their efforts had often resulted in failure: The men ended up playing the dominant leadership roles. Once more, Kanter raised her hand in protest. "There were often *more than twice as many men as women* in a kibbutz. Again, relative numbers interfered with a fair test of what men or women can 'naturally' do."

Kanter's insight is the kind of thing that, once you hear it, changes forever the way you listen to people's stories. Let me give you an example. Once — for a totally unrelated project — I spent an afternoon interviewing a remarkable woman named Ursula Burns. (I could easily have made this entire chapter about her.) She grew up in the 1960s in a tenement on Manhattan's Lower East Side. Her mother was a Panamanian immigrant. Her father was absent. Burns and her two siblings were raised in a tiny apartment on the ninth floor of a decrepit building.

"Nine was tough because…most of the time we couldn't take the elevator," she told me. "The junkies were in there and they slept there. And so we were not allowed. My mother had rules."

Burns went to Cathedral High School in Midtown

Manhattan, an all-girls Catholic school. She'd walk there, halfway up the island, to save subway fare.

"My mother had to pay $23 a month for the family to go [to Cathedral]. The most money she ever made in her life was $4,400 in a year. It's amazing. And she just did it."

At Cathedral, Burns met students who would talk about the vacations their families had taken. She said:

Now, I'm a reasonable kid. I know about things in the world. But I had never met anyone who had gone on a vacation like they were going on vacation, where you take the family, you get in some vehicle, and go somewhere else.

Burns went to college, earned an engineering degree, took a job at the fabled technology company Xerox, and in 2009 was named CEO — the first African American woman to run a Fortune 500 company.

You've heard a version of this kind of story before, I'm sure: An outsider makes her way to the top by virtue of her ambition, determination, hard work, and intelligence. But after reading Kanter, there was one part of Burns's story that I kept coming back to. At almost every step of her rise, she was the only one of her kind. At Cathedral, there weren't a lot of girls walking to school every day from the Lower East Side. In college, there were almost no other women in her engineering program, let alone other black women. When she came back for her sophomore year, her fellow engineering students said in astonishment, "You're still here!" Or, "My goodness, you really are good at calculus." They weren't dismissive or hostile to her. They were perfectly nice. They were just struggling to understand how someone who looked so different from them could be as smart as they were. (Or, as was frequently the case with Ursula Burns, *smarter*.)

The same thing happened at Xerox. When she started at the company, Burns had a huge Afro, in the style of Angela Davis, and a serious New York City accent. She would drive to work with the windows down, listening to the funk musician Rick James. This was in a prosperous, overwhelmingly white suburb of Rochester, New York. She did not fit anyone's stereotype of a brilliant engineer.

> People started to say to me things like — and this lasted for a while and took me a long time to figure out what they were saying — they said, "You're spectacular. You are really amazing."
>
> In the beginning, I kind of liked it. It sounded like a compliment. But after a while, it was like, *Something's up here.* And I realized later in my life what was troubling me. They had to figure out a way to characterize me in some special way because I was with them — and I was not meant to be with them.

By labeling her as exceptional, as some kind of singular genius, her colleagues didn't have to revisit their ideas about what women — and, in particular, *black* women — were capable of. They could keep their belief systems intact.

> The only way I could be with them was that I was that good. Because the regular people that look like me, they're not good enough to be with them. So Ursula must be this super person.

What she was getting was a lesson in Rosabeth Kanter's group proportions. There just weren't enough people like Ursula Burns at Xerox for Ursula Burns to be treated like… Ursula Burns.

Not long after I met Burns, I happened to read the memoir of a woman named Indra Nooyi. Nooyi arrived in America from India in 1978 with $500 in her pocket. In her thirties, she took a job at Pepsi at a time when white men held fifteen of the company's top fifteen jobs. "Almost all wore blue or gray suits with white shirts and silk ties and had short hair or no hair," she remembers. "They drank Pepsi, mixed drinks, and liqueurs. Most of them golfed, fished, played tennis, hiked, and jogged. Some hunted for quail together. Many were married with children. I don't believe any of their wives worked in paid jobs outside their homes." I think you can guess what happened next. In 2006, by some combination of ambition, determination, hard work, and intelligence, Nooyi was named the company's CEO — becoming the first woman of Indian descent to become the head of a Fortune 500 company. (I have a weakness for rags-to-riches stories.)

But once again, a very specific moment in Nooyi's story jumped out at me: the reaction to her appointment as CEO. The announcement was a cultural *event*. It made headlines. The press, she remembers, was "thrilled to celebrate my exoticism as a woman and an Indian immigrant" in a way that made no sense to her. She writes:

I was presented in a sari and sometimes enhanced by bare feet. I hadn't worn a sari to work since my Booz Allen Hamilton internship in Chicago twenty-five years earlier.

And bare feet? Only when, like anyone else, she kicked off her shoes at the end of a hard day.

One *Wall Street Journal* story when I took over, with the headline "Pepsi's New CEO Doesn't Keep Her Opinions Bottled Up," describes me in the first paragraph wearing a sari and celebrating Harry Belafonte by singing "Day-O."

Belafonte was the famous West Indian singer and actor, and the calypso song "Day-O" was his greatest hit. Indians? West Indians? Apparently, they were all the same. "In reality," Nooyi continued:

I briefly introduced Mr. Belafonte and, as a group, we all sang "Day-O" at a 2005 diversity-and-inclusion event. I was wearing a business suit with my trademark flowing scarf. Maybe they thought that was a sari.

When you are the only one of your kind, the world can't see you as *you*.

"How many of a category are enough to change a person's status from token to full group member?" Kanter wondered. We can't liberate outsiders from the pressures of being treated like a token, she said, unless we know when the dynamics of groups shift:

Quantitative analyses are called for in order to provide precise documentation of the points at which interaction shifts because enough people of the "other kind" have become members of a group... Exact tipping points should be investigated.

So let's investigate.

4.

In the late 1950s, the community organizer Saul Alinsky (in the day, one of the most important political figures in the country) testified before the US Civil Rights Commission. The group was investigating white flight, and Alinsky's entire speech was devoted to the importance of figuring out what the white-flight tipping point was.

> Everyone who has thought seriously about the matter knows that there must be a formula of some kind. They speak of a racial or an ethnic balance; sometimes they simply talk about "stabilizing" the community; sometimes they talk about ratios. "Balanced," "stabilization," "ratio," "percentage" all refer to a numerical percentage or "quota."... The fact is that call it what you will this percentage or quota procedure is agreed upon by many Negro and white leaders...

Everyone who has thought seriously about the matter talks about a numerical percentage.

"During the midst of a race riot a few years ago," he went on, "I had an opportunity to talk to some of the white leaders."

Alinsky worked in the Back of the Yards neighborhood in Chicago, for years an Eastern European stronghold.

> I said to them: "Suppose you knew that 5 percent of the population would be Negro, and you were sure the percentage would stay at that figure. Would you let Negroes live here peaceably, not segregated, but diffused throughout the neighborhood?"
>
> The men stirred. "Remember," I said, "about five percent and no more. Would you accept that kind of situation?"
>
> They exchanged confused looks. The mob's leader then spoke: "Mister," he said, "if we could have five percent or even a little more, but we knew for sure, and I mean for sure, that that was all there was going to be — you have no idea how we would jump at it! Buy it? It would be heaven! I've had to move two times already, pack up my family, move the kids to other schools, sell and lose a lot of money on my house — I know that when Negroes start coming into a neighborhood that means the neighborhood's gone; it is going to be all Negro. Yeah, your idea would be a dream."

So 5 percent was fine. That was safely below the tipping point. Could you go higher?

"Some white parents may reluctantly accept integration to the extent of 10 to 15 percent," a reporter for the *New York Times* wrote in 1959. So, maybe 15 percent was also fine. At the same hearing where Alinsky spoke, the commission asked the executive of a big real-estate firm for his opinion. He said his company had opened a nineteen-story apartment building called Prairie Shores that was three-quarters white and one-quarter black. "I can tell you without the slightest qualification," he said, "that this building is operating without any difficulty of any kind on this 75-25 white and Negro basis." So maybe 25 percent was still below the tipping point.

But could you go to 30 percent? People from Philadelphia and New York weighed in. The head of the Washington, DC, public-school system said no. From his experience, once a school hit 30 percent black, it went to "99 percent in a very short time." Finally, the chairman of the Chicago Housing Authority was consulted. He ran one of the biggest public-housing systems in the country. Surely he would know what the "right" number was to stop white flight? He was of the same mind as the head of the DC school system. "Take Cabrini on the North Side, which is one of our projects," he said. "When we started out, the percentage was about 70 percent white and 30 percent Negro. Today it is 98 percent Negro."

In the end, nearly everyone was in agreement. Something dramatic happened when a once-insignificant set of outsiders reached between one-quarter and one-third of the population of whatever group they were joining.

Let's pick the highest end of this range and call this the Magic Third.

The Magic Third turns up in all kinds of places. Take corporate boards, for example. They are among the most powerful institutions in the modern economy. Virtually every company of consequence has a group of (typically) around nine experienced businesspeople, who provide guidance to the chief executive officer. Historically, boards have been all male. But slowly doors have opened to women, and a body of research shows that having women on a board makes the board *different*. The research suggests that women on boards are more willing to ask difficult questions. They value collaboration more. They are better listeners. In other words, there's a "woman effect." But how *many* women do you need on a board to get the "woman effect"?

It isn't one:

[I was] the only woman in a room of guys. I'm not shy, but trying to get your voice heard around the table is not easy.

This is from a study where fifty female executives at major companies were interviewed about their experiences.

You can make a point that is valid. Two minutes later Joe says exactly the same thing, and all the guys congratulate him. It is hard, even at our level, to get your voice heard. You have to find a way to wedge in.

One woman remembers what happened when the board she belonged to invited a group of outside auditors to give a presentation.

They come into the room. They walk down one side of the boardroom and shake hands with everybody. Shook hands with the two guys on my left, skipped me, and then shook hands with the next guy. They left. The group started talking about their presentation, and I said, "I have to interrupt. Did you notice what happened?"

It's just like Kanter predicted. When a woman is all alone, she stands out as a woman, but she becomes invisible as a person.

"Adding a second woman clearly helps," the study goes on. But it still wasn't enough:

The magic seems to occur when three or more women serve on a board together.

Three out of nine people. The Magic Third!

I have to confess that I found this conclusion difficult to accept at first. Was there really that much of a difference between two and three outsiders in a group of this size? But when I started calling women who have served on major corporate boards, I heard exactly the same thing. This is the entrepreneur Sukhinder Singh Cassidy, who was so convinced of the value of numbers that she started a group called theBoardlist to help place more women on corporate boards.

"So is three the right number?" she said. "I'm not sure, but I do know there's a number where that person ceases to be distinct because of their differences, where there's so many of them in the room that you don't even think about it."

One person, she said, felt lonely. Two felt like a friendship. But three was a *team*.

So my gut is maybe three is the magic number. Because I think at three, you feel enough. Like, there is a subtribe within a tribe where you can be more fully yourself.... There's a certain tipping point at which it's enough.

Or here is Katie Mitic, also a veteran of a number of corporate boards.

I would say, absolutely, there is some tipping point in my experience.

She had served on boards with every iteration: one, two, three, and more than three women. Three was what made the biggest difference.

I feel more comfortable, more confident, saying what I would say. Doing what I would do...less special in a positive way. So I feel like I'm another voice in the conversation as opposed to Katie, the female...I'm more like Katie, the product expert, or Katie, the consumer internet expert.

If you observed a board of seven men and two women, it wouldn't seem — from the outside — all that different from a board of six men and three women, would it? But it is. That's what Mitic and Singh are saying — that there is a point where the culture of the board is suddenly transformed. Mitic says she once joined a board where she was the only woman, then watched as first one, then another, and then a third woman was added. Even she was surprised at how abruptly things changed.

I'll be honest, I didn't really understand the impact it was going to have.... It made sense that it would make it easier for me, but I don't think I had understood the level to which it would.

That's why we call it the *Magic* Third.

5.

I think we can go one step further. I think we can call the Magic Third a universal law. (Or at least something very close to universal.) One of the best pieces of evidence for this comes from the work of Damon Centola, who teaches at the University of Pennsylvania. Centola was one of the many scholars inspired by Kanter's call to "investigate" tipping points.

Centola dreamed up a very clever way to figure out where the crucial shift in group dynamics happens. He created an online game, which he played in countless iterations. A group of people — let's say thirty of them — is broken into pairs, making fifteen groups of two. Each pair is shown a photograph and asked to type in a suggested name for the person in the picture.

So, imagine that the pair is you and me. I see a photo and I type in *Jeff.* The way the game works, we enter our answers simultaneously, so you type in your answer without knowing what my answer is. We're effectively blind. You type in *Alan.* Then, immediately after we type in our answers, we see if we missed or matched and get randomly rematched with someone new. The process starts over again. It's on to a new pairing and then another pairing, and on and on until the game has run its course.

Now, as you can imagine, the chances of matching right away are infinitesimal. Even if the picture is a recognizable "type" — let's say a blond, blue-eyed woman, or an East Indian man in a turban — there are literally hundreds of names that we might think appropriate for someone who looks like that. So we probably aren't going to match in the first round, or the second round, or even the third round. It's going to take a long time, if it happens at all — right?

Wrong. Somewhere around fifteen rounds, a consensus emerges on the name.

"It's very quick," Centola says. "We ran this at multiple scales — at populations of twenty-four and fifty and one hundred [participants]. And this process of normal emergence was the same at all scales.... It's lightning fast compared to expectations."

Why does the game end so quickly? Because human beings are really, really good at figuring out norms — at the job of agreeing on how they should think about something.

So when I type in *Jeff* and you type in *Alan*, I know that I have planted *Jeff* in your memory and you know that you have planted *Alan* in mine, and both of us are now a little more likely to use one of those two names the next go-round. And so does everyone else we paired with in those early rounds. *Jeff* and *Alan* are now in the ether. And when you finally stumble on a match — when you type in *Jeff* and the person you're paired with likewise types in *Jeff* — you're never going back.

"As soon as there's something that works, you're likely to just keep typing *Jeff, Jeff, Jeff, Jeff*," Centola said. "Because it is the greatest likelihood that you'll experience success."

There is much, much more that could be said about this part of the experiment — and what it says about the way all of us are wired. (As human beings, we really want to agree on the rules of engagement!) But let's leave that aside and move to the second, crucial stage — because these kinds of experiments always have a catch.

Centola had a group of graduate students join the game with a very specific set of instructions: They were to act as dissidents. Once the group had agreed on a name and everyone was typing *Jeff, Jeff, Jeff,* the dissidents were told to break ranks. They were to buck the *Jeff* trend and all start using a different name, over and over again. Let's say it was *Pedro.* Here's what Centola wondered: How many dissidents would it take, typing in the name *Pedro* over and over again, to get the whole group to switch from *Jeff* to *Pedro*?

He added a handful of *Pedro* dissidents to the group. Did they make a difference? No. Then he tried more — eighteen percent of the group. No impact. Nineteen percent? Nothing. (I think you can see where I'm going with this.) Twenty? Nothing. But when the proportion of dissidents hit one-quarter — bingo! — something magical happened: Without fail, *everybody* switched to *Pedro.*

Centola ran this game over and over again, and always got the same result. The majority's consensus fell apart when the number of outsiders reached 25 percent. Centola says his favorite example was with just twenty participants. He ran two versions of the game simultaneously. The first had four dissidents, representing 20 percent of the whole. The second had five dissidents, representing 25 percent. The difference was one person! "We had them side by side," he remembers. "And, you know, four [dissidents] produces nothing. There was no change overall. But you add one more agent — you have five — and they jump up to like 90 percent conversion, *just like that.*" In Centola's laboratory version of reality, he ended up on the low end of the tipping-point range. He found the Magic Quarter!

Some observations about human nature are simply that — observations. They aren't invitations to action. Even in the case of Miami and Poplar Grove, we can imagine what an intervention would look like. Break up Poplar Grove High

School! Restore trust in Miami's institutions! But neither of those remedies is easy to implement.

Yet the idea that there is a magic moment somewhere between a quarter and a third is different. It practically begs us to intervene.

Let me give you an example. For years, there has been a significant gap between the test scores of white and African American students. Here's what it looks like. This data comes from the Early Childhood Longitudinal Study (ECLS).* The numbers show the difference between black and white scores on a 96-point math test. The data can be sliced up in a number of different ways. But these are the results for schools where black students make up less than 5 percent of the student population.

Kindergarten (fall): –4.718
Kindergarten (spring): –6.105
1st grade (fall): –7.493
1st grade (spring): –8.880
3rd grade (spring): –14.442
5th grade (spring): –20.004

By the end of kindergarten, the black kids in this group were six points behind — a small but not trivial number. But by the fifth grade, the gap was huge: *twenty points* out of a hundred. This is a perfect example of what has perplexed

---

* The ECLS was a landmark study started in the late 1990s that followed a national sample of children from kindergarten through the fifth grade, making note of their family background, test scores, schools, and anything else that would be useful in understanding their intellectual and psychological development.

American educators over the past several generations: Why is there such a big gap, and why does it grow?

But Rosabeth Kanter and all of the people who have looked at board rooms remind us that there is a world of difference between being one of a few in a group and being one of many. So maybe we should be asking a different question. This data was from classrooms where black students made up a tiny minority. What happens in classrooms where black kids are above the tipping point? Do increased numbers make a difference?

It turns out they do. When a group of educational researchers led by Tara Yosso looked just at classrooms where the percentage of minority students exceeded 25 percent, they found the test-score gap completely vanished.* The white students did as well as they always did. But now the black students had caught up.

I think it's important not to make too much of Yosso's findings. They are just about elementary- and middle-school performance on a single metric — one kind of standardized math-achievement test. I don't believe anyone thinks that we can make the achievement gap go away forever just by altering the composition of classrooms. But there's clearly *something* going on here, isn't there? And it's very hard to read that study and not want to at least *try* something new: rearrange school districts, advise minority parents about where to send their kids, conduct some kind of experiment. If you were an elementary-school principal with three classes of fifth graders, each with a sprinkling of students of color, you

---

* Yosso's group used data from the Early Childhood Longitudinal Study (ECLS).

might be tempted to consolidate all your minority students into one class, as difficult to explain as that move would be.

The point is that it doesn't always take a revolution to change the way a minority group is perceived. Think back to Ursula Burns and Indra Nooyi. Xerox and Pepsi didn't need a cultural transplant. The path forward was pretty simple and obvious. They just needed more women like Burns and Nooyi in top leadership roles, until they reached a point of critical mass.

Are we at that point now with black women? No. If another black woman from the projects becomes CEO of a fabled American company, you can bet it will lead to a parade of breathless news stories about brilliant, feisty, rule-breaking black women. But a tipping point *has* been reached with South Asians. In the nearly two decades after Nooyi took over at Pepsi, a flood of people who resembled her entered the upper levels of American corporations. One news outlet in 2022 added up *sixty* CEOs of Indian descent leading Fortune 500 companies, including IBM, Microsoft, and Google. Within the tech world, the percentage of Indian executives is even higher. After Starbucks named Laxman Narasimhan as its new CEO in March of 2023, the *Wall Street Journal* ran a profile, and not a word was said about the fact that Narasimhan was born in India. Between Nooyi and Narasimhan, something fundamental changed in the way American culture viewed Indian Americans. Something tipped.

6.

In the late 1940s, a group called the Palo Alto Fair Play Committee became concerned about the housing situation in their town. African Americans were moving into the area, and one of the few places they could live was an overcrowded stretch of Ramona Street, in the older part of the city. The members of the Fair Play Committee looked around and saw the emerging crisis facing other American cities, and wanted Palo Alto to be different.

"We had no illusions of solving the housing problem, but we wanted to do something," Gerda Isenberg, one of the group's leaders, would say many years later. "I had no more idea of how to set it up than the man in the moon. The meetings were so frustrating. My lawyers said we should give it up."

But the group persevered. Another Fair Play Committee member, a black graduate student at Stanford University named Paul Lawrence, was deputized to find some land. He located a parcel near a dairy farm on the outskirts of town. The price was $2,500. Ten members of the group put up $250 each. They divided the tract into twenty-four residential lots and one park, and drew up a set of rules.

The lots in the tract would be split three ways, in strict accordance with the Law of the Magic Third: equal parts white, black, and Asian. A black owner could sell only to a black buyer, a white owner could sell only to a white buyer, and so forth. Black people, it was agreed, would never constitute more than a third of the residents of the Lawrence Tract. The community would tiptoe up to the tipping point, but they would not cross it.

A row of small bungalows was built up and down the street. The first people to move in were Ethel and Reo Miles. They were black. The second family was Elizabeth and Dan Dana. They were white. The third family was Melba and

Leroy Gee. They were Asian. To maximize the amount of contact that different races would have, no two families of the same race could live next door to each other.

The families met monthly. They scheduled social events. The men went hunting together. "I was struck by the tract when I first moved in," one member said. "Neighbors of all colors came up, grabbed my furniture, and started moving me in. Neighboring women took my wife out to tea, while the men helped me fix up the house."

This was the 1950s: In some parts of the United States, white racists were burning down the houses of black people who dared to live near them, burning crosses on their lawns, throwing rocks through their windows. The Lawrence Tract was an attempt to show the world that different races could live in harmony.

As one of the original group members wrote:

> Those of us who are involved in causes leading to changes in social attitudes and structures often feel frustrated by the theoretical nature of our efforts…One successful demonstration is more effective than a hundred speeches. Some of us working in the field of civil rights had this in mind when we inaugurated a small housing project in Palo Alto.

But was the experiment sustainable? The neighbors on either side of Lawrence Lane didn't think so. The Lawrence Tract was trying to put whites, blacks, and Asians next door to one another. How long would that last? How would Palo Alto avoid white flight? "Some people were very opposed and said we were building a 'n—r-shack town,'" Isenberg remembered. "I received a few unpleasant phone calls." Some people in the surrounding streets threatened to put their homes up for sale. In response, the residents of the Lawrence Tract attempted to reassure their neighbors. This was not going to be a replay of what was happening in Detroit and Chicago and Atlanta, where whenever black people moved in, white people moved out. They had rules. And as long as those rules remained in place, the people on Lawrence Lane believed, their community would be stable.

"I was just a guy looking for a house," one of the tract residents, a black schoolteacher named Willis Williams, said. "Rentals were too high and the shacks they were offering me elsewhere because I was a Negro were terrible....I felt the tract was segregation itself, but a different type, a beneficial type. It was the practice of a mild discrimination so that a vicious discrimination might be prevented."

This is what it looks like to take tipping points seriously. If there really is a dramatic shift for the worse, right around a specific number, then you have to make absolutely sure you never reach that number.

Not long after their experiment began, the members of the Lawrence Tract were tested on this very question. One of the owners decided to sell one of the remaining empty lots along Lawrence Lane.

"The lot was owned by a white person and they decided to give it up," Nanosh Lucas said. Lucas grew up on the tract and is now writing a history of the experiment.*

---

* "A lot of the residents describe it as a place of safety, because school was definitely not a friendly place for any black folks, any Asian people during that time," Lucas said. "So in that lane, that's where people grew to understand one another." He went on:

They sold it to a real estate agent, and the Lawrence Tract Association goes to the real estate agent and basically says, "Hey, we want to just make sure that you're handling these proportions the way they're supposed to go. We basically need a white person in this lot."

The realtor was reassuring. But then the group got word that one of their own — a black family — had approached the realtor, wanting to buy the lot for a relative. It was all but impossible for black people to find housing in Palo Alto in those years. The relative was desperate.

And so the tract members gathered for an emergency meeting.

The sale would upset their proportions. It would push their African American proportion past the Magic Third.

In his research, Lucas found a term paper about the Lawrence Tract, written by a local student named Dorothy Strowger in 1955, that described the crisis:

A decision had to be made whether the Association felt the policy of "divided backgrounds" was being seriously undermined if not destroyed by this further addition to the unbalanced situation, and, if this were so, to weigh the value of the experiment against the need and welfare of the prospective buyer.

"The interesting thing about the parents is that they, you know, really seemed to try to create a post-racial society, where their children would grow up, not being so highly conscious of it. [They were] trying to get rid of that idea where one has to constantly think about one's identity all the time."

The question came to a head at a dramatic community meeting. The family that had approached the realtor favored the sale. Everyone else voted, in Strowger's words, "to put the total welfare of the tract first." The members then all chipped in to buy the lot back from the realtor.

"The meeting will long be remembered," Strowger's term paper continues. "Association members speak of it with passion and pride." But then she goes on to speak of the trauma left by the incident, in particular:

> the grief and guilt feelings which are still expressed by other Negroes who had some feeling of having had to sacrifice one of their own race to prove a principle which in a well ordered world should have needed no such proving.

The existence of tipping points creates an irresistible opportunity to engage in social engineering. It makes you want to tinker with the number of women on a corporate board or rearrange the minority students in an elementary classroom. But that doesn't mean it's easy.

The man passed over for a job because the number of women in the company isn't yet at the tipping point is unlikely to be satisfied by that explanation. The principal who lumps all of her minority students in one classroom will not have an easy time explaining her experiment to parents. The reason we avoid acknowledging the simple solutions offered to us by tipping points is that, in the end, the solutions aren't really that simple. That's what the members of the Lawrence Tract learned. They looked around them — at all the communities where white people had left for the suburbs — and decided that they could not in good conscience let their street go down

135

that same path. But in order to preserve that racial harmony, they had to harm the very people they were trying to help.

Lucas said the lot remained empty for a decade, like an open wound that no one wanted to touch. The whole episode was "a really harsh realization for the neighborhood [about] what you had to give up in order to make that neighborhood work."

He went on:

> In their mind the fate of the neighborhood was in the balance.... My analysis of it is that they were thinking that perhaps people from the outside were going to be looking at this and going like, "This tract association doesn't have any legitimacy because they're not enforcing the rules they said they would." And, that we'll reach this point where the neighborhood would fail.*

It's no wonder, then, that when most people attempt to play games around tipping points, they do so on the sly.

Just ask the Ivy League.

---

* In the late 1950s, as the idea of what came to be known as "benign quotas" spread across the country, everyone involved faced some version of this dilemma. Can you really discriminate in the cause of ending discrimination? The activist Saul Alinsky once gave a moving speech in defense of benign quotas, in which he admitted:
> I find it somewhat ironic that I, a person of the Jewish faith, should stand in public and speak favorably about a system of quotas. In the past, the quota has been used as a means of depriving individuals of my faith of opportunities and rights which were properly theirs, but the past is the past. What is an unjust instrument in one case can serve justice in another.
He was referring in part to the fact that a number of elite schools in the 1920s and 1930s had quotas on the number of Jews they would accept. Quotas were *awkward*. But Alinsky, like the members of the Lawrence Tract, didn't know of any other way to build integrated neighborhoods:
> For those who are shocked by the idea of the opening up of white communities to Negroes on a quota basis...I can only ask, what solution do they propose?

CHAPTER FIVE

The Mysterious Case of the Harvard Women's Rugby Team

"THE FEELING WAS THAT STUDENT ATHLETES BRING SOMETHING SPECIAL TO A COMMUNITY."

1.

On a blustery fall day not long ago, a rugby game was played on a lonely athletic field somewhere on the Princeton University campus. The home team was in black and orange. The visitors, from Harvard University, were in white. A few spectators stood on one side of the field, the teams on the other — each with a small, open tent for their equipment. For those who couldn't attend, there was a livestream available on YouTube.

Checking on the internet connection. It looks like we are good. We're live. Six viewers already. Welcome.

The announcers read the names of the players: Eva, Brogan, Maya, Tiahna, Skylar, Elizabeth, Zoë, Caroline — on and on. The spectators and players were warned about engaging in "racist, homophobic, or transphobic discrimination and other intimidating actions." The national anthem played. And they were off.

The Princeton women's varsity rugby program was only two years old. They were mostly converted high-school tennis and volleyball players: Only a handful had any real rugby experience. Harvard, the announcers pointed out, was different.

> The Harvard side has a lot of depth and a lot of people who have been playing rugby for a long time.

Harvard was undefeated coming into the game, having bulldozed their way earlier in the season through the likes of Quinnipiac University, American International College, and Queens University of Charlotte. When Harvard played Princeton the previous year, they won by a score of 102 to 0. Harvard was *good*.

It started to rain — first softly and then harder. The field turned slippery. The players were soaked. The spectators strung out along the sidelines huddled under umbrellas.

> Kick is taken by Courtney Taylor and carrying a good portion of the Princeton team with her toward the twenty-two…

The other announcer chimed in.

> …second phase attack.

The commentary was entirely in rugby-speak, incomprehensible to anyone who didn't already know the game.

Here goes Eva Rankin...taken down by Brooke Beers. There goes Jordan. The step, well supported, no, more attack, front footballed to Chloe Headland, taking a couple Tigers with her inside the five-meter line.

Two hours after it began, the game was over.

Good power and distance, just the direction a little bit off and goes to the right and wide and the ref calls it. That's the final action. Your final score today is sixty-one to Harvard, five to Princeton.

But again, folks, the final score is Harvard sixty-one and Tigers five.

If you happened upon the Princeton-Harvard game, it is possible you would have enjoyed the afternoon of spirited competition. Before long, though — as the rain poured down and you stood on the empty sidelines — you might also have asked yourself an impertinent question: *Why* does *Harvard have a varsity women's rugby team, anyway?*

Harvard offers an extraordinary number of athletic opportunities for its students. It has over fifty campus sports clubs. The school also competes in more Division I varsity sports than any other university in the country. At Harvard, an athletically minded young woman can compete in Division I Basketball, Cross-Country, Fencing, Field Hockey, Golf, Ice Hockey, Lacrosse, Heavyweight Rowing, Lightweight Rowing, Sailing, Skiing, Soccer, Softball, Squash, Swimming and Diving, Tennis, Track and Field, Volleyball, and Water Polo. We think of big state athletic powerhouses like the University of Michigan as institutions with lots of student-athletes. On a percentage basis, Harvard has *four times* as many student-athletes as Michigan.

Yet in 2013, Harvard decided that its female students needed still another option. Thus was women's rugby added to the already crowded top rung of varsity sports. That meant hiring coaches and trainers. And now athletes had to be recruited — a fact of special significance because not a lot of young women in the United States have ever played rugby. It's a foreign sport and a violent one at that, routinely causing such a long list of injuries — dislocated shoulders, broken collar bones, torn knee ligaments, concussions — that even on those rare occasions when an American high school offers rugby, many young women understandably shy away from the game. To field a varsity college rugby team takes some effort.

"Ultimately, we cast a large net in order to find the people who want to be at Harvard and who would be a great fit on and off the field," the team's coach, Mel Denham, told the *Harvard Crimson* student newspaper a few years ago. By "large net" she meant that her recruiting efforts spanned the globe.

The article continued:

High schools in California, Utah, Colorado, and some midwest states are regularly scouted, in addition to Canada.... "We have also started to work with some English players and are in the process of building relationships with coaches in England, New Zealand, and Australia as well," reported Coach Denham. "Our current team has players from Scotland, Canada, Hong Kong, Australia,

China, Germany and Honduras, which is incredible to have such diversity in our culture."

Why did Harvard want to go to all this trouble?

The question gets even more puzzling when you understand how the admissions system at Harvard works. Like many elite schools, Harvard effectively has a two-track process. The regular track is for smart students from around the world, who compete on their merits. The second track is for what the school calls ALDCs — that is, *A*thletes, *L*egacies (children of alumni), *D*ean's Interest List (children of rich people), and *C*hildren of faculty. ALDCs make up 30 percent of Harvard's student body. There are a lot of them. And their path to admission is very different.

In 2014, Harvard was sued by a group called Students for Fair Admissions (SFFA). The case would ultimately end up before the Supreme Court. And the strangest moments of the initial trial in federal court came when both sides attempted to explain the workings of the byzantine ALDC system.

Here is the lawyer for the plaintiffs, Adam Mortara, in his opening statement. He's put up a chart for everyone in the court to see. And he starts by analyzing what Harvard calls the "academic 1s." The intellectual accomplishments of acceptable applicants are graded on a 1 to 4 scale (over that, you've got no chance), 1 being highest. These are the superstars. In the normal course of events, academic 1s have a reasonably good chance of admission. But if you are a legacy — the child of an alum — and you're a 1, you're a lock.

Mortara points to a new chart, comparing admission rates stratified by ratings for regular students and for ALDCs.

You start to see how much better the legacy list does here. They do about 50 percent better. Virtually all of them get in at academic 1.

Then Mortara goes to the line that shows the acceptance rates for athletes. In their analysis of six years of admission data, Mortara and his team were able to find only a single athlete who scored an academic 1.

Of course the one athlete...got in.

Then Mortara looks at what happens to students one rung lower.

Then you see something interesting here in academic 2. A 10 percent admission chance for the regular folk with no connection to Harvard. A 50 percent admission chance at academic 2 for the legacy, dean's list, and children of faculty or staff. It's a 5x difference.

He pauses. Then adds:

Again, the athletes almost always get in. I told you that; I'll stop saying it.

He goes on:

At academic 3, 2.4 percent [get in], really pretty low chances for the regular folk. But if your mom or dad went to Harvard or your grandparent or uncle gave a lot of money to Harvard, then your chances of getting in are seven and a half times higher: 18 percent.

Down below at academic 4, almost nobody gets admitted in the regular group. But here we have the legacy, dean's list, and children of faculty or staff, still 3.5 percent of them got in.

Eventually, he concludes:

What that reflects is the academic rating is simply not as important to admissions for this group... And this effect is most profoundly seen with the athletes.... As I said, they almost universally get in.

The athletes always get in.
It is easy to construct a convincing — if cynical — explanation for why Harvard would give special preference to certain kinds of students. Alumni and rich people like to give money to schools such as Harvard. Harvard likes to have lots of money. As a result, it makes good business sense for Harvard to give the children of those two groups a leg up. Cutting a special deal for the children of faculty also makes a certain degree of sense: It's a simple way to keep your professors happy. What *doesn't* make sense is why athletes should be lumped in with those three other groups.

The *Harvard Crimson* contains paragraphs like this:

Victor Crouin '22, a member of Harvard's squash team who hails from France, said he was at the 2017 world junior squash championship in Tauranga, New Zealand, when he first connected with a University coach.

"The coach went all the way to New Zealand to watch the students, and then pick a few of them, and ask them, and give them a spot in case their grades were good enough," Crouin said.

Tauranga, New Zealand! What is so special about people who are good at squash that merits a trip to the other side of the world? And — what's more — that merits giving a break to squash players that is substantially greater than the break given to students who aren't gifted athletes? The advantage given to people who play squash and rugby and who sail boats is so large that the easiest way to get into the world's most prestigious university is not to be the best student at your school. It's to be the best athlete in your school.

At one point during the Harvard lawsuit, the school's longtime dean of admissions, William Fitzsimmons, was asked to justify his college's bewildering attitude toward athletes.

Q: There's been a lot of discussion about athletes. Why does Harvard give a tip for athletes?

Fitzsimmons looked and sounded every bit the Harvard man: He had a PhD in education, a distinguished bit of gray at the temples. He must have known the question was coming. It's hard to believe he wasn't coached about how best to respond to it. But just listen to his answer.

Fitzsimmons: For a couple of reasons. One is [that] having people, having all of our students gather together, you know, for athletic contests builds a spirit of community that I think many students expect and I think they deserve. It really unifies the institution in quite a specific and vital way.

This is the kind of answer one would expect from the athletic director at the University of Alabama or Ohio State, where 80,000 or more students, alumni, and community supporters routinely show up for college football games on a Saturday afternoon. *That's* community. But Fitzsimmons is principally talking about lonely sports like sailing and fencing and water polo. That rugby game at Princeton barely had any spectators. How could it build a "sense of community"? Fitzsimmons wasn't finished:

So now our biggest state often is California. Our fourth biggest is Texas. Our sixth biggest is Florida. So if you're a kid coming from some of these areas, you want to go to a place that is collegiate in the way Americans often think of colleges. So having a vibrant athletic tradition and ability to rally people around makes a big difference in our ability to attract all kinds of students.

Again. This makes no sense. Harvard doesn't need to worry about its "ability to attract" students: The college attracts so many students that it can admit only 3.4 percent of its applicants! More to the point, who is this imaginary person from California or Texas or Florida who would turn down an offer from Harvard because the sports scene wasn't sufficiently "vibrant"?

Fitzsimmons tries one last time.

The other part of it is that people who have achieved high levels of athletic expertise, if you want to use that word, often have a commitment, a drive, and an energy that often serves them well during college and then well beyond.

Fitzsimmons still isn't answering the question! No one would deny that you can learn valuable lessons on a playing field that will translate to success in your life and career. The issue here is simply why Harvard values the kind of "commitment" and "drive" that come from doing sports so much more than the commitment and drive that come from, say, writing a novel or solving a difficult quadratic equation. And, what's more, values the sporting version of that drive so highly that it will travel to the ends of the earth to find young women who want to play a dangerous game in the rain on an isolated field somewhere on the fringes of the Princeton campus.

Since none of the stated explanations seem to make sense, let me offer another. I think the rugby puzzle has nothing to do with character building and energy and drive and creating a unifying institutional experience. I think it has to do with the Magic Third and Rosabeth Kanter's ideas about group proportions.

But what Harvard is doing is very different from the kind of social engineering tried by the Lawrence Tract. The participants in that experiment made no secret of what they were doing. They wanted to manipulate their numbers, and they called their members together to work out the details. Social engineering takes on a very different face, however, when the engineers go about their business in secret. There is far too much of this second, hidden kind of manipulation going on. If we are to protect the integrity of our institutions, we need to be made aware of the games being played below the surface. And exhibit A? Harvard University.

2.

In the 1920s, the schools of the Ivy League faced a crisis. The problem was Columbia University, the most prestigious college in the nation's largest city. The children of the Jewish immigrants who had come en masse to New York at the turn of the century were now of college age, and they were making short work of Columbia's entrance exams. By the early 1900s, as much as 40 percent of Columbia's undergraduate population was Jewish, and the rest of the Ivy League looked at that number with horror. The newcomers from the farther reaches of the Bronx, Brooklyn, and the tenements of the Lower East Side of Manhattan seemed like aliens to the schools that had been educating the children of the WASP elite since the early days of the Republic.

In the words of a fraternity song of the period:

Oh, Harvard's run by millionaires
And Yale is run by booze
Cornell is run by farmer's sons,
Columbia's run by Jews
So give a cheer for Baxter Street,
Another one for Pell,

And when the little sheenies die,
Their souls will go to hell

(A "sheeny," in case you're wondering, was a derogatory term popular at the time for a Jewish person.)

Most alarmed was Abbott Lawrence Lowell, the stern patrician who served as Harvard's president from 1909 to 1933. Inspired by Columbia and NYU's efforts to limit Jewish enrollment, Lowell formed a "subcommittee to gather statistics" to determine exactly who was Jewish and who wasn't. The school started asking applicants for the first time to identify their "race and color," their mother's maiden name, the birthplace of their father. And to catch those who had cleverly changed their name to avoid being labeled Jewish, Harvard now asked: "What change, if any, has been made since birth in your own name or that of your father? (explain fully)."

Four admissions categories were created. J1 was assigned to candidates "when the evidence pointed conclusively to the fact that the student was Jewish." J2 was for those occasions when a "preponderance of evidence" suggested someone was Jewish. J3 was for when "the evidence suggested the possibility that the student might be Jewish." And "Other" was everyone else. Now Harvard could be certain of its Jewish enrollment, and when Lowell saw the results they left him in a panic. When he had taken over as president in 1909, Jews made up just over 10 percent of the school's population. By 1922, they made up more than twice that number. By 1925, the situation had reached a point of crisis. By Harvard's count, the freshman class was 27.6 percent J1 and J2, and an additional 3.6 percent was J3. The school was on the cusp of the Magic Third.

Harvard and the schools of the Ivy League had just spent several decades attempting to raise their academic standards. They had developed rigorous entrance exams and publicly committed to accepting all those who scored the highest.

"But now, just as these efforts were beginning to bear fruit, the 'wrong' students were passing the exams," Jerome Karabel writes in *The Chosen,* his landmark history of Ivy League admissions.

Harvard, Yale, and Princeton thus faced a painful choice: either maintain the almost exclusively objective academic standards for admission and face the arrival of increasing numbers of Jews or replace them with more subjective criteria that could be deployed to produce the desired outcome.

After much debate, Harvard decided to go the way of "more subjective criteria." The admissions office was given broad leeway to decide who did or did not get in. Now applicants were asked to provide letters of recommendation and list their extracurricular activities. It mattered, all of a sudden, what you did on your summer vacation and how compelling your application essay was, or which of your parents' friends could be persuaded to vouch for your character. Harvard created complex scoring systems to assess intangibles. It started conducting personal interviews, where Harvard people could size up applicants in person. And for the first time, it placed a strict limit on the size of the incoming freshman class — all to prevent, as college president Lowell put it, "a dangerous increase in the proportion of Jews."

Lowell went on: "It is the duty of Harvard to receive just

as many boys who have come, or whose parents have come, to this country without our background as it can effectively educate...," he explained. "Experience seems to place that proportion at about 15 percent."

That 15-percent mark was high enough that Harvard would not be seen as openly antisemitic, but low enough that it was in no danger of turning into Columbia. In her famous essay on her consulting experience, Rosabeth Kanter called a group where the minority numbered below 15 percent *skewed*:

> Skewed groups are those in which there is a large preponderance of one type over another, up to a ratio of perhaps 85:15. The numerically dominant types also control the group and its culture in enough ways to be labeled "dominants." The few of another type in a skewed group can appropriately be called "tokens," because they are often treated as representatives of their category, as symbols rather than individuals.

Kanter, of course, believed that skewed proportions were a problem: She wanted to increase the numbers of the minority group to the point where they could be themselves, and exert full influence over the culture of the group. Lowell, by contrast, was interested in keeping the minority group below that tipping point. He wanted to engineer the admissions process so that Jews stayed on the low end of a skewed distribution.

It is important to note that Lowell didn't want to close the door to all Jews, the way Southerners of his generation closed the door to all black people at their schools. He was interested in limiting the *number* of Jews. "The summer hotel that is ruined by admitting Jews meets its fate, not because the Jews it admits are of bad character, but because they drive away the Gentiles, and then after the Gentiles have left, they leave also," Lowell wrote to a friend. "This happened to a friend of mine with a school in New York, who thought, on principle, that he ought to admit Jews, but who discovered in a few years that he had no school at all." Let in too many Jews, and the Jews *drive away the Gentiles.* Lowell was essentially saying that he was trying to prevent white flight.

Over time, the special antipathy that Harvard held for Jews faded. In 2001, the school even appointed its first Jewish president. But the basic structure of Lowell's reforms remained unchanged. As *The Chosen* author Karabel puts it, Lowell "bequeathed to us the peculiar admissions process that we now take for granted." He taught his successors a lesson they have never forgotten: He showed them how to control Harvard's group proportions.

Take a look at the following two charts, which offer a glimpse of the enduring impact of Lowell's instructions to the administrators who followed him. They show the number of Asian Americans enrolled at Harvard and Caltech (one of the few schools in the world as hard to get into as Harvard) between the early 1990s and 2013. Let's start with Caltech.

1992 25.2%	1998 24.1%	2004 31.1%	2010 39.4%
1993 26.9%	1999 24.3%	2005 33.0%	2011 38.8%
1994 29.8%	2000 24.9%	2006 37.4%	2012 39.6%
1995 29.1%	2001 24.5%	2007 38.1%	2013 42.5%
1996 27.6%	2002 27.2%	2008 39.8%	
1997 27.4%	2003 31.1%	2009 39.9%	

Caltech is a school that uses a highly meritocratic admissions process. They don't play any under-the-table admissions games with athletes, legacies, or donors' kids. And if you rely on a much more meritocratic admissions process, you can't control your group proportions. That's why the Asian numbers at Caltech are all over the map. The Asian share starts out at a quarter of the student population. It jumps to almost 30 percent within two years, comes back down a bit and then, after the turn of the century, shoots back up. By 2013, it was at 42.5 percent. Today it's closer to 45 percent.

Is there any way to predict what the ethnic breakdown of Caltech's undergraduate population will look like a generation from now? No! Caltech doesn't try to control its group proportions. If a sudden flood of Nigerian immigrants were to come to the United States, and their children followed the same path as the Jewish and Asian sons and daughters before them, the West African population at Caltech may one day be as high as the Asian population. (This is not far-fetched: Nigerian immigrants currently have more graduate degrees per capita than any other group in America.) Caltech was hit by the same demographic shifts as every other elite school, but chose to shrug its shoulders.

Now look at Harvard's Asian-enrollment numbers over the same period.

1992 19.1%	1998 17.0%	2004 17.1%	2010 15.6%
1993 20.6%	1999 17.2%	2005 17.6%	2011 17.2%
1994 18.3%	2000 17.1%	2006 14.3%	2012 17.7%
1995 18.4%	2001 16.4%	2007 15.4%	2013 18.0%
1996 17.5%	2002 16.3%	2008 16.7%	
1997 17.4%	2003 16.2%	2009 17.0%	

Harvard Admissions (Percentage of Admitted Students by Race/Ethnicity)									
	2006	2007	2008	2009	2010	2011	2012	2013	2014
African American	10.5%	10.7%	11.0%	10.8%	11.3%	11.8%	10.2%	11.5%	11.9%
Hispanic	9.8%	10.1%	9.7%	10.9%	10.3%	12.1%	11.2%	11.5%	13.0%
Asian American	17.7%	19.6%	18.5%	17.6%	18.2%	17.8%	20.7%	19.9%	19.7%
Native American	1.4%	1.5%	1.3%	1.3%	2.7%	1.9%	1.7%	2.2%	1.9%
White and Other	60.6%	58.1%	59.5%	59.4%	57.5%	56.4%	56.2%	54.9%	53.5%

The Caltech numbers are what you get when an institution doesn't care about controlling its group proportions. The Harvard numbers are what you get when an institution *does*. The proportion of Asians at Harvard stayed basically the same for years. In fact, the proportions of everyone at Harvard have stayed basically the same.

Look, in particular, at the last row. Only one group at Harvard gets to exceed the Magic Third.

So, why did Harvard go to all the trouble of adding a women's rugby team? It's obvious. *Varsity sports are a mechanism by which Harvard maintains its group proportions.*

3.

A few years ago there was a bizarre court case devoted to this very question of elite colleges and sports. It involved a very rich man named Amin Khoury, who allegedly put $180,000 in cash in a brown paper bag and sent it to the tennis coach at Georgetown University, Gordon Ernst. Khoury wanted Ernst to recruit his daughter as a varsity tennis player. Khoury knew that at elite schools "the athletes always get in," so he believed, with impeccable logic, that this was the surest path for his daughter to be admitted to a prestigious college.

The trial was unusually entertaining, involving lots of embarrassing emails and texts, a boozy evening at a fancy restaurant, and various admissions and athletic officers squirming uncomfortably on the witness stand. As a case study in the corruption of higher education, *US v. Khoury* really cannot be beaten. The testimony heard at the trial also happens to be enormously helpful in understanding the way colleges use sports to manipulate their group proportions.*

Halfway through the trial, the prosecution called to the stand a former varsity tennis player at Georgetown. Let's call her Jane. She went to high school at an exclusive private school just outside Washington, DC, where tuition tops $50,000 a year.

Jane was a very good high-school tennis player.

Q: What was your national ranking?
A: My national ranking was 52 in the country.
Q: And you said you were from Maryland, correct?
A: Mm-hmm.
Q: How about just within Maryland?
A: I was number one in Maryland.

---

* Khoury was acquitted. And if you are curious why, I invite you to listen to the podcast I devoted to the subject.

If you are familiar with junior tennis, you'll know just how hard you have to work to be the number one player in your state.

Prosecutor: Where are you from? Where did you go to high school?

Jane: I went to Holton-Arms in Bethesda, Maryland. I left high school early every single day, and I went out to the tennis center at College Park out near the University of Maryland. There's an academy there. And I trained three hours a day on the court, and then I did an hour of fitness [afterward].

The unstated part of Jane's testimony was that devoting four hours a day to tennis requires an enormous amount of money. Jane's father was a partner in a law firm. He had to be. He had a daughter trying to succeed in junior tennis.

It's worth doing the math. All of the following numbers come from the tennis coach Marianne Werdel, who was herself a US junior tennis champion. Werdel conducted a focus group of twenty-three families with a child who played junior tennis to determine how much money they spent a year on the daughter or son's tennis game. This is what she found:

Focus-group families spent between $1,200 to $55,000 on memberships and court time. Outdoor annual costs average at $4,000 and indoor seasonal costs averaging at $35,000.

At the high end were private country clubs, which charge initiation fees of $20,000 or more, and monthly dues in the $750 range.

"Focus-group families spent between $7,500 and $45,000 annually for coaching," Werdel continues. Tournaments had entry fees and travel expenses. (The highest number quoted to her for that line item was $42,000 a year.) Most high-levels had a trainer. That's somewhere between $5,000 and $18,000 a year. Physical therapy ran as high as $7,000 a year. Then there was schooling. You can't really go to a public school if you are training four hours a day. So you need either an accommodating private school — such as Holton-Arms — or home schooling:

> Laurel Springs is the most common online school used by tennis families. It is approximately $4,000 to $6,000 for middle school and $7,000 to $9,000 for high school.... Families with children wanting to go to high-level universities averaged $7,000 for tutoring in conjunction with Laurel Springs tuition.

Tennis rackets came to somewhere around $900 a year for most families. Stringing those rackets ran somewhere between $800 and $2,500. Shoes were $500 to $1,800 a year, with another few thousand for clothes, racket bags, grips, towels, and so on.

Feel free to add all that up, but you get the point: It's really hard to be a national-caliber tennis player in high school unless you come from a wealthy family and live near a country club and have at least one parent with sufficient time on their hands to drive you all over the country for tournaments and handle the acquisition and management of the small army of coaches, trainers, physical therapists, and tutors you need to be successful.

And what was Jane's family's reward for spending that much on her tennis game? Jane would never play on the professional tour. She was never *that* good. But she did master a beautiful game that she can play for the rest of her life, which is not a trivial thing. More to the point, she got recruited by lots of very exclusive colleges. She chose Georgetown.

After Jane completed her testimony, the prosecution called Meg Lysy, the admissions officer at Georgetown who handled the tennis team.

Q: What was the typical process for the admission of tennis recruits?

A: Before the deadline...the coach would bring transcripts and would have SAT or ACTs and say, "These are the students on my radar to recruit." And it was my job to go through and look at the academic preparedness and say, "Yes, you can recruit the student. No problem." "No, you can't recruit the student."

In some cases, Lysy said, she doubted the academic qualifications of an athlete under consideration. But if they were good enough at tennis, she was willing to compromise.

A: Gordie [Gordon Ernst] would say, you know, "This player is going to change my team. This player is so strong." And in that scenario, we might admit someone whose academics were slightly lower, or lower than what we were looking for, because it would have such an impact.

Q: What, if anything, did you do to verify a recruit's tennis ability?

A: I didn't do anything.

Q: What did you rely on to assure yourself of a recruit's tennis ability?

A: It was the coach's word.

Q: Why did you rely on the coach's word?

A: Well, because his job [is] to be the tennis coach, recruiting the talent, and bringing the talent. And my role was to look at the transcripts and the academic preparedness.

For ordinary prospective college students, the process of admission involves a painstakingly detailed round of review and consideration — essays, transcripts, letters of recommendation, long arguments in the admissions conference room. But not if you are a tennis player. In that case it all comes down to what the coach wants. Would Jane have gotten into Georgetown if the coach hadn't thought she was a great tennis player? Probably not. Lysy was clear on this.

Q: How did a tennis recruit's grades compare to the typical Georgetown admitted students?

A: They were much lower.

Q: And how did a tennis recruit's standardized test scores compare to the typical Georgetown admitted students?

A: Much lower.

Q: Why was Georgetown willing to accept students with lower grades and standardized test scores as tennis recruits?

A: The feeling was that student athletes bring something special to a community, like a university like Georgetown. You know, they bring talent. They bring pride. You know, everyone wants teams to do well. And Georgetown's had national recognition with their sports programs, which is exciting for students and for alumni.

It's the same utterly unconvincing answer that Harvard's Dean Fitzsimmons gave! *Student athletes bring something special to a community.* Really? Listen to Jane describe the demands of being on the tennis team.

Q: How many days a week did you practice at Georgetown?
A: Monday through Friday.
Q: Do you all practice hard?
A: Absolutely. Practices included, you know, on the court and also off the court. So that included, like, weight lifting two to three times a week, as well as tennis practices every single day, Monday through Friday.
Q: Did you play year-round, or was it seasonal?
A: It was pretty much year-round. We did have a break post-Thanksgiving through the end of the holiday season. So right when we started second semester, the spring season was our main season.
Q: Did you sometimes travel for games?
A: Yes. Very heavily in the main season and during the spring. And then also in the fall, we had several tournaments across the country.
Q: Did you ever have to miss classes to practice or go to a game?

A: Absolutely. We would occasionally miss practice — or sorry, miss classes, depending on where the tournaments or the matches were, for days or just a day. It depended on where it was.

It's difficult to believe that tennis players "bring something special to the community" if they never spend any time in the community. Why is Georgetown so happy to compromise its own admissions standards for people who will spend all of their spare time hitting backhands on a practice court somewhere? *What's so special about a really good tennis player?* I've already given you the answer: What's special about really good tennis players is that the only way to be a really good tennis player is to *come from a wealthy family and live near a country club and have at least one parent with sufficient time on their hands to drive you all over the country for tournaments and handle the acquisition and management of the small army of coaches, trainers, physical therapists, and tutors you need to be successful.*∗

The first witness called in the Khoury trial was a man named Timothy Donovan. He was the one who served as the go-between between Amin Khoury and the Georgetown tennis coach, Gordon Ernst. Donovan had played tennis at Brown University, along with Gordon Ernst and Amin Khoury, back in the late 1980s. They all knew each other. Now he ran something called Donovan Tennis Strategies, a

---

∗ When we think of big-time college athletics, we focus on high-profile sports such as basketball and football. Those obviously aren't country-club sports, with the latter's same economic barriers to competition. But football and basketball account for only a fraction of the sports played at schools like Harvard.

consulting firm dedicated to getting all those tennis players, whose parents had spent hundreds of thousands of dollars developing their forehands and backhands, into one of the coveted slots carefully set aside by elite schools for tennis players.

Q: Approximately how many clients do you have each year?
A: It can vary a little bit, but roughly on average seventy-five to eighty per class.
Q: How much do your services cost?
A: There's a range. We have three different packages, so it starts at $4,600 currently. It goes up to roughly $10,000.
Q: And how else have you been compensated?
A: On three occasions, I received a success fee.
Q: What is a *success fee*?
A: It's basically a bonus where the client will come to us and say, you know, "We'd like to incentivize you. If you can be helpful in our son or daughter ending up at this school, we would be willing to pay you a bonus essentially of a certain amount."
Q: And in what amount have you received success fees?
A: So, in the three fees, one of them was $15,000, one of them was $50,000, and one of them was $200,000, of which $160,000 was actually paid.

On his website, Donovan lists all the schools where his clients have been accepted.

Amherst College
Bates College
Bowdoin College

Carleton College
Carnegie Mellon University
Columbia University
Cornell University
Dartmouth College
Duke University
Georgetown University

Wait for it...

Grinnell College
Hamilton College

Wait for it...

Harvard University

Harvard has a tennis team that it fills every year, just as Georgetown does. But tennis teams are small. They add only a handful of new players each year. To really move the needle on group proportions, you need a sport with the same comfortable exclusivity but with many more participants. Fencing is a good start: fourteen athletes on the men's side, eleven on the women's. Sailing works well too. That's another thirty-four roster spots. Rowing is the gold standard. There is heavyweight rowing and lightweight rowing, and there are forty women on the heavyweight roster and another twenty on the lightweight roster — and the same thing on the men's side. In a perfect world, Harvard would just add middleweight rowing, freeing up another twenty or thirty slots for students who go to high schools with enough money to field competitive rowing programs. But the middleweight category in collegiate rowing does not exist — *yet*. Harvard needed something new. And in 2013, Harvard realized that the answer was right in front of them, in the country's boarding schools and suburban sporting clubs: women's rugby.

There are thirty-three players on the Harvard women's rugby roster!

And if you looked at the biographies of the young women playing for Harvard that rainy day at Princeton, it was easy to see how the sport was tailor-made for a little extra bit of social engineering. This team — like most other sports teams at Harvard — was overwhelmingly white. The members came from some of the nicest upper-middle-class communities in the world: Shaker Heights, outside Cleveland; Marin County, just north of San Francisco; Herzliya, outside Tel Aviv; Upper St. Clair, one of Pittsburgh's fanciest suburbs. There were two players from Summit County in Colorado, an exclusive ski area where the average single-family home costs well over $1 million. The team's star outside back went to one of the best girls' private schools in Toronto. The star scrum half hailed from an elite boarding school in British Columbia. One player had grown up in New Jersey but trained every year at a national rugby "development program" in California; another had played for a rugby club that practiced at a complex on the perfectly named "Country Club Road"; still another was the daughter of a former US Senator. Two sisters had played club rugby for a group in suburban Sacramento — which, like so many of its fellow athletic hothouses servicing the elite schools of the United States, helpfully lists on its website the colleges where its players have been accepted to play varsity rugby.

Bowdoin College
Brown University
Dartmouth College
UC Berkeley
UC San Diego
West Point

Wait for it…

Harvard University

4.

In October of 2012, the US Supreme Court held oral arguments in the case of *Fisher v. University of Texas.* Oral arguments are at the heart of every Supreme Court case. They take place in the Court's central chamber on First Street, across from the United States Capitol — an imposing room in the grand neoclassical revival style, with forty-four-foot ceilings and twenty-four Doric columns in Italian marble. Lawyers for both sides stand up and are grilled by the nine justices, all seated at the front behind a long, raised, mahogany table.

The case involved a student named Abigail Fisher, who had been denied admission to the University of Texas. She sued, claiming "her" place had been given to a minority student with lesser qualifications. The school responded with an argument straight from Rosabeth Kanter: It wouldn't do any good to have only a token number of outsiders, Texas argued. The university needed to enroll enough minorities so that those groups could contribute meaningfully to the school's diversity. It needed to reach a "critical mass" of blacks and Hispanics — and it could not achieve that, it said, if it admitted students like Abigail Fisher.

Fisher was one of the most serious legal challenges to the practice of affirmative action that had been in place in many American schools for decades. The courtroom was packed. Fisher's lawyer spoke first. He barely got a sentence out before the justices interrupted him with question after question. The stakes in the case were huge.

Then it was the university's turn. The school's attorney was Gregory Garre.

> **Mr. Garre:** Thank you, Mr. Chief Justice, and may it please the Court: For two overriding reasons, the admissions plan before you is constitutional under this Court's precedents....

Garre got out one more sentence before he too was interrupted. If the University was going to make a Rosabeth Kanter argument, then the justices had a Rosabeth Kanter question. Kanter famously wrote that "exact tipping points should be investigated." That was the directive that led to people trying to figure out how many women it took to transform a corporate board, or how many dissenters it takes to overturn a consensus. So when Texas said it needed a critical mass of minority students, the justices immediately wondered: *How are you defining critical mass?*

> **Chief Justice Roberts:** What is that number? What is the critical mass of African Americans and Hispanics at the university that you are working toward?
>
> **Mr. Garre:** Your Honor, we don't have one…
>
> **Chief Justice Roberts:** So how are we supposed to tell whether this plan is narrowly tailored to that goal?

The University of Texas believed in critical mass. But it didn't want to say what it thought critical mass might be.

> **Chief Justice Roberts:** I understand my job, under our precedents, to determine if your use of race is narrowly tailored to a compelling interest. The compelling interest you identify is attaining a critical mass of minority students at the University of Texas, but you won't tell me what the critical mass is. How am I supposed to do the job that our precedents say I should do?
>
> **Mr. Garre:** Your Honor, what — what this Court's precedents say is a critical mass is an environment in which students of underrepresented —
>
> **Chief Justice Roberts:** I know what you say, but when will we know that you've reached a critical mass?

Roberts asks a couple more times. There's an awkward pause, and Justice Anthony Kennedy jumps in.

> **Justice Kennedy:** Suppose we — that you, in your experience identify a numerical category, a numerical standard, a

numerical designation for critical mass: It's X percent. During the course of the admissions process, can the admissions officers check to see how close they are coming to this numerical —

Mr. Garre: No. No, Your Honor, and we don't.

Why didn't Texas want to define what they meant by *critical mass*? Once again, the answer is obvious: Because they knew that if they did, it would become clear that they were miles from ever achieving that threshold with their minority populations. In 2008, when Abigail Fisher first sued the University of Texas at Austin, African Americans made up about *4 percent* of the school's population. That translates to roughly one black student in every class of twenty-five students; it's going to be hard for a minority student in that situation to reach the Rosabeth Kanter threshold of feeling comfortable and confident.

Now, if Texas wanted to be honest, they would say something like:

At the University of Texas we believe in the principle of diversity. But unfortunately we cannot offer an environment that gives minority students the best chance of feeling comfortable and confident. If that kind of experience is important to you, we recommend you attend another school.

Or how about:

At the University of Texas we believe in the principle of diversity. As an expression of that commitment, we will be donating a significant sum to another institution in Texas where minority groups can more effectively achieve critical mass.

But of course in the real world no university is ever going to say something like that. So instead the University of Texas sat its lawyers down and gave them strict instructions: *Tell the Supreme Court that we are deeply committed to enrolling a critical mass of minority students. But for goodness sake, don't answer any questions about what we mean by that term, because then it will be clear that we aren't in fact committed to giving minority students the benefits of critical mass.*

So Gregory Garre — the former Solicitor General of the United States, a former Supreme Court clerk, a pallbearer at the funeral of a former Supreme Court Chief Justice, the lawyer you call when you are trying to climb the very highest of mountains — sat there, mutely, pretending he did not have an answer. In frustration, the justices finally called on the Solicitor General of the United States, Donald Verrilli, who was there that day to give moral support to the University of Texas.

Chief Justice Roberts: General, how — what is your view on how we tell whether — when the university has attained critical mass?

General Verrilli:...I agree with my friend that critical mass is not a number. I think it would be very ill-advised to suggest that it is numerical. So —

Chief Justice Roberts: Okay. I'm hearing a lot about what it's not. I'd like to know what it *is*, because our responsibility is to decide whether this use of race is narrowly tailored to achieving, under this university's view, critical mass.

General Verrilli: ... I don't think there is a number, and I don't think it would be prudent for this Court to suggest that there is a number...

Finally the Court's most acerbic member, Antonin Scalia, spoke up.

Justice Scalia: We should probably stop calling it *critical mass*, then, because *mass*, you know, assumes numbers, either in size or a certain weight.
General Verrilli: I agree.
Justice Scalia: So we should stop calling it *mass*.
General Verrilli: I agree.
Justice Scalia: Call it a *cloud* or something like that.*

At which point the entire courtroom erupted in nervous laughter.

More than half a century earlier, the members of the Lawrence Tract met and debated whether to sell their vacant lot to a white or a black family. The Tract had to "weigh the value of the experiment against the need and welfare of the prospective buyer." Deciding between those two goals was far

---

* Here is what the lawyers for Texas might say in their defense: "The Supreme Court forbade us in (a case called) *Regents of the University of California v. Bakke* from using racial quotas. So if we commit to a number, we will be in clear violation of that ruling. We'll lose the case."

This is nonsense. First of all, the Court was asking for that number — and it wouldn't ask for a number if it felt that its own previous rulings prohibited it from requesting one. The university also simply could have cited Kanter's work, or any other research on group proportions, and said they were in the process of investigating how it applied to them. But they didn't. They behaved like fools.

from easy. But if you want to use tipping points in the service of engineering a social outcome, that is what you have to do. You have to decide how far you will go to defend a number. And you have to be honest about what you are doing.

But in *Fisher,* the exact same issue comes before the highest court of the land, in a case about the constitutionality of one of the most controversial issues facing higher education. Now the stakes *really* matter. And the very brilliant lawyer for one of the country's leading educational institutions just... shrugs.

In 2022, the Supreme Court heard another affirmative-action case, *Students for Fair Admissions v. President and Fellows of Harvard College.* By this point the Court had lost patience with American colleges and their pretense that a number they refused to specify could serve as the basis for an entire admissions system. So the Court threw up its hands and ruled all race-based affirmative-action programs unconstitutional.

Can you blame them?

The irony here is overwhelming. The game that Harvard is playing with rugby and that Georgetown is playing with tennis is, of course, *also* affirmative action. Except that instead of admitting underprivileged students with lower academic credentials, athletic affirmative action admits *privileged* students with lower academic credentials. It is only the first kind of affirmative action, however, that universities were unwilling to defend. And only the first kind that was considered so controversial that it ended up before the Supreme Court. The United States decided that it had no place for a special deal intended to benefit people who have been subjected to discrimination and hardship. But it was fine with a special deal intended to benefit people who can afford to spend hundreds of thousands of dollars on their children's ground strokes. I have no idea how you feel about the subject. But we can all agree — can't we? — that the wrong affirmative action was brought before the Court.

When the US Supreme Court issued its opinion, Harvard University released an angry statement. "We affirm that," the school said:

> To prepare leaders for a complex world, Harvard must admit and educate a student body whose members reflect, and have lived, multiple facets of human experience. No part of what makes us who we are could ever be irrelevant.
>
> Harvard must always be a place of opportunity, a place whose doors remain open to those to whom they had long been closed, a place where many will have the chance to live dreams their parents or grandparents could not have dreamed.

It would take a Jesuit to make sense of the many layers in that statement. But let us try. When the university says that "no part of what makes us who we are could ever be irrelevant," we can assume it is referring to its determination that Harvard should always be a place where only one group gets to be above the Magic Third. When it calls Harvard an institution where "many will have the chance to live dreams their parents or grandparents could not have dreamed," we can assume it is making a small, inside joke about the special deal it grants to the children of alumni. (What they really mean is the opposite: Harvard is a place where many have the chance to relive the dreams their parents and grandparents *already* dreamed.) And when Harvard says it wants a student body that represents "multiple facets of human experience," we can assume it is referring to the extraordinary lengths the school goes to, to ensure that a healthy proportion of its student body has been properly prepared for the Harvard experience on the country-club playing fields of the United States.

If you don't think that social engineering has quietly become one of the central activities of the American establishment, you haven't been paying attention.

CHAPTER SIX

Mr. Index and the Marriott Outbreak

"WE ASSUME IT WAS INTRODUCED BY ONE PERSON."

1.

On February 26, 2020, the biotechnology company Biogen held its annual leadership retreat at the Marriott Long Wharf hotel near downtown Boston. Biogen is based in nearby Cambridge. The company has around 8,000 employees, 175 of whom were invited to Boston, flying in from the company's facilities around the world. The meeting began on a Wednesday morning with breakfast in the Harbor View Ballroom, with sweeping views of the water. Colleagues who hadn't seen each other in months, or who had met only over the telephone or email, shook hands, hugged, leaned in closely to hear each other talk over the conversational din. That night, dinner and cocktails were held at an event space a few blocks away, the State Room, where the company gave out awards for outstanding service. The mood was buoyant. Profits and earnings were up. A slate of promising treatments was under development. On Thursday afternoon, the meeting ended and the attendees scattered — to the airport or to their homes around Boston.

In retrospect, everyone associated with planning and running the meeting realized it never should have happened. But this was late February of 2020. The virus known by the awkward name of SARS-CoV-2 was brand new. It had emerged in the city of Wuhan in central China the previous December, and had just begun to show up, here and there, throughout Europe and the rest of the world.

Could it turn into something big? Almost twenty years earlier, a close cousin of COVID — known as SARS — had surfaced in southeastern China, terrifying health officials. But SARS petered out before it could do widespread damage in the rest of the world. And it was possible to believe that this was just another false alarm. The signature events of the early stages of the pandemic — the mass lockdowns, the mask mandates, the social-distancing rules that upended life around the globe, the endless sirens in the night — were still weeks and months away. In February 2020, there were optimists and pessimists, and the leadership team at Biogen was among the optimists. That is, until the weekend after the conference, when one of its executives went to Massachusetts General Hospital in downtown Boston complaining of flu-like symptoms. Then, in short order, someone else who had gone to the conference felt that way, and then someone else and someone else, until around fifty people had fallen sick.

By Monday, the Biogen leadership was alarmed. An email was sent to everyone who had been at the conference, telling them to see a doctor if they were feeling unwell. On Tuesday, the team contacted the Massachusetts Department of Public Health. Then, on Thursday, after two employees in Europe tested positive, Biogen alerted all its employees that the company had an outbreak on its hands. That night, the company advised everyone in Boston not to go to Mass General to get tested. Biogen employees "are overwhelming the emergency room," and the hospital police were warning that they would deny entrance to anyone coming from the company.

Everyone was desperately trying to contain the spread, but by now it was too late. Several people who had attended the Marriott meeting went straight from there to an investment conference at another Marriott in Boston, at Copley Place. Now people from that conference, too, were getting sick. Another executive had flown from Boston to a conference in Naples, Florida, hosted by the consulting company PWC. While he was there, he got sick too: headache, fever. Had he infected others?

Then there was North Carolina, where Biogen had 1,450 employees working out of a facility in the Research Triangle, outside Raleigh. The Research Triangle contingent came back from Boston, went to work on Monday, and started getting sick as well. How many people had *they* infected? Emails began flying back and forth between state health officials and Biogen. The governor of North Carolina got involved.

From there things only got worse, as it dawned on everyone that because so many of the people at the Marriott meeting had gotten infected with COVID, and because so many of them had immediately boarded planes and gone elsewhere — not just Florida and North Carolina but everywhere, this being a multinational company with people all over the world — what had happened during those two days in downtown Boston was nothing less than a public-health disaster.

The Lawrence Tract and Harvard's rugby team are examples of social engineering. Tipping points create an irresistible temptation to intervene in the world. But with that temptation come very difficult questions. How do we balance the needs of the individual against those of the group? This chapter is about a third, even more difficult, social-engineering challenge — the one raised by the Biogen meeting at the Marriott Long Wharf. It has to do with the unsettling reality of how epidemics spread. In all of the exhaustive (and ultimately exhausting) commentary on the COVID pandemic, this particular issue rarely came up — perhaps because it raises too many awkward questions, or perhaps because the assumptions that most of us carried into the COVID pandemic were simply wrong. But the next time around, when another deadly virus sweeps the globe, I promise you it will be front and center.

2.

The Boston region's first known COVID case was detected on January 31. A Chinese student studying at the University of Massachusetts flew back to Boston from Wuhan in China, the city where the epidemic began. He returned just before quarantine rules and a ban on foreign travel from China took effect. That's around thirty hours in transit at the very least: Wuhan to Shanghai, Shanghai to Paris, Paris to Boston's Logan Airport. After he landed in Boston, he tested positive for COVID.

This was the early days of the pandemic. No one was taking the kind of precautions that would become commonplace a month later. The student landed at Logan. Stood in line in immigration. Made his way from Logan to his apartment in Boston. Did he have roommates? Maybe he did. If so, they almost certainly weren't wearing masks or practicing social distancing. This was surely a public-health disaster in the making.

But it wasn't. The student infected no one else. In fact, the whole incident was so ho-hum that the executive director of the city's public-health commission went out of her way to tell people not to worry: "Right now, we are not asking Boston residents to do anything differently," Rita Nieves said. "The risk to the general public remains low."

Five weeks later, a group of scientists at the Broad Institute in Cambridge figured out how to create one of the first diagnostic labs for processing COVID tests. This allowed them to analyze the genetic signature of the COVID virus in every patient they diagnosed, which allowed them to create a giant road map of how COVID moved through the Boston region. On no fewer than 120 occasions in those early months, they found, someone brought a new strain of COVID into the Boston metropolitan area. Of those, however, only a small fraction went anywhere. And even those that did spread mostly hit a wall.

One of the worst outbreaks happened about a month after the Biogen meeting, at a local nursing home. Virtually all ninety-seven residents of the home came down with COVID. Twenty-four of them died. A third of the staff got sick as well. The facility was *ravaged.* But did that particular strain do any damage beyond the nursing home? Not really. This was a place full of people coming and going, yet a strain so infectious and so lethal that it could wipe out an entire floor of a nursing home barely made a dent in the outside world. It spread. But it didn't *tip*. Only one outbreak in those months in Boston fit that description: the Biogen meeting at the Marriott Long Wharf.

Jacob Lemieux, an infectious-disease specialist who was part of the COVID research team at the Broad Institute, said:

> This information was coming out about the connectedness of the initial cases, and we started putting two, two, and two together, and…this feature of the data was staring us in the face, that so many of these early cases were connected to each other and connected to this conference.

The cases that arose from the Marriott meeting had a distinctive genetic signature — a mutation called C2416T. It had not been seen in the United States until the Biogen meeting, and in fact had been previously seen only in two elderly patients in France. So, just by tracing the path of C2416T — the Biogen strain — through the population, Lemieux and his colleagues could get a sense of how much of an impact that single event had.

"As we were releasing our results, the *Boston Globe* called us and said, 'Wow, that's really interesting,'" Lemieux went on:

> "But, you know, how many people could be impacted by this?" And we said, "Well, gosh, we don't know. I mean, it's a lot." And they said, "Well, how many is a lot?" And we said, "Well, you know, *a lot*…" We had an internal estimate and we shared it with [them] and the next day [it was on] the front page of the *Boston Globe:* "Scientists say 20,000 people infected by business conference" or something.

As it turned out, that estimate was woefully conservative. As scientists around the world reported the genetic signature of the COVID strains in circulation, the map they had drawn of the spread of the Biogen virus grew larger and larger. C2416T spread everywhere: twenty-nine American states; countries as far afield as Australia, Sweden, and Slovakia.

People were uploading sequences from around the world, and we could see this signature.... And it turned out that the initial estimate, which seemed so high, was actually really low. And in fact, probably hundreds of thousands of people were infected as a consequence of chains of transmission that had begun at this event.

The final estimate was that the Biogen meeting resulted in well over 300,000 infections. And how did it start?

"We assume," Lemieux said, "it was introduced by one person."

More than 300,000 infections from a single meeting, all traced back to a single person. What was so special about that one person?*

3.

We have looked, so far, at two elements of epidemics. The first is the overstory. The overstory casts a shadow over whatever is happening on the ground. The second element is

---

* One logical possibility is that the particular strain that spread from the Biogen meeting was unusually infectious. This was not the case. Later strains — Omicron, for example — were far more transmissible.

group proportions. The mix of people in a group determines when and if that group tips. Both of those elements were on display in the Poplar Grove suicide epidemic. Poplar Grove has its own particular overstory — an extreme ethic of achievement — that had devastating side effects. And its group proportions were all wrong. It was a monoculture. It needed alternative identities in which students overwhelmed by the norms of the school could find safe haven.

But there was a third factor. Remember what one of the sociologists studying Poplar Grove, Seth Abrutyn, said:

> In at least three of the four clusters, there was a high-status student that was very visible, who very much embodied the ideal of Poplar Grove's youth.…A lot of the youth who had died by suicide seemed like they were perfect, and then were just gone. So it was sort of like, "Well, if they can't survive in this context, how can I?"

One of the engines of the Poplar Grove epidemic was that the students who started the school's suicide cluster had special status: They occupied a significant position in the school's hierarchy. I talked about this idea in *The Tipping Point*. I called it the Law of the Few. Many of the social problems we deal with are profoundly asymmetrical — meaning that a small number do all the "work." And when I say *small*, I mean really, really small.

Let me give you an example. Years ago, I went to see a remarkable man named Donald Stedman. (He died in 2016.) He was a chemist at the University of Denver, and a brilliant inventor. One of his many creations was an elaborate contraption that used infrared light to instantly measure and analyze the emissions of cars as they drove by on the highway. I flew to Denver to meet him, and we drove to an off-ramp of I-25. There, right at the Speer Boulevard exit, Stedman had hooked up his invention to a big electronic sign. Whenever a car with properly functioning pollution control equipment passed, the sign flashed GOOD. When a car passed with what was over the acceptable emissions limit, the sign flashed POOR.

We must have sat there, watching, for an hour. What quickly became apparent was that a POOR rating was incredibly rare. Yet, Stedman said, those few cars were the primary cause of Denver's air-pollution problem. For whatever reason — age, ill repair, deliberate tampering by the owner — a small number of automobiles were producing carbon-monoxide levels as much as *one hundred times* higher than the average.

"Let's say a car is fifteen years old," Stedman told me.

Obviously, the older a car is, the more likely it is to become broken. It's the same as human beings. And by *broken* we mean any number of mechanical malfunctions — the computer's not working anymore, fuel injection is stuck open, the catalyst died. It's not unusual that these failure modes result in high emissions. We have at least one car in our database which was emitting seventy grams of hydrocarbon per mile, which means that you could almost drive a Honda Civic on the exhaust fumes from that car. It's not just old cars. It's new cars with high mileage, like taxis.

In Denver in 2006, Stedman discovered, 5 percent of the vehicles on the road produced 55 percent of the automobile pollution. That's the Law of the Few: It's a very large problem caused by a very small number of actors.

Stedman's argument was that once you understood the asymmetry of auto pollution, it became clear that the existing system of smog checks made no sense. Onsite smog checks, he told me, do a pretty bad job of finding and fixing the few outliers. Car enthusiasts with high-powered, high-polluting sports cars have been known to drop a clean engine into their car on the day they get it tested. Others register their car in a faraway town that lacks emissions testing or arrive at the test site "hot" — having just come off hard driving on the freeway — which is a good way to make a dirty engine appear to be clean. Still others randomly pass the test when they shouldn't, because dirty engines are highly variable and sometimes burn cleanly for short durations. Meanwhile, hundreds of thousands of motorists in Denver had to go to an emissions center every year — take time from work, wait in line, pay $25 — for a test that almost none of them needed. Why bother?

Stedman's idea was that someone should just set up his devices around Denver, and have a police officer pull over anyone who fails. A half-dozen of his roadside smog checkers, Stedman estimated, could test thirty thousand cars a day — which, in a few years, would translate to a reduction in emissions in the Denver area of 35 to 40 percent.

Since Stedman's pioneering work, other researchers have conducted similar kinds of tests all over the world. And the results are always the same: Somewhere around 10 percent of vehicles are, at any given time, responsible for over half the automobile-based air pollution. The distribution of polluting cars is — to borrow a phrase used in one study of drivers in Los Angeles — "extremely skewed."

In another study, a group of Italian researchers calculated how much Rome's air quality would improve if 10 percent of the city's cars were electric-powered. As you would imagine, it would make a big difference. But then they did a second calculation: What would happen if the city required just the top 1 percent of polluters to go electric? Pollution would fall by the same amount.

Nearly forty years after Donald Stedman invented his magic contraption, almost everyone agrees with Donald Stedman. So what has happened in Denver since Stedman started putting up his roadside testing sites? Nothing.* The state of Colorado still makes most drivers get a regular emissions check, and Denver's air quality — which was pretty good in the 2000s — has gotten worse in the past decade.

Urban air pollution is a perfect example of a problem caused by the Few. But we behave as if it's a problem caused by all of us. No one wants to act on the asymmetry, and it's not hard to understand why: Singling out a handful of big-time polluters would make the job of the people who worry about Denver's air quality a lot harder. What if the people pulled over were disproportionately poor? What if they couldn't afford to get their cars fixed? Do you confiscate their cars if they don't comply? What if the police balk at being asked to enforce antipollution laws? What if environmentally minded groups take matters into their own hands, buy a Stedman box, and start shaming motorists as they pass by?

Moving from the position that a problem belongs to all of us to the position that a problem is being caused by a few of

---

* The one nod Colorado has made in Stedman's direction is to exempt newer cars from regular emissions testing.

us *is really difficult.* And we are so intimidated by that difficulty, apparently, that we'd rather breathe dirty air.

In this section of the book, we've dealt with well-meaning attempts at social engineering that run into impossible problems: What if the only way to save a community devoted to helping black people is to turn black people away? Harvard's rugby team is an example of a second kind of social-engineering problem: What do we do when institutions quietly manipulate their numbers in order to sustain the privilege of a few? But here I want to describe an even more daunting problem that is very much in our future. Technology is going to give us the ability to figure out who the special few are — not just on roadsides in Denver but in all kinds of places, including big hotel conference rooms at the outset of a pandemic.

What will we do with that information?

4.

Viruses and epidemics are studied by many different groups, with many different perspectives. People in the public-health field are interested in how a disease affects a given population. Virologists are interested in the specifics of the actual infectious agent. Immunologists are interested in how the body responds to a foreign agent. And that's just the beginning. From there the various specialties divide into subspecialties, and the subspecialties divide in turn into microspecialties. There are tens of thousands of academic journals in the world, which gives you a sense of just how splintered science has become. Sometimes these various fields speak to each other and read each other's work. More often they do not, and what goes on in one corner can go unnoticed by the scientists who work in another. In the case of COVID, that was very much what happened with the small band of scientists who study aerosols.

Aerosols are tiny particles that float through the air. There are billions of them. Some are natural. Others are man-made. Aerosol scientists tend to be engineers or chemists. Donald Stedman was an aerosolist. He was interested in measuring the microscopic particles that come out of the exhaust of your car. That's a classic aerosol inquiry. Another would be: *When you cook bacon in a frying pan, what is that wonderful odor made of? Are all the particles that rise from the frying pan harmful? How big are they? Where do they go? If you turn on your exhaust hood, does the hood do its job?*

A leading journal in this field is *Aerosol Science and Technology.* And just over a month after the Marriott outbreak, the journal invited several leading aerosolists to weigh in on the mysterious epidemic sweeping the world.

Their paper was published at the beginning of April 2020, alongside an article headlined "Humidity, density, and inlet aspiration efficiency correction improve accuracy of a low-cost sensor during field calibration at a suburban site in the North-Western Indo-Gangetic plain." The paper was entitled "The coronavirus pandemic and aerosols: does COVID-19 transmit via expiratory particles?" It's safe to say that few people outside the aerosol world read it — which is a shame, because *Aerosol Science and Technology* was one of the first major scientific publications to correctly describe the COVID epidemic.

The instigator of the paper was William Ristenpart, who teaches at UC Davis, in northern California. A chemical engineer by training, Ristenpart got into studying human diseases by chance in 2008. "I found a paper by a pretty distinguished epidemiologist looking at airborne disease transmission between guinea pigs [of] influenza," he said. The paper was interesting but, to his mind, incomplete. It analyzed the whole problem, said Ristenpart, without ever asking the kinds of questions that came naturally to an aerosolist. "You know — is there a fluid flow? Is there velocity? Which way is it going? Things like that."

What he meant was that the epidemiologist was interested in *whether* guinea pigs could give one another the flu without any close physical contact. But they didn't seem to want to know *how* that might happen — and the *how*, to an aerosolist, was the crucial part. So Ristenpart began to dabble in the world of human disease, but from a chemical engineer's perspective. When you talk or breathe or sneeze, you exhale air. How does that process work?

"Have you ever seen your vocal cords? Until I dug into this, I didn't know," he said. "But laryngologists all use a laryngoscope, [meaning] you stick basically a fiber optic cable up your nose and it goes down here and then you can see your vocal cords in action."

He showed me a picture of his own vocal cords, taken by a laryngoscope. They are inside the larynx (the voice box): two strips of tissue, side by side, that slide open and shut like pocket doors.

It's pretty fascinating every time the vocal cords come together. So when you're [talking]…You know, I have kind of a deep voice, it's about 110 hertz. So 110 times per second, the vocal cords are slamming into each other.

Every time the cords open, little strings of fluid form. In the picture Ristenpart showed me, the strings looked like tiny fluid bridges stretching across the opening between the two pocket doors.

"And when those [bridges] break, little droplets are formed," he went on.

When you exhale, that's what is coming out of your mouth — these little droplets of saliva. Think of blowing bubbles from a bottle of syrupy fluid. You stick the wand in the bottle, and there's a thin film of liquid across one end. Then you blow on it and bubbles go everywhere. That's exactly what's happening inside your mouth, only there are millions of bubbles, not dozens, and they are microscopic.

So the COVID virus emerged, and *Aerosol Science and Technology* asked Ristenpart and three of his colleagues to comment. Their first question was, *What do we know about these droplets?* You may remember what we were told in the earliest days of the pandemic. On March 28, 2020, the World Health Organization posted the following on its social-media platforms:

FACT: #COVID-19 is NOT airborne.

The #coronavirus is mainly transmitted through droplets generated when an infected person coughs, sneezes or speaks.

To protect yourself:
-keep 1m distance from others
-disinfect surfaces frequently
-wash/rub your 🖐
-avoid touching your 👀👃👄

When the WHO said the virus wasn't airborne, what it meant was that the droplets coming out of your nose and mouth were too heavy to float in the air. That's why you could protect yourself by keeping your distance from someone who was infected: The droplets would travel only as far as the force of a sneeze or a cough would carry them. The message was "Avoid physical contact."

But the aerosolists thought this made no sense. If virus particles in those liquid bridges are being turned into tiny bubbles every time your vocal cords open and shut, then it's foolish to focus just on coughing and sneezing. The real issue is *talking*. You can exhale far more particles in a ten-minute conversation than you can in two or three sneezes. Ristenpart says:

> I think people — you know, doctors, everybody — have focused on the coughs, the sneezes, 'cause…they're big dramatic events. You can see things flying out.…And if you can see it, you can be…worried about it. But speech is ubiquitous. We talk with everybody all day long, right?

And, more importantly, we shouldn't assume that those little bubbles that come from talking are too heavy to float in the air. Ristenpart and his three coauthors thought that COVID belonged to the same class of aerosols they had been studying their entire lives. The bubbles are light. They float around like cigarette smoke. They can stay aloft in a room for as long as an hour — long after the person who exhaled them has left.

"Given the large numbers of expiratory particles known to be emitted during breathing and speech," Ristenpart and his colleagues wrote:

and given the clearly high transmissibility of COVID-19, a plausible and important hypothesis is that a face-to-face conversation with an asymptomatic infected individual, even if both individuals take care not to touch, might be adequate to transmit COVID-19.

The Biogen case had been a mystery to the public-health researchers who first investigated it because they couldn't figure out how a virus that spread through direct contact could infect an entire room. "This was the thing that was so hard for us to fathom," said the Broad Institute's Lemieux. "Hundreds of people in this two-day conference were infected. It's socially awkward to cough on someone, so how could one person cough on hundreds of people?"*

But if COVID was airborne, then it all made sense. All you had to do to transmit COVID was breathe and talk. The person at the heart of the Biogen case was just someone giving a speech in the Marriott's big, stuffy conference room. "The louder one speaks," Ristenpart and his coauthors wrote, "the more aerosol particles are produced." A person in the thick of a COVID infection stands up in front of the entire meeting and for a good forty minutes emits aerosolized

---

* One of the things the COVID virus did over the course of the pandemic was to get better and better at playing the aerosol game. Here's what one study concluded about the Alpha variant, which took over as the dominant strain in late 2020: "The Alpha variant was associated with a 43-fold…increase in fine aerosol viral RNA" — meaning there was 42 times more Alpha virus in airborne particles than there had been in previous strains. The article went on: "Our observation of increased aerosol shedding…suggests that evolutionary pressure is selecting for SARS-CoV-2 capable of more efficient aerosol generation."

particles loaded with a deadly virus. We've explained our superspreader event.* Or have we?

Because if the virus is spread by something as simple as talking and breathing in an enclosed room, then why weren't there a thousand cases like the Marriott meeting? We know about the Biogen outbreak because it was a singular event.

Why was it singular?

5.

In the early 1970s, there was a measles outbreak at an elementary school outside Rochester, New York. And because sixty children fell ill, the local health officials felt compelled to launch an investigation. They collected medical records, analyzed maps of the school, studied how the ventilation system worked, figured out who rode the bus home and who didn't, and determined where every infected child sat in their classroom. From that, they were able to reconstruct the path of the virus. The outbreak, they learned, came in two waves. Twenty-eight students got infected in the first wave, and

---

* If you are wondering, by the way, if the WHO ever formally admitted that COVID was airborne, the answer is yes. After months of dancing around the word *airborne,* they finally changed the language on their website. Someone can acquire COVID, they wrote, "when infectious particles that pass through the air are inhaled at short range (this is often called short-range aerosol or short-range airborne transmission)." Transmission can also happen in crowded indoor environments through "long-range airborne transmission," the WHO website says, "because aerosols can remain suspended in the air or travel farther than conversational distance." The change appeared on their website almost two years after the aerosolists said few other explanations were plausible for what they were seeing all around them.

those twenty-eight eventually passed on the virus to another thirty-one kids. That much was normal. You catch the measles from someone else. Your parents keep you at home until the infection passes. Sooner or later, the outbreak dies out.

But then they stumbled onto something strange. It had to do with how the first wave of twenty-eight schoolchildren got sick. *It was from one person:* a girl in second grade. And her case made no sense. She didn't ride the bus to school, which the investigators thought was one of the likeliest places for transmission to happen. Nor did she infect students just in her own classroom, which is also the likely scenario for the spread of an infectious virus. Instead she infected children across *fourteen different* classrooms. In the models that epidemiologists used to understand the spread of diseases such as measles, the assumption was that every infected person had roughly the same chance of passing on their virus to someone else. But this little girl made a mockery of that assumption: The only way to make sense of that inexplicable first wave was if she exhaled *ten times* more virus particles than the typical measles patient.

"We are intrigued by the possibility of an order of magnitude difference between the infectiousness of the index case and the subsequent cases," the investigators wrote.

Intrigued, it's safe to say, was an understatement.

It took a long time for this idea — that some people might excel at infecting others — to take hold in the scientific world. For years in the medical literature there were scattered reports, the epidemiological equivalent of UFO sightings. But no one knew quite what to do with cases like this. They didn't fit easily into the existing models about how epidemics work. The term *superspreader* didn't come into regular use until the end of the 1970s, but even then the concept remained theoretical. There were too many unanswered questions. Everyone understood that, say, a six-foot-five man weighing 275 pounds would pose more of a threat in spreading a respiratory virus than a 100-pound woman. His lungs were much bigger! But height and weight alone could not explain away the fact that a second grader was exhaling ten times more measles particles than her classmates.

The doctors in Rochester were flummoxed. They knew who their superspreader was, yet they couldn't figure out what made her any different.*

Enter the aerosolists.

One of the most important tools in the aerosol world is an aerodynamic particle sizer, or APS machine. It's a box, fed by a funnel. It's the human equivalent of the magic box that Donald Stedman invented for measuring the emissions of cars. If you breathe into it, it runs the air that comes out of your mouth through a series of lasers, which count the

---

* Here's another example. In the 1950s, a group of doctors in the VA hospital in Baltimore jerry-rigged their hospital ventilation system so that the air drawn from the tuberculosis ward was pumped into a room full of guinea pigs. They wondered, would the guinea pigs get sick just from breathing the same air as the patients? This was very early in our understanding that sometimes infectious agents are airborne. The answer was — they did. It was a landmark finding. You can trace a straight line from that experiment to the work of aerosolists today.

Then came the baffling part. Different TB strains have distinctive signatures, so the doctors compared the TB carried by the newly-infected guinea pigs to the patients back in the ward. This was a routine step: They had to make sure the guinea pigs got their infection from the patients in the ward. "It was not anticipated that the detailed bacteriology involved would be of special interest," the doctors wrote. But to their complete surprise, they discovered that nineteen of the twenty-two guinea pigs who caught TB, and whose strains were measured, were infected by just two of the patients.

number and measure the size of every aerosol particle in your breath. In one crucial early experiment, William Ristenpart's lab gathered a group of volunteers and had them breathe into an APS. The study subjects repeated vowel sounds. They shouted and whispered. They performed "vocalizations." And the researchers confirmed what all those UFO sightings over the years had suggested: A small group of their sample was off the charts.

"That's what we call *superemitters*," Ristenpart said. "Some people just released about an order of magnitude more aerosols for the...same given observed loudness." He went on, "We had no idea. If I had to go back to the beginning, I probably would've hypothesized: *Different people have different-sized distributions.* But I didn't guess it would be an order-of-magnitude difference between people."

Another leading aerosolist, Harvard's David Edwards, found the same pattern. He traveled to Asheville, North Carolina, and Grand Rapids, Michigan, and measured the breathing of a group in each city. He ended up testing 194 people. The overwhelming majority were low spreaders. They would be hard-pressed to infect anyone. But there were thirty-four whom Edwards called high producers. Of those thirty-four, eighteen were super-high spreaders, and within that elite group was one person who exhaled on average an astonishing 3,545 particles per liter — over *twenty times* more than the largest group of low spreaders.

Finally, near the end of the pandemic, came the decisive bit of evidence. As part of a "challenge study," British researchers deliberately infected thirty-six willing volunteers with COVID. All of them were young and healthy. They were all exposed to the exact same dose of the exact same strain at exactly the same time under exactly the same conditions. All were then quarantined in a hospital, enabling the researchers to put them under a medical microscope, monitoring and testing every symptom and vital sign. Ristenpart and Edwards were measuring ordinary people who weren't infected with a virus. The British study, by contrast, was the first to look at what happened to people *with* COVID. And what did they find? A full 86 percent of all of the COVID virus particles detected in their group of infected volunteers came from... two people.

Airborne viruses do not operate according to the Law of the Few. They operate according to the Law of the Very, Very, Very Few.

6.

What the aerosolists had identified was not something that happened at random, from time to time, to one person or another. "For unclear reasons, certain individuals are 'speech superemitters' who emit an order-of-magnitude more aerosol particles than average," Ristenpart and his colleagues wrote in their *Aerosol Science and Technology* manifesto. In other words, a certain kind of individual — like that little girl in Rochester — produces lots of aerosol particles as part of their genetic makeup.

William Ristenpart thinks that superspreaders might be people who, by some quirk, have saliva with unusual properties: Their saliva is more elastic and more viscous — thicker and stickier — than normal. So when they break through those liquid bridges across their vocal cords, more aerosols are produced.*

David Edwards, for his part, believes that whatever individual differences exist — at least when it comes to particles emitted by breathing — might be amplified by something as simple as hydration.

"Your upper airways are like a car wash," he explains, "and the air that comes into your upper airways is like a car."

When the car wash is working properly, the vast majority of the little bits and pieces in the air you breathe gets washed away.

"If you stay well hydrated, your upper airways will capture pathogens all the time, and they move them — within twenty minutes or an hour — out into your gut and you swallow…and they're eliminated that way," Edwards said. "But when you're dehydrated, there's no water in the car wash." And with the car wash broken, things like virus particles get past the cleansing operation in your upper airways and into your lungs. That's why being dehydrated makes you more vulnerable to colds and the flu and COVID: When you exhale, those virus particles come back out — and now you are more likely not just to contract a virus but to spread it. The particles hit your dry airways and break up into a concentrated, foamy spray, like a big wave hitting a beach. That's how you get to 3,545 particles per liter.

So, which people tend to have dehydrated upper airways?

---

* Ristenpart: "You can see this very clearly, if you like. Take some saliva and take your fingers and pull it apart. You'll see like a little string. It's called *beads-on-a-string instability*. And you don't get that with plain water, but you do get it with fluids that are viscoelastic. So the hypothesis is that maybe these superemitters have anomalous viscoelastic properties in their saliva."

When Edwards looked at his breathing data, he found that the biggest predictors of high production of aerosols were age and body-mass index (BMI).

> The older you get, the more dehydrated you tend to be. The more body mass you have, the more dehydrated you tend to be. And when you become infected [with COVID-19], you often become dehydrated. And so it turns out that the common denominator in these three groups of people is a dehydration issue.*

We don't yet know which — if any — of these explanations is correct. But it seems certain that one day scientists *will* know, and that discovery will create an industrial-size version of the dilemma we faced with Donald Stedman's roadside-emissions plan. The temptation to use this knowledge to control the course of future epidemics will be as great as it was for the Lawrence Tract and Harvard University. Only this time around, the resulting complications will be even worse.

What if age and obesity really *are* the two biggest predictors of superspreading? Does that mean in the middle of a pandemic passengers will refuse to sit beside an overweight person on a plane? What if the answer is viscous saliva, and someone comes up with a ten-second test to measure if someone is in the 99th percentile? Would a restaurant or a movie

---

* Here is the conclusion from a study that looked at the hydration levels of a large sample of Americans: "Our findings…suggest that individuals with higher BMIs may behave in ways that lead them to be inadequately hydrated. Obese individuals have higher water needs than nonobese individuals, because water needs depend upon metabolic rate, body surface area, and body weight. Water turnover rates increase with BMI based on higher energy requirements, greater food consumption, and higher metabolic production."

theater or a church be justified in asking everyone to take a saliva test at the door — and then turn away those whose results fall at the extreme end?*

Stedman would have said, in answer to his detractors, that all of these objections are well and good, but at a certain point the city of Denver has to decide how serious it is about cleaning up its air. This will be true of the next deadly aerosolized virus as well. We will have to decide how far we are willing to go in order to save lives.

In the summary of their findings, the British research group wrote this:

> Predicting or identifying people who might be high virus emitters, perhaps even before they are infected, is of interest because they could be prioritized for interventions to block transmission.

That sentence — that finding the superspreaders will be "of interest" the next time around — is an understatement. It will most definitely be of interest.

7.

I think we can now venture a theory of what happened at the Marriott Long Wharf on February 26, 2020.

---

* In his book *The Rules of Contagion: Why Things Spread and Why They Stop*, epidemiologist Adam Kucharski writes: "Viewing at-risk people as special or different can encourage a 'them and us' attitude." Focusing on superspreaders, he says, is dangerous, "leading to segregation and stigma." He's right! The problem is that nature does not follow the politically convenient course.

We have someone, in the thick of a COVID infection, attending a crowded meeting. We do not know the real name of the index case at the Marriott, but for simplicity's sake let's assume it was a man and call him Mr. Index. (The term used to describe the person at the root of any disease outbreak is the *index case*.)

Mr. Index is a superspreader. He doesn't realize this, of course. No one does. And for the most part, it hasn't mattered much over the course of his life, or at least no one has ever noticed that, say, when he got the flu, everyone got the flu. But now he harbors a deadly virus.

C2416T — the virus he carried — was first spotted in France. So let's further assume that Mr. Index worked in one of Biogen's Western European operations. He got infected just before he left for Boston. He was still in his incubation phase, so he didn't infect anyone on the plane. But it was a long flight: almost nine hours. And he didn't drink enough water, because he didn't want to get up repeatedly to use the bathroom. Maybe he had a glass of wine — alcohol speeds up dehydration — and went to sleep. The fact that the air on planes is notoriously dry didn't help matters. He landed. He waited in a long line to pass through immigration.

It takes about twelve hours of breathing dry air to "downregulate" the hydration systems in your upper respiratory tract, and between his flight and the long wait to have his passport checked, Mr. Index was well past that point by the time he got to his hotel. He was older and heavyset, which meant that he needed to be drinking much more water than everyone around him. But he didn't realize that, and now his surging infection and his dehydration have made his natural inclination to overproduce aerosols much, much worse. His upper respiratory tract is now a long, parched, desert highway. His saliva is thick and syrupy. There are so many saliva bridges across his vocal cords that his voice box looks like the Thames winding through London.

He arrives at the Marriott Long Wharf. Mr. Index has breakfast with the group in the Harbor View Ballroom. (In hindsight, it would have been a big help if the ballroom's floor-to-ceiling windows had been open. But they weren't, and in any case no one in those early days of COVID was thinking about the importance of ventilation.) After breakfast, Mr. Index leaves with everyone else for the Grand Ballroom downstairs. The lobby outside the ballroom is long and narrow. During coffee breaks, it will be congested. Let's suppose that his is the first presentation of the day: an update on Biogen's European business. He stands up in front of the entire group. He speaks loudly, as people addressing a big room naturally do, and because the news from Europe is unusually good and he's excited, out come millions of aerosolized particles.

Mr. Index talks and talks. He answers questions. Afterward his colleagues come up to give him a hug (or a handshake, or a kiss on both cheeks) for a job well done. Mr. Index leaves the meeting on a high.

Until, that is, he wakes up a couple of days after the conference with a raging fever, a crippling headache, and the sudden realization that he is very, very sick — followed by a second, even more terrifying realization that perhaps as a result, lots of other people are about to be very, very sick as well.

Part Three

The Overstory

CHAPTER SEVEN

The L.A. Survivors' Club

"AND I DIDN'T TALK ABOUT THE HOLOCAUST, NOT EVEN TO MY OWN CHILD."

1.

At the outbreak of the Second World War, Fred Diament was sent to the Sachsenhausen concentration camp outside Berlin, and from there to Auschwitz. He was fifteen. He was what was known as a "low number," meaning one of the first to be sent to the camps. Fred's father was beaten to death. His brother was hanged. He endured five winters in the camps, fought in Auschwitz's underground resistance, survived the death march out of Auschwitz in 1945, met his future wife on a boat to Palestine, served in Israel's war for independence, fought again in the Sinai campaign of 1956, then moved to Los Angeles, finished his undergraduate degree at night, and rose to be CEO of a women's clothing company. He was five-foot-four. He acted like a giant. Everyone called him Freddie.

"Freddie was very angry," Rachel Lithgow said. She met Freddie and the circle of Holocaust survivors around him in Los Angeles when she was working for Steven Spielberg's Shoah Foundation. "He was also hilarious. He had an incredible sense of humor. Dark. You know, he would call it 'the country club known as Auschwitz.' "

Freddie's best friend was Siegfried Halbreich. They had been in Sachsenhausen and Auschwitz together. "Sig" was one of the leaders of the Auschwitz resistance, and because he had been a pharmacist before the war, he served as a doctor to the prisoners. He moved to Los Angeles in 1960 and opened a custom frame shop in Santa Monica. He and Freddie were inseparable. "It was like watching Ralph Kramden and Norton go at it. All they did was spend every day together arguing," Lithgow said. "It was ridiculous. Sig was this very clipped, proper German guy. The most casual I ever saw him was when he didn't wear a tie once."

Freddie died in 2004.

And so we go to the funeral and it's a full house. You know, everybody's there, right? The whole community's there. Even the people who hated Freddie and he hated showed up to, you know, pay their respects. And Sig Halbreich, his best friend for life, gives the eulogy.... And Sig gets up there and he's very dramatic. He's dressed in his best suit. And Sig says — in his thick German accent — "What can we say about Fred Diament?"

And then he turned around to address the coffin of his dearest friend.

And waved his hands at him. Waving, just like, pointing and waving, but his back to us. Wild gesticulation. We couldn't hear a damn word of it. And then he turned back around...gripped the podium, and very dramatically said,

Und dat vas Fred. The whole place lost their minds. We couldn't stop laughing.

Then there was Masha Loen. Masha was Lithuanian. She survived Stutthof, the concentration camp the Nazis set up just outside Gdańsk in Poland. She got typhus, twice. (Thereafter, she called the experience "the typhuses.") When the camp was liberated Masha was buried in a pile of bodies, but was spotted waving her hand in the air. She married the love of her life, moved to Los Angeles after the war. She was indomitable.

"Oh, you have no idea," Lithgow said. "She was my secretary and we were doing a mailing one Pesach and we're all there."

Pesach is Passover, during which Jews do not eat leavened bread. Masha was an observant Jew.

"Where's Masha? Where's Masha? And I go to one of the unused offices — *Pesach,* by the way — I open up the door and there, she's like this with a cheeseburger."

A cheeseburger is just about the most nonkosher food imaginable.

"And I went like this" — Lithgow made a gesture of horror — "and she goes, 'Shut the door.' So I come in and I shut the door behind me and she goes, 'Listen, you. I'm a good Jew. I survived the death march and the typhuses....I should be constipated two weeks because our ancestors wandered in the desert?' I just stared at her and she said, 'Now get the hell out of this office. And if you tell anybody you saw me in here, including my husband, I'll kill you.' And I just backed out slowly."

Freddie, Sig, and Masha were the heart of the Los Angeles

survivors' club. They took English classes together at night at Hollywood High School. Word got out. More and more survivors from around the city joined them. A teacher noticed, and gave them classroom space.

"They kind of slowly started to see [themselves in] each other, you know," Lithgow said.

> They would sit after the class was over and just talk. Then they started to show up with stuff. Like, "This is the last photograph taken of my mother." "This is the [prisoner] uniform I wore when I was liberated from Bergen-Belsen. I can't throw it away, but I can't have it in my house for one more second. We don't know what to do."
>
> And so Fred Diament called up some guy he knew at the [Jewish Federation of Los Angeles], and this is what he asked him: "Can we borrow a closet to keep our stuff in? Because we want to save it, but we don't want it in our house[s]."

But whoever it was that Diament called — Lithgow could never figure out who it was — told them they should instead make a little display out of their mementos.

> And they took all their sort of artifacts and they took out a tiny little ad in the *L.A. Times* saying, you know, "People from the Holocaust are showing their things. And if you'd like to come to the Federation on Sunday between X and Y, they'll be on display." Thousands of people showed up. And then the survivors thought, "Gosh, we have something here."

The Jewish Federation of Los Angeles gave the survivors some space on the ground floor of its building on Wilshire Boulevard. They called it the Martyrs Memorial Museum. It opened in 1961. It was the first Holocaust museum in the United States. Years later, Lithgow would become its executive director.

Over the next few decades they became, in Lithgow's words, the "nomads of Wilshire Boulevard," moving from one tiny space to the next. They were always low on money or behind on rent, but they persisted. And in time, their idea spread across the United States, to the point where there are now Holocaust memorials or museums in virtually every major American city: New York, Dallas, Chicago, Houston, Miami, and on and on.

The Martyrs Memorial Museum is now called Holocaust Museum LA. It's in a beautiful new building in Pan Pacific Park in Hollywood's Fairfax neighborhood. If you are ever in Los Angeles, you should visit. Go to one of their events. The museum's events, Lithgow explained, "don't end with the national anthem and they don't end with 'Hatikvah' [the Israeli national anthem]. They sing…" And she began to sing, in Yiddish, "Partisan Song," the unofficial anthem of Holocaust survivors, written in 1943 by Hirsh Glick, a prisoner of the Vilna Ghetto.

Zog nit keyn mol, az du geyst dem letstn veg,
Khotsh himlen blayene farshteln bloye teg.
Kumen vet nokh undzer oysgebenkte sho,
S'vet a poyk ton undzer trot: mir zaynen do!*

---

* Never say that you're going your last way / Although the skies filled with lead cover blue days / Our promised hour will soon come / Our marching steps ring out: "We are here!"

"It's what they would sing in the woods or at night in the barracks to keep their spirits up."

When you leave the museum, a question might occur to you — trivial in comparison to what you have just experienced, but important in its own way: *Why did it take until 1961 — over fifteen years after the end of the Second World War — for there to be even a single monument to the Holocaust in the United States?* And, more puzzlingly, *Why did it take so long for the idea to spread across the country?* I mean, take a look at the list of all the museums inspired by what Freddie and Sig and Masha created, and pay attention to the dates when they opened.

DATE CREATED	STATE	NAME
1961	California	Martyrs Memorial Museum
1984	Illinois	Illinois Holocaust Museum and Education Center
1984	Michigan	The Zekelman Holocaust Center
1984	Texas	Dallas Holocaust and Human Rights Museum
1984	Texas	El Paso Holocaust Museum and Study Center
1986	Florida	Holocaust Memorial Resource and Education Center of Florida
1989	Washington	Holocaust Center for Humanity
1992	Florida	The Florida Holocaust Museum
1992	New York	Holocaust Memorial and Tolerance Center of Nassau County
1993	California	Museum of Tolerance
1993	Washington, DC	United States Holocaust Memorial Museum

1995	Indiana	CANDLES Holocaust Museum and Education Center
1995	Missouri	St. Louis Kaplan Feldman Holocaust Museum
1996	Texas	Holocaust Museum Houston
1997	New York	Museum of Jewish Heritage — A Living Memorial to the Holocaust
1997	Virginia	Virginia Holocaust Museum
1998	New Mexico	New Mexico Holocaust and Intolerance Museum
2000	Texas	Holocaust Memorial Museum of San Antonio

The first opened in 1961. The second opened in 1984. But not until the 1990s — half a century after the Holocaust ended — did the idea of memorializing it take root across the country. Why?

In *Revenge of the Tipping Point* so far, we have explored the idea that we are responsible for the fevers and contagions that surround us, that it is our actions — intentional or unintentional, open or surreptitious — that determine the shape of an epidemic. But the cases we've looked at so far have been tied to a place or a community: Miami, Poplar Grove, the Lawrence Tract, Harvard. All of those places had their own very specific overstories.

In the next two chapters I want to expand our discussion of overstories to the kind that can hover over entire cultures and countries. This kind of overstory is closer in meaning to what the Germans call the *Zeitgeist*, which translates literally as *time-spirit*. Zeitgeist overstories are wider and higher. They cast a far longer shadow on the ground beneath them.

And the questions I want to ask are: *What does it take to change a zeitgeist overstory? Can a story on that scale be rewritten and reimagined, in a manner that changes the way those below think and feel?*

I believe the answer is *Yes*. We can even name the people who were responsible for one of the great overstory revisions of the last century.

But we are getting ahead of ourselves.

2.

Our memories of the Holocaust — in the words of the historian Peter Novick — have a strange "rhythm."* The defining novel of the First World War was probably Erich Maria Remarque's *All Quiet on the Western Front*. It sold millions of copies and was translated into dozens of languages. It came out in 1928 — ten years after the war ended. That "rhythm" of memory is typical. The United States pulled out of Vietnam in 1973. The two most culturally influential movies about the war — *The Deer Hunter* and *Apocalypse Now* — came out in 1978 and 1979, respectively. By 1982, there was a full-scale memorial to the Vietnam War on the Mall in Washington, DC.

But the Holocaust wasn't like that. There was a popular — if oddly upbeat — Broadway production of *The Diary of Anne Frank* that ran for almost two years in the 1950s, followed by a movie version. In the 1960s, Sidney Lumet made a

---

* Novick's book on the subject, *The Holocaust in American Life*, came out in 1999. It was an enormous critical success.

critically acclaimed movie — *The Pawnbroker* — about a survivor of the concentration camps. But the film was only a modest success at the box office, and some Jewish groups called for it to be boycotted. There were a handful of other novels and movies, here and there, but nothing culturally consequential. The problem was not that people were denying the Holocaust, claiming it never happened. It's because they didn't know about it. Or they knew about it but didn't want to talk about it.

In 1961, the distinguished Harvard University historian H. Stuart Hughes published *Contemporary Europe: A History,* a lengthy account of what happened in Europe between 1914 and the end of the 1950s. Over the course of 524 pages, Hughes never once uses the word *holocaust.* He mentions what happened in the concentration camps just three times: in a sentence on page 229, a paragraph on page 237, and two paragraphs on page 331. Hughes devotes far more space to classical composer Arnold Schoenberg and the rise of atonality and the twelve-tone scale.

The following year, in 1962, Samuel Morison and Henry Commager released the updated edition of their two-volume textbook, *The Growth of the American Republic.* Morison won two Pulitzer Prizes over the course of his career. Commager was considered one of the most important American historians of the postwar era. If you were a college student anywhere in the United States in the 1950s and 1960s, chances are that *The Growth of the American Republic* was the book you read in history class. As you can imagine, Morison and Commager had much to say about the Second World War. It happened during both of their lifetimes. But the Holocaust? It gets a few sentences in a single paragraph, with no particular emphasis on the explicit antisemitism driving it. "These atrocity camps had been established in 1937 for Jews, gypsies, and anti-Nazi Germans and Austrians," they write. "With the coming of the war the Nazis used them for prisoners of all nationalities, civilians and soldiers, men, women, and children, and for Jews rounded up in Italy, France, Holland, and Hungary."

A few sentences of further description follow, then:

> But the evidence is conclusive that the total number of civilians done to death by Hitler's orders exceeded six million. And the pathetic story of one of the least of these, the diary of the little German girl Anna Frank, has probably done more to convince the world of the hatred inherent in the Nazi doctrine than the solemn postwar trials.

And with that, they are finished with the issue and off to a description of President Roosevelt decamping to his winter house in Warm Springs, Georgia. Never mind that "Anna Frank" is actually *Anne* Frank. And although it is technically accurate that she was born in Germany, she was living in Amsterdam when she was writing her diaries, because her family had fled the Nazis, which would seem to be a relevant bit of information. And for goodness' sake she was *Jewish* — and if you omit that part, you miss the whole point of the "Anna" Frank story.

"References to 'Auschwitz' or 'Concentration Camps' are rare," the historian and Holocaust survivor Gerd Korman wrote in 1970, after reading through more than a dozen of the top contemporary history books of the postwar era.

One textbook writer of American history took the trouble to add "(Cuban)" next to his "Concentration Camps" and was then consistent enough never to mention the word or camp names while surveying American and European affairs during World War II. Another book reproduces a photograph of a Jewish storekeepers' window, whitewashed with symbols and the key word Dachau, but neither index nor text ever reveals what the Dachau is to which the merchant had "been sent on leave."

Even within the Jewish community — and among survivors, in particular — there was a reluctance to talk publicly about what had happened.*

Here is Renée Firestone, another of the stalwarts of the L.A. survivors' club, talking in her testimony to the Shoah Foundation about the long path she took to openly acknowledging what had happened to her.

I lived a very glamorous life as a fashion designer until one day I had a phone call from the Simon Wiesenthal Center asking me would I come to tell my story. And I laughed at Rabbi Cooper and I said, "Come on. After all these years, why should I now start talking about those terrible days, those terrible weeks and years?"

---

* Novick writes, "In 1957 the *New Leader* ran a series of eighteen personal essays to see 'what's going on in the minds of the five million Americans who have graduated college since Hiroshima.' At least two thirds of the respondents were Jewish. In writing of what had shaped their thinking they mentioned a variety of historic events, from the Great Depression to the cold war. Not a single contributor mentioned the Holocaust."

And he proceeded to tell me that that night a Jewish cemetery was desecrated in the valley and — and a temple was spray-painted with swastikas. And when I heard the word swastika I went crazy and I hung up on him. I said I have to think about it.

And that night I was back in [the] camp all night in my nightmare. Next morning, I woke up and I called him back and I said "I'm ready to talk."

I want you to understand that when we came here and I started my business and I realized that I have to really concentrate on a family, that we were a very unique little group of people from the age of fifteen to the age of forty, maybe, that we had no children and no elders. That we have to re-create a new nation. So that's what we concentrated on and that's what I did.

And I didn't talk about the Holocaust, not even to my own child.

Here's another member of the L.A. club, Lidia Budgor. Budgor survived the Lodz Ghetto, Auschwitz, Stutthof, the death march, a bout of typhus, and saw virtually everyone in her family killed by the Nazis. She had just about the most harrowing war experience imaginable. The interviewer asks about her son, Beno.

Interviewer: When Beno was growing up, did you tell him about the Holocaust?
Budgor: Yeah, we talked about it. Yeah.
Interviewer: What age?
Budgor: High school.
Interviewer: What did he have to say?

Budgor: He knew that I was always involved. He knew it…
Interviewer: What do you think — how did he handle it, being a child of a survivor?
Budgor: No reaction. No, it didn't affect him.*

No reaction? What version of events did she tell him? "When I first started [speaking out]," said Stutthof survivor Masha Loen, "there were people who didn't even know there was a Holocaust."

Some Jewish people didn't know, like I told you.…It was like…you know, something out of the blue. They were shocked that there was a Holocaust. And these were very close friends of mine.

Today we speak of the genocide that happened in Europe during the Second World War as the "Holocaust" — capital *H*. The atrocity has a *name*. It's a loose translation of the Hebrew word *shoah*, which in Israel has long been the word used to describe the Nazi genocide. But in the years after the war, if the subject came up at all, what happened in the

---

* Before Budgor talks about Beno, and what she did (or didn't) tell him about her experience, she says this about her son. (She's a Jewish mother, after all.)
    Budgor: And I knew that my son will get a double-curriculum education, that his brain will — will work. And sure enough, he finished yeshiva, and with flying colors, with all honors, and valedictorianship, and so on, went into UCLA. And his future was made. And he certainly has achieved a lot.…
    Interviewer: What is he doing now?
    Budgor: He is a nuclear physicist, very —
    Interviewer: Married?
    Budgor: Married, with two beautiful children. And married a very fine young woman from Santa Barbara — Jewish.

concentration camps was referred to as "the Nazi atrocities" or "the horrors," or by the term the Nazis themselves used, "The Final Solution" (always in quotation marks, to establish some kind of moral distance). Had you said the word *Holocaust* in ordinary conversation in the postwar years, no one would have known what you were talking about.

Take a look at the following chart from *The New Republic*, showing how often the terms *holocaust* and *Holocaust* appeared in print over the past two hundred years. The lowercase, generic version goes from a trickle to a stream. The uppercase version is almost never used until the late 1960s — and even then, in modest numbers.

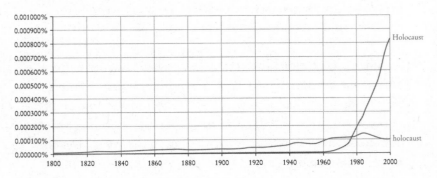

But wait. Right around 1978, something dramatic happens, doesn't it? The *Holocaust*-usage line goes almost vertical. So what happened in 1978 to make things tip?

3.

In 1976, two senior executives from the broadcast network NBC were walking by a bookstore when they saw a book in the window about the Jewish experience during the Second World War. One of the executives was Paul Klein, who ran programming for NBC. The other was his boss, Irwin Segelstein, who headed the company's planning group. They were the two people who decided what went on the air at the network.

Segelstein looked at the book, turned to Klein, and said, "Why don't we do it?"

And Klein replied, "We should."

Segelstein had a reddish beard and square, oversize glasses. He was chubby and irrepressible. He dressed in leisure suits with floral shirts, buttoned low. He had gotten his start in advertising. Once, early in the run of NBC's *Saturday Night Live,* the show's creator, Lorne Michaels, went to Segelstein and threatened to quit. Endless battles with his bosses over what he could and couldn't do had left Michaels feeling frustrated and exhausted. Segelstein listened quietly. Then, in one of the great television rants, he told Michaels he wasn't going anywhere:

> If you read your contract closely, it says that the show is to be ninety minutes in length. It is to cost X. That's the budget. Nowhere in that do we ever say that it has to be good. And if you are so robotic and driven that you feel the pressure to push yourself in that way to make it good, don't come to us and say you've been treated unfairly, because you're trying hard to make it good and we're getting in your way. Because at no point did we ask for it to be good. That you're neurotic is a bonus to us. Our job is to lie, cheat, and steal — and your job is to do the show.

Klein picked up Segelstein every morning in his Mercedes. (The doorman thought Klein was Segelstein's chauffeur.)

"Paul and I agree on everything but the basics," Segelstein once said of Klein. Klein was the more intellectual of the two. He was famous for saying that half of the American viewing audience were "morons"; when pressed on his estimate, Klein doubled down and suggested that maybe they were *all* morons. He was known for promoting what he called the Least Objectionable Programming theory, or LOP, which held that a television show's success was a function of how few people it offended. Klein also coined the term *jiggly* to describe the overly sexualized content of his competitor, ABC.

These were not men with principled ideological agendas. They were people who understood the American zeitgeist. Their job was to know what the public wanted — and they were very good at it. Segelstein had also lost an uncle, an aunt, and three first cousins at Auschwitz. He *knew* what had happened in Europe. And what Irwin Segelstein meant when he gestured at the book in the window and turned to Paul Klein was, *Do we think the American public is finally ready to hear about it too?* And Klein's response meant, *I think they are.*

The result of that conversation was a miniseries called *Holocaust: The Story of the Family Weiss.* It told the story of the Weisses — a family of prosperous Berlin Jews — and Erik Dorf, a rising Nazi official. It starred James Woods and a young Meryl Streep. It cost $6 million to make — a small fortune at the time — and required more than 100 days to shoot. Much of it was filmed at the site of the Mauthausen concentration camp in Austria.

Meryl Streep would later say that filming at the actual site of a death camp was "too much for me." It was grueling. She went on:

Around the corner there was a *hofbrau*, and when the old soldiers got drunk enough, and it was late enough, they would pull out their souvenirs of the war; it was very weird and kinky.

The director, Marvin Chomsky, hired a group of extras to play the camp inmates. He warned them they would have to take off their clothes and be machine-gunned to death.

"And while we were shooting this scene, one of the young, very young cameramen came up to me," Chomsky recalled.

And he said, "Mr. Marvin, you are making this up for the movie, this didn't really happen." And we had with us a gentleman who had a permit for weapons…a military man, and I said, *"Herr Graff,"* in my best German, I say, *"Ist das war oder nicht war?"* 'Is it true or not true?' And all eyes went right to him, and he thought and he said, *"Ja, das ist war."* All the kids, the young ones, just ran off crying their hearts out.

Again and again, Chomsky had to confront disbelief among the local crew. They had traveled all the way to northern Austria to film on the site of an actual concentration camp, but the crew still couldn't believe the story was real. They would look at photographs taken when the camps were liberated and shake their heads. Chomsky remembers them saying:

This was all doctored by American photographers, or British photographers. All doctored, made up, it never happened. Never happened. The piles of bodies in Bergen-Belsen [concentration camp] never happened.

The final cut of the miniseries was nine and a half hours, much longer than NBC intended. The network was nervous because it had aired another long miniseries earlier that year, about Martin Luther King Jr., and it had been a ratings fiasco. *Holocaust* aired on NBC over four consecutive nights. Here is a scene from the second episode. The show did not sugar-coat the Nazi Final Solution.

Two German officers walk to a grassy area, where a large pit has been dug. We see a group of twelve men huddled together, naked and shivering.
    A soldier turns to one of the officers, Colonel Blobel.

Soldier: Not much today, sir. The villages have been cleaned out.

The second officer, Captain Erik Dorf, points to a group of townsfolk standing not far away. He's high up in the SS, visiting from Berlin to do an inspection.

Dorf: Sergeant, are those civilians?
Soldier: Ukrainians, sir. They like to watch.
Dorf: And the photographer and the man taking motion pictures, who are they?
Colonel Blobel: For the battalion archives....
Dorf: I don't like this, any of it.
Blobel: You don't like it? What the hell do you think this is, a ballet? You're getting your Jew-free Russia, aren't you?
Dorf: It isn't tidy.
Blobel: It isn't tidy. I'll show you what's tidy.

Blobel turns to the soldiers.

Blobel: Line them up!

Two of the soldiers move the men into a line. We hear shooting and cries before we see what is happening. The camera shifts to a gunman shooting nonstop, then we see the men falling to the ground.

The Holocaust survivor and activist Elie Wiesel, writing in the *New York Times,* called NBC's *Holocaust* "untrue, offensive, cheap" and "an insult to those who perished and to those who survived." In a way, he was right — it was television's version of history. But Wiesel missed the point: This was the first time most Americans had ever heard about the Holocaust.

The scene with Blobel and Dorf goes on for an uncomfortably long time. We see soldiers casually looting the dead bodies, the onlookers drinking and smoking as if they were attending a soccer match. Dorf turns on Blobel.

Dorf: The orders were for secrecy and orderliness in these matters, and you're running a carnival.

Blobel responds by grabbing Dorf's gun and pressing it into his hand.

Blobel: Damn you. Go down there and you tidy it up.
Dorf turns and walks to the rim of the pit.
Blobel: It's like eating noodles, Dorf. Once you start, you can't stop.

The camera turns to a pile of lifeless bodies dripping with blood.

Blobel: Ask the men what it's like, Captain. You shoot ten Jews, the next hundred are easier. Shoot a hundred, you'll want to shoot a thousand.

As Blobel lectures him, Dorf walks down into the pit. We hear moaning. At least one man is still alive and in pain. A soldier points to him, though we don't see the man.

Soldier: That one, sir.

Dorf raises his gun, lowers it, looks around, and then shoots twice.

Blobel: Good, good. Two shots are plenty…Captain Dorf. The Zulu warriors say a man is not a man until he's washed his spear in blood.

The chart showing usage of the term *Holocaust* showed that sometime early in 1978, that word goes from almost never having been used to being used all the time. When did the *Holocaust* miniseries air? April 16, 1978.*

---

* The researcher who has done the most work trying to track the use of the term *holocaust* in reference to the Nazi atrocities is Jonathan Petrie. Petrie finds scattered use of the term beginning in November 1938, in the private correspondence of Jewish leaders and among scholars. The October 3, 1941, issue of *The American Hebrew*, for example, has a picture of two French Jews carrying a Torah scroll, with the caption "Before the Holocaust." The term appeared with increasing frequency after that, largely in Jewish magazines or academic articles. But what was the tipping point? Petrie writes:

> In the spring of 1978 over 100 million Americans viewed some part of NBC's mini-series titled *The Holocaust* [sic] — the screening was a major cultural event. As an immediate consequence, the capitalized and unmodified "Holocaust" became the recognized referent to Hitler's Judeocide in an American society newly sensitized to that tragedy.

4.

It is hard today, I realize, to accept the idea that the world could be changed by a television show. Audiences have been sliced up a hundred ways among cable, streaming services, and video games. The most popular comedy of the 2010s, for example, was *The Big Bang Theory,* a show about a group of brainy young people living in Pasadena. It ran for twelve seasons, and in seven of those seasons it was the highest-rated sitcom on television. When *The Big Bang Theory* series finale aired in the spring of 2019, it drew 18 million viewers, or 5.4 percent of the American viewing audience. 5.4 percent? There are as many Americans who think that the moon landing was a hoax as watched the end of *The Big Bang Theory.*

But a generation ago, television was a very different story. The 1983 series finale of the sitcom *M*A*S*H* — the *Big Bang Theory* of its era — drew *106 million viewers.* That was over 45 percent of the American public. If you walked anywhere in the United States during primetime on February 28, 1983, when the final *M*A*S*H* episode, "Goodnight, Farewell and Amen," aired, the streets would have been empty.* *That's* power.

"This was the period in which popular culture was dominated by three networks, each of which routinely got audiences for their top programs that dwarf anything anybody

---

* Program/ Year/ Viewers (in millions)/ Share of audience for finale:
  M*A*S*H/ 1983/ 106/ 45.5
  Cheers/ 1994/ 80.4/ 30.9
  Seinfeld/ 1998/ 76/ 27.5
  Friends/ 2004/ 52.5/ 17.9
  Big Bang Theory/ 2019/ 18/ 5.4

gets today," says Larry Gross, a scholar at USC who has studied the power of television for half a century.

> The most popular shows on television would do better than the Super Bowl does today. Just routinely, they would just amass these audiences — old and young; and educated, not educated; and men, and women, minorities, so forth. It was a melting pot....It was like preindustrial religion, entire communities gathered together to absorb the same messages.

Gross and several of his colleagues once did a fascinating bit of research to demonstrate what television of that era was capable of. He analyzed the responses of a large group of people who were asked how they felt about the biggest hot-button racial issues of the 1970s, such as: *Should students be bused to new schools in order to integrate them? Should it be permissible to discriminate on the basis of race when it comes to renting or selling homes? Should there be laws against interracial marriage?* On each of those issues, liberals, moderates, and conservatives were far apart. No surprise there. But then Gross singled out the responses of the members of these groups who watched a lot of television. This changed everything. Liberals, moderates, and conservatives, in most cases, disagreed strongly on hot-button issues *only if they didn't watch a lot of television.* But the more television people of all ideological persuasions watched, the more they started to agree. When a large group of people watch the same stories, night after night, it brings them together.

"It's not the media pushing this button to get that effect," Gross says. "It's the media creating the cultural consciousness about how the world works…and what the rules are." The stories told on television shaped the kinds of things people thought about, the conversations they had, the things they valued, the things they dismissed. And that shared experience was so powerful and transformative that knowing how much television someone watched was a better predictor of how they saw current issues than knowing who they voted for in the last election. "I always like to quote this line from a Scottish writer, Andrew Fletcher," Gross said. " 'If I can write the songs of a nation, I don't care who writes their laws.' "*

We need to pay more attention to the songs we're singing.

5.

So: Back to the L.A. survivors' club at Hollywood High in the late 1950s. They were a group of people — still young — who had survived a harrowing experience. It is easy to imagine a scenario where that group of survivors would have a million different reactions to what they had been through. Some would want to tell the world; others would want to move on. But here there was no such variation: In the postwar years there was a kind of common agreement not to speak of it.

This was what historian Novick meant when he mentioned the strange "rhythm" of Holocaust memory. He was talking about the effects of an overstory. What was that overstory

---

* The exact quote is: "Let me make the songs of a nation, and I care not who makes its laws."

about? Novick writes about a conference convened by the American Jewish Committee (AJC) just as the Second World War was ending. They invited some of the top scholars of the day in an attempt to learn how to combat the kind of hatred of Jews that had just played out with horrifying consequences across Europe. The consensus of the expert committee was that antisemitism was driven by a perception of Jewish weakness: The antisemite was, in this view, a kind of vindictive bully, preying on the helpless. As the head of the AJC explained, Jewish organizations should, as a result:

> avoid representing the Jew as weak, victimized and suffering.... There needs to be an elimination or at least a reduction of horror stories of victimized Jewry.... We must normalize the image of the Jew.... War hero stories are excellent.... The Jew should be represented as *like* others, rather than unlike others. The image of Jewish weakness must be eliminated.

In the late 1940s, there was a proposal to build a Holocaust memorial in New York City. "On three separate occasions — in 1946, 1947, and 1948 — the representatives of the...American Jewish Committee, Anti-Defamation League, American Jewish Congress, Jewish Labor Committee, and Jewish War Veterans, unanimously rejected the idea — and effectively vetoed the initiative," Novick writes. "They were concerned that such a monument would result in Americans' thinking of Jews as victims: it would be a 'perpetual memorial to the weakness and defenselessness of the Jewish people'; it would 'not be in the best interests of Jewry.'"

This attitude is completely understandable. It was *necessary.**** Sig Halbreich moved to Los Angeles from Cleveland in 1959, in part to get away from what he felt was an oppressive interest in his past. "Questions, questions, so many questions. I didn't want to talk much about what I had been through," he once said. Can you blame him? When the survivors' club first got together, their discussions about the Holocaust were private. It was the kind of conversation you can have only with someone who has shared the same experience.

"They spoke about it with each other," museum director Lithgow said. "But there was still lingering fear and there was still some…I hate to say it, but they were embarrassed by it to some degree. They were embarrassed by their accents. They were embarrassed by their tattoos. They were embarrassed that their children didn't have grandparents or family members at the school plays that every other kid had. I don't know why it turned inward for them, but it did. They felt shame about it for some reason."

That was the overstory held by the survivors: That what had happened in the camps was too overwhelming, too far outside even the most extravagant imagining of horror, and that the only emotional path available was forward. At the same time, those who hadn't gone through the experience had their own overstory. The textbooks from the 1960s that

---

* There was a hugely popular television show in the 1950s called *Queen for a Day,* where women told a hard-luck story to the audience, which then voted on the "winner" and crowned her queen. In one episode, the winner was a survivor of the Birkenau concentration camp who said: "Each time I look down at my left arm and see my tattoo I am reminded of my terrible past.…If only my tattoo could be removed." She won, and the show paid to have her tattoo removed.

relegated the Holocaust to a few sentences were written by historians who knew how to write about politics and economics and statistics and the other raw materials of their profession. But they didn't have the language or the imagination to capture the experience of the camps.

After the war Halbreich served as an interpreter for General Dwight Eisenhower — then the Supreme Allied Commander in Europe. Eisenhower noticed Halbreich's concentration camp tattoo — *68233* — and asked: "Did it hurt you very much when they tattooed this number on your arm?"

Halbreich thought: "My gosh, what kind of people are the Americans? They see what's going on here, full of bodies, dead people…and he asked if this was hurting? But later on, I understood, he had no idea. The Americans, it was strange to them to face something like this." Eisenhower didn't know how to talk about what was all around him either.

The silence was deepest in Germany. The Germans had their own shame to deal with. At the Bisingen concentration camp near the French border, local authorities had a long debate after the war about what to put on the sign in front of the cemetery holding some of the camp's victims. They settled on *Ehrenfriedof — Honorary Cemetery* — since, as the local government explained, "It was absolutely appropriate to keep the memory of the crimes of National Socialism alive among the local population." However, the government went on, it saw no reason to point out "the crimes of National Socialism to the foreigners who drive in large numbers on the federal highway 27, which serves as an international thoroughfare."

The community then planted thousands of trees and hedges, which soon overran parts of the camp. The Bisingen football club built a playing field over a charcoal kiln that the inmates had been forced to fill with shale. A small stone pyramid was placed nearby with the inscription: *Wanderer, if you pass here, remember those whose lives were taken before they had lived it meaningfully.* They could hint at what happened, but they couldn't say it out loud.

Imagine what it must have felt like in the mid-1970s to be someone who wanted the world to know about the Holocaust. Thirty years had passed since the end of the war. The window in which past events were typically considered and digested was closed. Historians were ignoring the subject. The survivors didn't want to talk about it. Hollywood was largely silent. In Germany, soccer teams were practicing on the sites of abandoned concentration camps. All the United States had was a makeshift museum off Wilshire Boulevard in Los Angeles, where a group of refugees had deposited mementos they couldn't bear to keep in their homes. The Holocaust didn't even have a *name.* What had happened in Germany during the war looked for all the world like it was going to end up as a footnote — and it seemed little could be done to change that fact.

But then again, Miami went through three shocks in 1980 and was never the same. Poplar Grove was a safe haven and then it wasn't. The cardiologist from Boulder goes to Buffalo and suddenly becomes a very different cardiologist. Perhaps a better question to have asked at that moment was not *if* the way the world thought about the Holocaust could be changed but *how.*

6.

And so, in that little corner of Wilshire Boulevard, the survivors' club opened the doors to their tiny museum.

"I think they were shocked that anyone gave a damn," Lithgow said. "I think they were really stunned that people cared. And that anybody was interested in listening to them."

But people *were* interested, and the Holocaust survivors learned that it really was possible to speak of the unspeakable. The numbers tattooed on their forearms were not embarrassing. Reliving a memory was not a sign of weakness.

Over the next two decades, that idea began to slowly spread, from Wilshire Boulevard clear across the country. Outside Chicago, an Auschwitz survivor named Zev Weiss started trying to persuade colleges to teach courses about the Holocaust. He was met at first, he remembered later, with "evasion, postponement, and general disinterest." But he wouldn't give up. He traveled around the country to lobby colleges, at times even sleeping in his car. He showed up at the offices of professors, insisting that they cover the Holocaust in their classes. "Some of his requests were a bit extreme," a friend remembers of Weiss, "and he wasn't a guy that was easy to argue with. It was easier to simply say yes to Zev before he even asked the question."

In the mid-1970s, Jewish groups worked with Congress to pass the Jackson-Vanik Amendment, a law that pushed the Soviet Union to do what would have once been thought unthinkable: loosen its emigration rules, allowing hundreds of thousands of Russian Jews to emigrate to Israel and the United States. It was, in the words of one historian, a triumph for a "proud, muscular Jewish particularism." Then in 1977, a group of neo-Nazis applied for a permit to march through Skokie, Illinois, a heavily Jewish suburb of Chicago. The town didn't ignore the march — its first impulse — but instead fought back. Something in the American Jewish community had turned, and it was that shift that had led Paul Klein and Irwin Segelstein to pause in front of the bookstore window and make their fateful decision.

The two TV executives didn't wait to see if they could find evidence of those same stirrings outside the Jewish community. They didn't hedge their bets and tiptoe around the subject. They created one of the most devastating and unflinching history seminars in modern history. It aired for four consecutive nights, starting on April 16, 1978, and 120 million people — *half the country* — tuned in.

In Germany, where *Holocaust* aired in January of the following year, the effect was even more electric. The program ran late at night, ending close to midnight, on a little-watched network of regional television stations — and *still,* 15 million West Germans, around a quarter of the country, had tuned in by the end. It was called "*the* German TV event of the 1970s." Magazines and newspapers ran special issues and sections on *Holocaust.* Thousands of viewers, some of them in tears, called in to their local television stations. Neo-Nazi groups planted bombs at TV stations in Koblenz and Münster to try to stop the show from being aired. Guilt-stricken veterans threatened suicide. A former SS officer reported that his wife and four children called him an "old Nazi" after watching the second installment, and deserted him. In Germany, the statute of limitations for prosecuting former war criminals was about to expire. After *Holocaust,* the West German parliament changed its mind and abolished the statute of limitations. In the words of one German journalist:

> "Holocaust" has shaken up post-Hitler Germany in a way that German intellectuals have been unable to do. No other film has ever made the Jews' road of suffering leading to the gas chambers so vivid....Only since and as a result of "Holocaust" does a majority of the nation know what lay behind the horrible and vacuous formula "Final Solution of the Jewish Question."

Today in Bisingen, there is a proper museum at the site of the former camp, one of thousands of Holocaust memorials and museums that have since been built across Germany.

7.

Many years after *Holocaust* aired, Herbert Schlosser, the former head of NBC television, was interviewed about how the show made it onto the air. He was Klein and Segelstein's boss. Schlosser gave credit where it was due — he was just the guy upstairs — except for one thing. In the earliest discussions of the series, the script had been titled *Holocaust*. But when the scripts were finished, that word had been dropped. It had no special meaning in the mid-1970s, after all.

"One day there arrived at my door a stack of scripts *this* high," Schlosser remembered. "And I made one contribution to it....I read the scripts. But I noticed the show was not called *Holocaust*. It was called *The Family Weiss*, which is the name of the family that goes through the Holocaust in the series. So I called [the producer] and I said, 'You don't want to call it *The Family Weiss.*'"

Schlosser wanted to go back to the name the script had been given originally. "Call it the *Holocaust,*" he instructed the producer.

And that's why everyone calls the holocaust, the *Holocaust.* Look back at that list of American museums: After 1978, *everyone* used the term *Holocaust* in their name. Even the original museum on Wilshire Boulevard went from *Martyrs Memorial Museum* to the *Los Angeles Museum of the Holocaust.* The mass atrocity that no one knew how to talk about now had a name. And why? Because a television executive thought it sounded better than *The Family Weiss.*

That's what storytellers can do. They can change the overstory.

CHAPTER EIGHT

Doing Time on Maple Drive

"I DROVE THE CAR OFF THE ROAD ON PURPOSE."

1.

In 1995, just four years after the collapse of the Soviet Union, the political scientist Timur Kuran wrote a famous essay entitled "The Inevitability of Future Revolutionary Surprises."

"Intellectuals disagree about many things, so there is nothing unusual about the numerous controversies that have followed the fall of East European communism," Kuran began. "What is remarkable is our nearly unanimous agreement on the fact that this momentous overturn caught the world by surprise."

Kuran went through the list of everyone who might have seen the revolution coming but did not. First were the "journalists, diplomats, statesmen, futurologists, and scholars," the experts whose job it was to make sense of world affairs. They were caught flat-footed. What about the ordinary people of Eastern Europe? Shortly after the fall of the Berlin wall, a poll was taken in East Germany: "A year ago did you expect such a peaceful revolution?" Five percent — a pittance — said yes. Eighteen percent said, "Yes, but not that fast." And the balance — three-quarters of those polled — said they were totally surprised.

Kuran went on and on. What about the communist leadership, whose power and livelihood depended on understanding the state of their own countries? They were oblivious. Even the dissidents — the people who had been fighting to overcome the Soviets for a generation — were blindsided. Kuran pointed out that the playwright Vaclav Havel, who would go on to become one of the first leaders of the democratic Czech Republic, wrote an essay in 1978 called "The Power of the Powerless" in which he predicted — correctly — that the Soviet empire was not nearly as impregnable as it seemed. It could be overthrown, he said, by a "social movement," an "explosion of civil unrest," or a "sharp conflict inside an apparently monolithic power structure." Havel's conclusion was astonishingly prescient: "What if [the brighter future] has been here for a long time already, and only our own blindness and weakness has prevented us from seeing it around us and within us and kept us from developing it?"

But what happened when the very revolution that Havel had predicted actually started? He didn't see it. When the Soviet leader Mikhail Gorbachev came to Czechoslovakia to speak, in what was one of the first real signs that Russia was willing to relax its grip on its satellite states, Havel was livid that his countrymen cheered Gorbachev.

"I feel sad; this nation of ours never learns. How many times has it put all its faith in some external force which, it believed, would solve its problems?...And yet here we are again, making exactly the same mistake. They seem to think that Gorbachev has come to liberate them..."

These were people who knew the history and culture of

Eastern Europe as well as anyone. The intellectuals had read all the books that mattered, and measured everything that could be measured. The people of Eastern Europe lived every day under Soviet rule. The dissidents had been fighting for their freedom as long as they could remember. There was nothing, as a group, they did not know. But Kuran's point was that there is something about a revolution — large or small — that baffles us: When a group of people come together, in a fever, and abruptly change the way they behave or what they believe, we are suddenly at a loss for words or understanding. "Just weeks before the Russian Revolution of February 1917," Kuran writes, the architect of that fight, Vladimir Lenin, "suggested that Russia's great explosion lay in the distant future and that he himself would not live to see it." This was his own revolution!

The stories of Miami and the *Holocaust* miniseries, I think, give us a partial answer as to why we are perpetually surprised. Overstories are far more volatile than they appear. But in this chapter I want to explore a second reason — which I think goes further in making sense of our perennial bafflement. We miss the signs of change because we are looking for them in the wrong places. And anyone who came of age in the early twenty-first century lived through an almost textbook example of this blindness: the battle over gay marriage.

2.

After Evan Wolfson enrolled at law school in the early 1980s, he read a book by the historian John Boswell, a scholarly text called *Christianity, Social Tolerance, and Homosexuality.* Wolfson was in his early twenties, just back from a stint with the Peace Corps in West Africa. There he had come out. "I mean, I'd always known I was gay," he said, "but [that's] when I began actually having sex and really imagining what a life [of being openly gay] would be like." The Boswell book opened his eyes. "I grabbed it and wrapped it in a fake cover and took it with me on the beach to Florida, where I was visiting my grandparents."

What Wolfson learned from Boswell was that "it had not always been this way for gay people, that different societies had treated homosexuality and understood sexuality and arranged sexuality differently." He found that message profoundly hopeful: "If it had once been different, it could be different again." He began to think about what it would take to change the way the world looked at gay people.

> I asked myself, *Why is it that gay people experience discrimination and oppression in our society in a way that they didn't in other societies?* And I decided that it could really be understood as a rejection — discrimination against how we love, who we love...
>
> And then I asked myself, *Okay, so what is the central structure...in which our society teaches and understands and supports love?* And of course, in our society, like virtually every other, it's marriage. So then I decided that by fighting for marriage, by claiming marriage, we would be making the most powerful possible statement that we are equal and central and worthy.

Marriage, Wolfson believed, would serve as the "engine of transformation that would change how non-gay people understood who gay people are."

This was the early 1980s. It may be difficult today to appreciate how deeply radical Wolfson's conclusion was at the time. Gay marriage simply wasn't a part of any social or political agenda. The overstory was miles away from the idea that marriage ought to be extended to same-sex couples. If you talk to your parents (or grandparents), for example, they will almost certainly remember a book from the late '60s called *Everything You Always Wanted to Know About Sex* (**But Were Afraid to Ask*) by California psychiatrist David Reuben. Reuben's book was the first modern sex manual. It was a number-one bestseller in fifty-one countries, and sat atop the *New York Times* bestseller list for over a year. Woody Allen made a hugely successful comedic film based on the book. Reuben was a guest on Johnny Carson's *Tonight Show* a dozen times, playing the role of the nation's avuncular sex therapist. *Everything You Always Wanted to Know About Sex* defined the zeitgeist, and here is what Reuben had to say in his chapter devoted to "Male Homosexuality":

> The majority of gay guys, when they cruise, dispense with the courtship. They don't even have time for footsie or love notes on toilet paper. Homosexuality seems to have a compelling urgency about it.

Reuben described furtive meetups in bathrooms as typical. He said men often have as many as five sexual encounters in an evening, each lasting "about six minutes." Homosexuals "thrive on danger," he said. They "have a compulsion to flaunt their sex in public." He went on and on about their love of costume, their obsession with food, their proclivity for blackmail, their adventurous sexual practices.

And then there was this. Reuben's narrative method, in the book, is to ask a series of questions, then give brief answers:

What about all the homosexuals who live together happily for years?

What about them? They are mighty rare birds among the homosexual flock. Moreover, the "happy" part remains to be seen. The bitterest argument between husband and wife is a passionate love sonnet by comparison with a dialogue between a butch and his queen. Live together? Yes. Happily? Hardly.

The other part of these "marriages" that doesn't fit in with happiness is that the principals never stop cruising. They may set up housekeeping together, but the parade of penises usually continues unabated. Only this time jealousy, threats, tantrums, and mutual betrayal are thrown in for good measure. Mercifully for both of them, the life expectancy of their relationship together is brief.

If this is how an entire generation looks at the lives of gay men, how on earth do you fight for marriage equality? Why would the rest of society let you share their most important social institution if they thought this is what you would do with it? Wolfson decided to write his law-school thesis on gay marriage. But he couldn't find a faculty adviser who would work with him.

"I went to some of the big liberals and more sympathetic faculty members. They to a person [said] no," he remembers.

They had all grown up on David Reuben. What Wolfson was talking about sounded ridiculous. "They thought it was either going to be too difficult...or not a worthwhile goal."* Wolfson left law school and toiled for years, fighting to change laws at the state level. But whatever progress gay activists made was met with backlash, culminating with President George W. Bush giving one of the most famous speeches of his presidency in February of 2004:

> **President Bush:** The union of a man and woman is the most enduring human institution, honored and encouraged in all cultures and by every religious faith. Ages of experience have taught humanity that the commitment of a husband and wife to love and to serve one another promotes the welfare of children and the stability of society.

Bush stood before the country and said — enough.

> Marriage cannot be severed from its cultural, religious, and natural roots without weakening the good influence of society.
>
> Today, I call upon the Congress to promptly pass and to send to the states for ratification an amendment to our Constitution defining and protecting marriage as a union of a man and woman as husband and wife.

One state legislature after another passed amendments to their constitutions making gay marriage impossible. Among

---

* Finally, Wolfson found a thesis adviser in the form of "a bread-and-butter, non-liberal, non-gay-identified...professor named David Westfall, who was basically just a regular family-law guy." Westfall gave him a B.

activists, a sense of gloom descended. "There were many calls to retreat, to give up, to stop, to slow down, including from some of the key players in the movement," Wolfson remembers. The leaders of the Human Rights Campaign urged caution. So did US Senator Dianne Feinstein of California, a longtime ally of the movement. "That whole issue has been too much, too fast, too soon," she said.

2004 was when years of work fell apart.

"There were a lot of people [in the movement] who were really despairing," says Matt Coles, who was a leader in the gay-rights fight at the time.

> The organizations that focused primarily on Congress or focused primarily on state legislatures were really, really thinking this was going absolutely nowhere.

The activists convened a summit in Jersey City, New Jersey, across the river from Manhattan. Together they hammered out a long-term plan for their movement. Careful. Cautious. Deliberate. They decided to move slowly, working at the state level and starting in the places where they felt they had a toehold. They would start from the least-controversial ideas — recognition of domestic partnerships, then civil rights. Only when they had won those two battles would they fight for the biggest prize: the freedom to marry.

Coles says that if you had asked him then how long he believed it would take to win marriage equality in every American state, he would have answered without hesitation.

"In 2005...I would've said twenty to twenty-five years." He paused. "But maybe thirty or forty."

He and all his fellow activists were wrong. Within a

decade, opposition to gay marriage had just withered away. Sasha Issenberg, who wrote *The Engagement,* the definitive history of the marriage-equality fight, calls the victory "the most significant shift in American public opinion on an issue in my lifetime." He goes on:

> In fifteen, sixteen years, support has gone up over one and a half times. And it's happening across demographic and political groups. It was young people, old people, white, black, Latino, evangelical, just all in one direction.

In the heat of battle, the activists did not understand that victory was in fact just around the corner. To paraphrase Timur Kuran: *Intellectuals disagree on many things, so there is nothing unusual about the numerous controversies that have followed the battle for gay marriage. What is remarkable is our nearly unanimous agreement on the fact that this momentous overturn caught the world by surprise.*

They were looking for signs of change in all the wrong places. So let's go back and look again.

3.

The made-for-TV movie *Doing Time on Maple Drive* aired in 1992, on the Fox network. It was nominated for three Emmys, which meant it was considered a cut above normal television fare. It tells the story of the Carters, a wealthy family living in a beautiful neighborhood. Dad is a successful restaurateur. He and his wife have three grown children: a married daughter and two sons — the youngest of whom,

Matt, is the golden child, handsome and brilliant, and a Yale graduate. In the movie's opening scenes, we see Matt bringing his fiancée home to meet his family for the first time. She is beautiful and wealthy and very much in love with him.

If you've ever seen a made-for-TV movie from that era, you know what happens next. The Carters turn out to be far from perfect. The older brother is an alcoholic. The father is overbearing and tyrannical. The mom is in denial. The married daughter tries to have an abortion without telling her husband. And Matt — we soon learn — is hiding a terrible secret.

The first to learn the truth is Matt's fiancée. She discovers an incriminating letter in his bedroom. She tearfully confronts him, then jumps into her BMW and drives off. We never see her again. Matt's bachelor party is that evening. He puts on a brave face. But at the end of the night, while driving home, he suddenly veers off the road and crashes headlong into a telephone pole. He tells his parents an elaborate story about swerving to avoid hitting an animal. But as the questions start to pile up, Matt's mother confronts him in the Carters' elegant living room.

> **Mom:** You'd better start explaining yourself, young man. You owe me an explanation!
> **Matt:** You already know. You know exactly why. You want me to say it?
> **Mom:** Don't talk to me that way.
> **Matt:** No! You want me to say it? You want me to say it, Mom? I didn't swerve to avoid hitting a dog, I swerved to avoid living this life!

I think you can guess what Matt's secret is, can't you?

Matt: Because I thought it would be better to be dead than to tell you...

Mom: All right, I've heard enough...

Matt: No, you haven't, Mom! No, you haven't. I tried to kill myself.

Mom: No, you didn't. You had...you had an accident.

Matt: No! No! No! I thought it would be better to be dead...

Mom: No! No, you had...

Matt: Mom! I thought it'd be better to be dead than...

Mom: No...

At this point the millions of people watching *Doing Time on Maple Drive* started to choke up.

Matt: Yes! Than to tell you I was gay! I drove the car off the road on purpose. I did it on purpose, Mom. On purpose.

What did all those viewers get from *Doing Time on Maple Drive*?

In the case of *Holocaust,* it is easy to see how a cultural event could change the overstory. A powerful and unflinching history lesson was watched by half of the United States, simultaneously, over the course of four consecutive days. What *Holocaust* did was give permission for the world to talk and think about something that had to that point been considered off-limits. But I think this kind of process works in much more subtle ways as well. In the previous chapter, I described the work of USC scholar Larry Gross, and I think it's worth repeating something Gross said: "It's not the media pushing this button to get that effect. It's the media creating the cultural consciousness about how the world works…and what the rules are," and up in the overstory, these kinds of rules are constantly being rewritten and revised.

For example, in the same era as *Holocaust,* a slew of "feminist" shows ran on television. *The Mary Tyler Moore Show* was the pioneer. Then came *Phyllis, Maude, Rhoda, One Day at a Time, Cagney & Lacey,* and *Murphy Brown* — and on and on. The explicit message of these shows was clear. They were about tough, competent, professional women. They made it plain that women could be every bit as capable as men. But remember, the power of television isn't telling us *what* to think. It's telling us *how* to think. And what were the implicit rules of those shows? That a successful woman is almost always someone who is older, white, straight, and *single.*

"So if you were a feminist, you couldn't be married," argues the scholar Bonnie Dow, who wrote a brilliant book analyzing this wave of TV programs.

> If you were a feminist, you couldn't have children.…The assumption is that if you have those kinds of politics…if you're willing to be out front about believing in women's equality, it's going to be very difficult for you to have a functional relationship. That's one of the rules.

The shows defined progress for women strictly in terms of career success, in terms of "making it like a man." Dow went on:

> It's about having the same opportunities as men. It's about achieving the same things that men are allowed to achieve,

which of course sort of erases all the possibilities for acknowledging the ways that women are different because they reproduce, for one thing, and might need a different kind of workplace.

The overstory created by these shows was something muddy and ambivalent, a way of thinking about women's rights that emphasized the overwhelming sacrifices women had to make to succeed professionally. To be immersed in *The Mary Tyler Moore Show* or *One Day at a Time* did not turn you into a feminist; it could just as easily turn you into someone who thought that feminism was an impossibility if you wanted kids and a family.

So let's go back to *Doing Time on Maple Drive*. Here we have a television movie that comes out just as people like Evan Wolfson are starting the battle for gay marriage. Did stories like that one — and there were, in that era, a surprising number of made-for-TV movies that touched on homosexuality as a subject — help or hurt the cause?

Bonnie Dow did an analysis of this question as well. And she found a set of embedded rules in the gay narratives of the 1980s and 1990s, just like the rules found in feminist sitcoms.

Rule #1: *Gay people are never at the center of shows that are ostensibly about gay people.* As a practical matter, that means the gay character has a one-time appearance — a bit part — in a recurring series. And when they do play a bigger role, writes Dow, "the narratives tend to be about how their revelation about their sexuality affects their relationships with straight characters, friends and family, co-workers."

Rule #2: *A gay person's sexuality is not an incidental fact. It is the single defining and complicating fact about their lives.* As Dow says, gay characters "become a sort of problem that has to be solved in the lives of their straight friends." The film historian Vito Russo once made a list of all the ways gay characters died in films released from the 1910s to the early 1980s. He counted forty-three dead gay characters. Twenty-seven of them were murdered. Thirteen died by suicide. One was executed. One died after being castrated, and another died of old age. That's what is meant by homosexuality as *a problem to be solved.*

Rule #3: *Gay characters are seen only in isolation.* "The gay characters are very rarely seen in community with other gay characters," Dow says. "So they tend not to have gay friends. They tend not to go to gay events." This might be the most important of the three rules, because it is the great obstacle that Evan Wolfson and other gay activists spent years battling: Gay characters are seen only in isolation because the culture did not accept that gay people were capable of real relationships. As David Reuben put it, gay life was just a "parade of penises."

So what do we find in *Doing Time on Maple Drive*? At first glance, the movie would seem to have helped the cause of gay marriage: It was about a family dealing with Matt's secret identity, honestly and painfully and lovingly. But in fact it didn't help, because it's actually the embodiment of Bonnie Dow's three rules:

First, *Doing Time on Maple Drive* isn't a movie about what it means to be gay. It's a movie about what it means to be straight and find out someone you know is gay. After Matt has his accident, the plot essentially involves him telling everyone in his life, one by one, about his secret identity. And the plot is driven by how *they* react to Matt's news, not how Matt reacts to them.

Second, being gay is a problem to be solved. Matt tries to kill himself because he can't handle the fact of his sexuality. In a scene where he says to his mother, "I didn't choose this. I am this," Matt goes on to say:

> Do you think I'd choose to be this different from everyone else? That I'd choose to make you and Dad this upset? And I'd choose to lose someone as beautiful and wonderful as Allison? And what about AIDS? I mean, suppose somebody wanted to be gay. Would they want to be gay now?

Even Matt thinks of his gayness as a problem to be solved! Who on earth would choose to be gay?

By the way, that single line about AIDS is the only mention of what might be going on with other gay men in the broader world — fulfilling Dow's third rule, "Gay characters are seen only in isolation." We learn that Matt has a former boyfriend, Kyle. But all we see of Kyle is a fleeting moment when he comes to visit Matt in the hospital.

Dow's point is that through the 1970s, 1980s, and 1990s, this was how the most powerful medium in popular culture handled gay sexuality. Movies like *Doing Time on Maple Drive* weren't as openly hostile to gay life as *Everything You Always Wanted to Know About Sex,* but they still denied the ability of gay people to hold real relationships. If you wanted to know whether the world was ready to think about gay people — and gay marriage — in a different way, you couldn't look exclusively at the results of elections, or legal verdicts, or public-opinion polls.

All those things were useful, in their own way. But they didn't get at the heart of the matter. *You had to look and see if the rules of the overstory were changing.* As it turns out, they were. You may have heard of the instigator. It was called *Will & Grace.*

4.

Will & Grace was the brainchild of two screenwriters who had grown up in Los Angeles together: David Kohan and Max Mutchnick. They were veterans of the sitcom world. But there was a story problem they had never managed to solve. Here's Mutchnick:

> Sydney Pollack, who was a mentor of David's, taught us a lot about writing…a love story. We were in his office one day. He knew we were writing sitcoms at this point, and he said, "A love story is over after the boy and the girl kiss. So, if you can figure out a way to tell a love story where they don't kiss, you can have a show that would run for a very long time."

Pollack was one of the greatest film directors of his generation. His point was that love stories require *friction.*

"Right?" This is Kohan. (The two of them finish each other's sentences.) "It's only as good as the obstacles that prevent them from getting together. I remember Sydney struggling with it. I remember him saying, 'Boy, race isn't the obstacle anymore. Class isn't an obstacle anymore.' You couldn't make, like, *Guess Who's Coming to Dinner?* in 1990. And where are the obstacles? When Max and I started working together, it was like, 'I got one.' "

Their idea was to explore the relationship Mutchnick had with his "high school girlfriend," Janet Eisenberg.

Max: She was a girlfriend that I met at Hebrew school. Oddly, a little sidebar story, her father was the surgeon who amputated my diabetic grandfather's legs. And so we had a very bizarre connection to each other, but we were instantly friends.

David: He would walk into her house and say to her father, "Where are the legs? What have you done with them?"

Max: Dr. [Eisenberg] never liked that too much. But it was an undeniable thing. [Janet] was very, very committed and interested in me, and I adored her. And I wasn't ready to deal with my truth at that time.... Yeah, so [Janet] and I, it was just.... It was the big secret, and in fact in those days, when you were gay and closeted, you actually thought, "Okay, how am I going to figure this out, where I'm going to live a double life?" ... When I told her I was gay, she said, "I have to rethink everything..."

Hollywood had always resolved this kind of story — between a closeted gay man and a straight woman — in a standard way. As Mutchnick explains, "When the gay guy reveals to the female that this is what he is, and he loves what he loves, he is banished and punished, and she is the victim."*

But as Mutchnick and Kohan thought about it, they realized there was another way to do the story of the gay man and straight woman who loved each other: What if the woman wasn't the victim, and the man wasn't punished?

Will & Grace appeared on NBC, in its first iteration, from 1998 to 2006, as part of NBC's vaunted "must see TV" on Thursday nights.† It was one of the most popular and widely watched television shows of its generation. Will was a gay lawyer. Grace was a straight interior designer. They shared an apartment in New York City and were joined by Grace's assistant, the irrepressible Karen, and Will's gay friend, Jack. Together the four of them argued, started relationships, ended relationships, and kissed each other in endless comedic combinations, all based on the premise laid down in the very

---

* By the way, that's exactly what happens in *Doing Time on Maple Drive*. The letter that Matt's fiancée, Allison, stumbles across is from Matt's old boyfriend, Kyle. It's a *love* letter. Devastated, she confronts him in tears:

Allison: I don't know how to begin this. Matt, I love you.

Matt: I love you too.

Allison: But we can't do this. I haven't slept all night. I've just been up... and I've been sitting and I've been thinking...and I've been going over stuff, and I'm sorry, but we can't.

Matt: Whoa, whoa, whoa, Allison...

Matt tries to comfort her. It's no use.

Allison: You know, the funny thing is in the back of my mind...I always thought that...I always thought that you might be gay. And I hated myself for thinking it...because I thought it was my fault.

† It had a second, less-successful run from 2017 to 2020.

first episode: Grace is about to get married, and Will talks her out of it. She leaves her groom at the altar. She and Will go to a bar to drown her sorrows. She's still in her wedding dress — and the patrons at the bar are egging them on.

> **Patron #1,** to Will: Hey, what about a toast to your lovely new bride?
> **Crowd, cheering:** Yeah! Yay!

They make up vows in the moment.

> **Patron #1:** Come on, you two, how's about a kiss?
> **Crowd, chanting:** Kiss! Kiss! Kiss! Kiss! Kiss! Kiss!

They look at each other and think, *Maybe this could work.* Will kisses Grace.

> **Grace:** Nothing? Anything?
> **Will:** Sorry. No, it's....Hmm.

Now, if you've watched *Will & Grace,* I'm sure you'll agree that Kohan and Mutchnick's premise was clever. And the show itself was very funny. But on the surface, there doesn't seem to be anything revolutionary about it. It's a sitcom about a bunch of single young people in a Manhattan apartment — just like *Seinfeld* and *Friends,* the two other hugely popular television sitcoms of that generation. In the planning and execution of the show, Kohan and Mutchnick sanded down every rough edge, so as not to offend advertisers and the viewing public. They cast Eric McCormack as Will, their gay lead. McCormack, in real life, is straight. He's conventionally handsome. His character, Will, is a corporate lawyer — hardly a profession, according to the stereotypes of the late 1990s, that coded as gay.*

The director of the first season was Jimmy Burrows, a Hollywood veteran who had directed episodes of virtually every sitcom from the '70s on: *Phyllis, Rhoda, 3rd Rock from the Sun, Friends, Frasier.* Burrows recalled later:

> I knew how difficult homosexuality would be to middle America. So I told Max and David, *I think we should try the first year to make America believe that Will's gonna recant and marry Grace.* Because that's what the show is. The show is a relationship, a sexual relationship without any sex. Let's have those scenes with Will and Grace where they talk and… they look like husband and wife. Let's have a kiss in the pilot.…Let's have a kiss in the final episode, under a chuppah.

Will & Grace was a show about a gay man. But Burrows wanted to make sure that in the beginning Will didn't seem *too* gay.

When *Will & Grace* first aired, some people in the gay community hated the show — for this exact reason. Critics dismissed it. One critique, in an academic journal, was entitled "Nothing Queer about Queer Television," pointing out that we never see Will in bed with another man. For that matter, the show rarely mentioned the AIDS epidemic, even though it aired when the crisis was in full force. When the show first launched, the *New York Times* called it "absolutely ordinary." The review went on:

---

* "Carson Kressley couldn't have played Will," Max says. Kressley is the outgoing, hilarious, campy TV personality who rose to prominence on the television show *Queer Eye for the Straight Guy.*

These actors are enormously congenial, but are stranded by scripts that assume it's clever to have Will and Grace play "The $25,000 Pyramid" really well together. And they are surrounded by annoying sidekicks, including Will's gay friend Jack (Sean Hayes), a prancing fool who sings show tunes while playing poker. Jack displays every stereotypical mannerism possible so that Will can avoid them altogether; how daring is that?

Exactly. That was the verdict on *Will & Grace* — that the show's daring premise had been so watered down that it was indistinguishable from any number of other frivolous television sitcoms. But the consensus on *Will & Grace* turned out to be wrong. The show was actually deeply subversive. Why? *Because it broke every one of Dow's overstory rules.*

Gay characters central to the narrative? Check. The story is impossible without Will and Jack.

Homosexuality not "a problem to be solved"? Check.

Gay people hanging out with other gay people? Check.

The message of Will and Grace was, in effect: *Look at Will. A funny, successful, endearing man. He is capable of loving and being loved. He is defined by the enduring strength of his relationships with those around him. He is normal. And he happens to be gay.*

"We knew that we had a win in the fact that there was an out, gay man at the center of our show," Mutchnick said. "And so that's how we slowly fed this gay conspiracy to the American public."

He was joking. But only kind of.

5.

In Chapter 4, I talked about the strange dynamics of tipping points found in Damon Centola's name game. Centola wanted to know how many "dissidents" it would take to disrupt a consensus reached by the majority. And his answer was, *It doesn't take a lot*. Once 25 percent of the members of any group start pushing for a new name, the rest of the group quickly folds its cards and goes along. But the change isn't gradual. It wasn't that you had some defectors at 20 percent, then a few more at 22 percent, and finally at 25 percent you got everyone. Nothing happened until you got to 25 percent — and then everything happened.

Think about the psychology of that kind of change. "If you're just below that tipping point — you're at 20 percent — you have no idea how close you are," Centola says. In one of the versions of his game, with twenty people, having four dissidents didn't make the slightest difference. But when he added one more — bringing the outsiders up to the magic 25 percent mark — the consensus abruptly shifted. "You don't know that [with] one or two more people, you could trigger that tipping point," he said. If change happened gradually, you could see that you were getting closer and closer to your goal — and you wouldn't be surprised when you reached it. But if nothing happens and then everything happens, you are in the strange position of being discouraged during the long stretch when nothing is happening and stunned at the point when it all shifts.

That's exactly the situation that the marriage activists were in, in the gloom of their meeting in Jersey City. They were getting closer and closer to victory. But it *felt* like they were losing. They couldn't see that up in the overstory things were quietly aligning in their favor. The irony of that, of course, is that many of those same activists — like millions of other people — were tuning in every Thursday night to watch *Will & Grace*. The evidence that the tide was turning was being broadcast right in front of them. But you have to be able to connect the dots between the story on the screen and the attitudes of the people watching. The activists couldn't do that — and I don't blame them, because I don't think *anyone* managed to do it at the time. The idea that there is some amorphous, distant canopy overhead that casts a shadow on all of us down below — and that the clue to that overstory can be found in a television sitcom — simply seems too hard to accept. But if four nights of the *Holocaust* miniseries can change the zeitgeist, why can't eleven seasons of Will just being…a normal guy?

Evan Wolfson, the de facto leader of the gay-marriage fight, says that the tipping point for their cause was 2012. Up to that point, when gay marriage had appeared on the ballot in one state or another, they had lost thirty different times. But that year, they started winning.

We finally figured out how to do it, and we won four outta four, and Maine was one of them. Maine was a state where we had lost a ballot measure…in 2009, and we decided not to take that "no" for an answer. And we spent three years on the ground knocking on doors, persuading — identifying the people who had not yet been with us but were reachable, and figuring out how we can move them.

They put forward their own ballot measure, asking the citizens of Maine if they were willing to overturn what they had said three years earlier, and legalize same-sex marriage. This time they won. Afterward, Wolfson's team started conducting focus groups. They sat down with people who had voted against them in 2009 and for them in 2012, to figure out why they had changed their minds so quickly.

> We asked them, where did you hear most about this question? You know, where were you thinking about it and hearing about it? And by far, the number-one answer was television.

All those years of watching *Will & Grace* had begun to add up.

"I was in politics for sixteen years and I realized something particularly on the moral and cultural issues...," the Republican Senator Rick Santorum said in a speech after the dust had settled. "It's that politics does not shape those issues. *Popular culture* shapes those issues, particularly the issue of [gay] marriage.... When it came to the issue of marriage, and changing the definition of marriage, there was no change. None, zero, for thirty years. And then a television show came on the air called *Will & Grace.*"

Gay marriage *tipped*. That surprised us. It shouldn't have.

Part Four

Conclusion

CHAPTER NINE

Overstories, Superspreaders, and Group Proportions

"OXYCONTIN IS OUR TICKET TO THE MOON."

1.

The opium poppy is a beautiful flower with a long stalk. After it blooms, the petals fall away to reveal a pod the size of a small egg filled with a thick yellowish sap. And for thousands of years, that sap has been the object of human fascination — a chemical cornucopia, in the words of one historian, "containing sugars, proteins, ammonia, latex, gums, plant wax, fats, sulphuric and lactic acids, water, meconic acid, and a wide range of alkaloids."

Dry the sap and smoke it, and you get opium: Kingdoms have risen and fallen over opium. But extracting the alkaloids from the sap's cocktail of compounds yields something even more valuable. In the early-nineteenth century, the German pharmacist Friedrich Sertürner isolated the first of the poppy's alkaloids. He called it *morphium* or *morphine*, after Morpheus, the Greek god of dreams. Morphine dulled pain and produced a pleasing euphoria. It was also highly addictive.

The next of the poppy's gifts was codeine, isolated in 1832 by a Frenchman named Pierre Jean Robiquet. About forty years after that, the English chemist C. R. Alder Wright boiled a mixture of morphine and acetic anhydride over a stove for several hours, looking for an opiate that wasn't addictive. His concoction ended up being called *heroin*, and for a time it was heralded as the great safe alternative to morphine.

And then in 1916, two German chemists took a similar alkaloid to codeine named thebaine, resynthesized it, and came up with something they called *oxycodone*. Oxycodone never gained the notoriety of its cousins heroin and morphine — until eighty years after its discovery, that is, when it was reimagined by a company named Purdue Pharma. Purdue packaged oxycodone in a high-dose extended-release tablet. The company marketed its invention around the world with more enthusiasm and audacity than anyone had ever marketed a painkiller before, calling its creation *OxyContin*. I'm betting you have heard of it. It has become the most infamous prescription drug in history.

This book began with the testimony before a Congressional committee of three executives from an unnamed company. If you haven't guessed by now, the executives belonged to the family that started Purdue and gave the world OxyContin: the Sacklers. And it was Kathe Sackler, daughter of one of Purdue's three founding brothers, who when asked about her family's role in the opioid crisis said:

> I have tried to figure out, was — is there anything that I could have done differently, knowing what I knew then,

not what I know now. And I have to say, I can't — there's nothing that I can find that I would have done differently . . .

The other Sackler to speak before the Congressional committee was David Sackler, grandson of a founding brother. And what did David Sackler say, after Kathe Sackler disavowed any responsibility for the opioid crisis?

I take a deep moral responsibility for it, because I believe our product, despite our best intentions and best efforts, has been associated with abuse and addiction.

Has been associated.

He used the passive voice.

Over the course of *Revenge of the Tipping Point,* I've argued that this kind of dissociation and denial is all too common. We retreat to the position that epidemics are mysterious, that we are powerless to affect them and bear no responsibility for the course they take. The parents in Poplar Grove retreat into their grief. We look at Miami and convince ourselves that it is no different from any other city, and look in surprise at the about-face of the American public on the subject of gay marriage. But in each instance it turns out we are wrong.

So let us return to where we started, the opioid crisis. And let's use the lessons from Poplar Grove and Miami and the Lawrence Tract and Harvard and *Holocaust* and *Will & Grace* — the lessons of superspreaders, group proportions, and overstories — to try to make sense of the chaos unleashed by OxyContin.

Can we now understand the decisions and circumstances that led to the opioid epidemic? I think we can.

2.

In the March 2019 edition of the academic journal *Population and Development Review*, there is an article by a demographer named Jessica Y. Ho: "The Contemporary American Drug Overdose Epidemic in International Perspective." Midway through, there is a chart. It shows how many people died of drug overdoses in high-income countries from 1994 to 2015. This is the figure showing the rate of male deaths per hundred thousand.

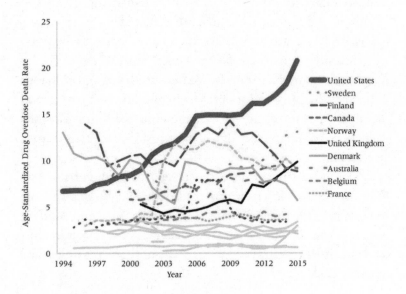

Denmark and Finland, the chart tells us, started out with one of the worst problems in the group, but then things got better. Canada, the United Kingdom, and Australia have a steadily worsening crisis, but their overall numbers still lag behind the world leaders. And do you see that tangle of gray lines at the very bottom that barely rise above the zero mark? That's Austria, Italy, Germany, Japan, the Netherlands, Portugal, Spain, and Switzerland. They never had an opioid crisis at all. Only one country has had a truly catastrophic experience with opioid overdose — the country represented by that thick line rising well above all the others.

The United States.

Jessica Ho's chart tells us that the opioid crisis is not really an international problem. It's fundamentally an *American* problem. It's small-area variation — an epidemic that operates within a particular set of borders — but in this case the area involved isn't that small. Maybe it's better to call it large-area variation.

But wait. Are we sure it's not small-area variation after all? Let us turn now to a March 2019 analysis of the opioid crisis published by a group led by Lyna Z. Schieber of the Centers for Disease Control: In the paper's appendix, there is a chart that details the annual amount of opioid painkillers prescribed in every US state from 2006 to 2017. For the sake of simplicity, let's focus on the 2006 numbers, because that's when the epidemic was first gaining steam. The numbers represent "morphine milligram equivalents" per capita, which is a fancy way of saying how many doses, per person, were consumed in a given year. Here are the first few rows of the chart.

Alabama 808.8
Alaska 614.4
Arizona 735.0
Arkansas 765.7
California 450.2
Colorado 495.4
Connecticut 648.3
Delaware 881.5

There is *a lot* of variation from state to state. Alabama has almost twice the number California has. Delaware is sky-high. But Colorado isn't. This now looks very much like the phenomenon that the father of small-area variation, John Wennberg, discovered in Vermont, or the way Miami is different from the rest of the country when it comes to Medicare fraud. And the further you go down the list, the more pronounced the variation becomes.

Illinois 366
Indiana 756.6

Illinois and Indiana are neighbors. They have very similar poverty rates, unemployment levels, and income figures. Why does Indiana have twice the problem Illinois does?

The opioid epidemic is commonly described as the result of a combination of social and economic crises afflicting the American working classes: the loss of manufacturing jobs, the hollowing out of communities, the breakdown of families, and the confluence of soaring rates of depression, mental illness, and despair. All those problems are important. But none of them explain Ho's chart. Italy is much poorer than the United States, and it has much more unemployment. Where is their opioid crisis? The United Kingdom has more than its share of social problems. Why is its line so much lower than America's? And those theories definitely don't account for why Indiana was devastated by opioids while its next-door neighbor, Illinois, wasn't.

What we've learned so far is that the way to make sense of variation is to look for overstories. Miami had its own overstory. The way we talked about the Holocaust shifted when NBC's miniseries changed the overstory. So is there a corresponding overstory that helps us make sense of this strange pattern of variation in opioid use? It turns out that there is. It involves a man largely lost to history. His name was Paul E. Madden.

3.

Paul E. Madden was a lawyer from San Francisco who had served in the city's District Attorney's office. In 1939 he was named director of the California Bureau of Narcotic Enforcement, a state agency dedicated to controlling the use of dangerous drugs.

Madden was in his early forties, and full of righteous energy. He had a big head, double chin, blond hair swept back: imperious, ponderous, puritanical. He climbed the political ladder by force of ambition and moral conviction.

A person under the influence of marihuana [sic] may believe himself so small that he is afraid to step off the curbstone into the street, or he may feel himself of enormous size and of superhuman strength and passion and in that condition commit crimes altogether foreign to his nature.

That's Madden writing about one of his favorite topics: the perils of illicit narcotics.

Time and space and distance are obliterated; he may be driving an automobile at the rate of eighty miles per hour and believe he is going only twenty, a red light may appear green, and the [car bearing] down upon him or coming toward him may seem a mile away. Results of [a] person in that condition driving a machine may easily be imagined.

Madden liked to speak with a certain amount of hyperbole. Things were never *bad*; they were *evil*. Illegal drugs did not *compromise* the user; they *destroyed* him. The opium and heroin addict "loses all sense of cleanliness, and, mentally, the power to differentiate between right and wrong." Inside California, Madden played the same role as his famous contemporary, J. Edgar Hoover, the head of the FBI. He was the public face of law enforcement. You could find his picture in the newspaper, posing next to a big pile of contraband cocaine. You could hear him on the radio, warning of the invasion of California by illicit drugs from Mexico, China, or Japan.

Good evening, ladies and gentlemen. There may be harder jobs than breaking up a narcotics ring, I don't know. I've never seen one. Especially difficult is the job of rounding up a band of narcotic peddlers, including the brains of the gang.

Madden busted people for buying morphine-based veterinary drugs in large quantities, which he suspected they were reselling on the street. He raided Japanese freighter ships moored in the port of San Francisco, confiscated bags of cocaine, and urged the higher-ups in Washington to take diplomatic action. He heard about farmers growing poppy seeds and wondered: What if those seeds *aren't* for kaiser rolls? What if they are being diverted for opium production? Madden was a whirling dervish, a zealot of the highest order, one of the first of what would turn out to be a long line of histrionic American anti-drug crusaders.

Paul E. Madden's true obsession, however, wasn't illegal drugs from overseas. It was the painkillers being prescribed by doctors. Madden's big concern was that legal drugs were being diverted for illegal purposes. Unscrupulous doctors were handing out opioids indiscriminately. Criminals were forging prescriptions and reselling the drugs on the street. So Madden came up with an elegant solution: He made a list of all the fruits of the poppy — morphine, opium, codeine, plus a few other drugs for good measure — and persuaded the California Legislature to add an amendment to the state's Health and Safety Code, known as Assembly Bill No. 2606, which passed the Senate on June 6, 1939. The key language is in Section 11166.06. Every time a doctor wrote a prescription for one of those opioids, he or she had to use a special prescription pad supplied by Madden's Bureau of Narcotic Enforcement:

The prescription blanks shall be printed on distinctive paper, serial number of the book being shown on each form, and also each form being serially numbered.

Each prescription blank shall be printed in triplicate with one blank attached to the book in such a manner that it will be readily removed, while two of the blanks shall be perforated for removal.

The key word was *triplicate*. Every prescription page in Madden's special pad came attached to two carbon copies. The bottom copy had to be kept by the prescribing physician for a minimum of two years. The second copy was for the pharmacy's records. The final copy had to be mailed directly to the Bureau of Narcotic Enforcement by month's end.

Shortly after the triplicate measure became law, Madden found his first high-profile case. It involved a doctor in San Francisco named Nathan Housman. Housman was a playboy from a wealthy family, who kept an office in the swanky Flood Building on Market Street — to this day, one of the most beautiful office buildings in downtown San Francisco. Housman was shady. His name had come up in a sensational case a few months earlier involving a large inheritance trust and a wealthy widow found dumped in the street in a staged hit-and-run. But the case that caught Madden's attention centered on Alma Elizabeth Black, whom the newspapers described as "a patient [Housman] treated for seventeen years for an ailment which an autopsy — performed at his own demand — failed to detect." Nathan Housman's "treatment" for Black was morphine. And upon her death, Black left her entire estate — worth, by some reports, over $1 million in today's dollars — to...Nathan Housman.

Madden's agents descended on Housman's local pharmacy, on Eddy Street in the city's Tenderloin district. They found

Housman there, frantically copying from the pharmacist's list of his morphine prescriptions. "Our agents found 345 prescriptions made out by Dr. Housman for 200 different patients," Madden announced. "A check of our records disclosed that only four of these had been made known to our office. That is an intolerable situation." So Housman was arrested and charged. But not for murder or malpractice — for failure to file Mrs. Black's morphine prescriptions in triplicate.

"I asked Doctor Housman several times for the records, and each time Doctor Housman said he had none," one of Madden's investigators testified at the trial. "He said he didn't know he was supposed to keep them."

Housman ended up in San Quentin Prison, and to every doctor in California, his conviction sent a message: Paul Madden was *serious.* He didn't think that all of California's doctors were as bad as Nathan Housman. But Madden felt there were enough doctors in California as unusual as Housman to cause a lot of damage, and he wanted to use Housman to send a message to those dangerous few: You could not escape the government's watchful eye. He had a carbon copy of every opioid prescription written in the state of California in rows and rows of filing cabinets at his headquarters. All he had to do was look at the file for *Housman, Nathan* of the Flood Building in downtown San Francisco. If the file was bulging, it was time to pay Dr. Housman a visit. And if Madden learned that one of the doctor's patients had died of an overdose of prescription morphine, and he looked under *H* and saw nothing at all in the doctor's file — well, then, Dr. Housman had an even bigger problem.

So far in this book, we've looked at a wide variety of ways

that overstories emerge. In Poplar Grove, the overstory arose from years of upper-middle-class parents pushing their kids to succeed. Miami became Miami because of an extraordinary confluence of events at the end of the 1970s: the influx of Cuban refugees, the rise of the cocaine trade, and a race riot. When it came to our understanding of the Holocaust, a television miniseries seems to have played an enormous role.

Paul Madden's row of filing cabinets don't seem, at first glance, to be in the same category. But the more Madden talked about his new plan in his many speeches and public appearances, the more his simple idea began to morph into something bigger. The act of writing a prescription had been a private transaction between physician and patient. Now it was a public act, with real consequences. As he wrote in a letter to the journal of the California Medical Society, "The great amount of good to be derived from this system is that the State Narcotic Enforcement Division will, every thirty days, have a complete report of the narcotics dispensed" in the state. With those two carbon copies, Madden was making doctors pause and think.

In 1943, Hawaii passed a version of Madden's triplicate rule. Illinois followed suit eighteen years after that, followed in short order by Idaho, New York, Rhode Island, Texas, and Michigan. What began as one man's idiosyncratic crusade turned into a national phenomenon. States around the country began reaching into their doctors' medicine cabinets and telling them that when it comes to this drug and this drug and this drug, *You cannot be left to your own devices.* A policy turned into an overstory.

Fifty years passed. And then a second overstory emerged.

4.

Russell Portenoy grew up in Yonkers, just outside New York City, in a working-class family. He was the first in his family to go to college, and he was brilliant: charismatic, driven, innovative. Just after medical school, he did a residency at Albert Einstein College of Medicine in New York City, where one of his mentors was a physician named Ron Kanner.

"I remember very distinctly meeting him, and he's a dynamic guy," Portenoy said in a 2003 oral history years later for the International Association for the Study of Pain. "I asked him what he did, and he said he does pain. I laughed, and I said, 'That's silly, because pain is a symptom, it's not a disease. You can't do that.' He assured me that no, indeed, you could actually do a symptom."

Portenoy's initial reaction to Kanner was then the mainstream position in medicine. If someone was in severe pain with a bad back, you tried to fix their back. If a cancer patient was in pain, you focused on treating the cancer. Pain was just a manifestation of an underlying problem. But Kanner was part of a group who believed that approach was backward — that if someone was in pain, for whatever reason, *you should treat the pain.*

For Portenoy, that first meeting with his mentor was an epiphany. He became convinced that, because medicine was thinking of pain as a symptom rather than a problem in and of itself, his profession was letting patients suffer needlessly. Doctors needed to take pain seriously, which meant, Portenoy believed, that they should not be afraid to prescribe opioids.

In interviews Portenoy would tell stories like this, about a patient suffering severe "cluster" headaches:

He spent eight years totally disabled in severe pain. Multiple emergency-room visits, multiple hospitalizations. He was then referred to me, and I gave him an opioid and I pushed the dose up, and he became pain-free. He's been pain-free now for two years. It was like he lived through hell and now is back.

One of the emotions that he can't suppress is anger. He keeps on talking about his prior neurologist, who, actually, is a headache specialist and knows a lot but doesn't know opioids and didn't know that opioids could be used. I know this person, a wonderful person who in no way wanted this man to suffer, and in no way said he should tough it out. He just had a set of tools that was limited and didn't know that he could refer for the others. I think that that's a very real phenomenon out there.

Portenoy *loved* opioids. He called them a "gift from nature." These drugs, he told the *New York Times* in 1993, "can be used for a long time, with few side effects and…addiction and abuse are not a problem." Later he would temper that enthusiasm, but only slightly. His fundamental belief was that you couldn't treat pain the way you treated, say, strep throat — with a protocol you could find in a textbook. Pain was amorphous and subjective and idiosyncratic. Treating pain is "a little science, a lot of intuition, and a lot of art," he would say. Did he think that high doses of opioids, taken over a long period of time, posed a risk of addiction? Sure — in *some* patients. But he was convinced that group was very small — less than 1 percent of all patients — and a thoughtful physician, he felt, ought to be able to distinguish between the kind of patient who would thrive on opioids and the kind who wouldn't.

Portenoy's 2003 oral history with the International Association for the Study of Pain ran almost three and a half hours, and to read it — through the lens of what would happen over the following two decades — is fascinating.

Say, for example, you have a person come into your office. He's twenty-two years old, he has post-traumatic pain in the knees since surgery a year ago.

You ask him some questions. You find out that he had a problem with marijuana in college and he's still using it on weekends, he's got a family history of alcoholism in his father and his brother, he's got tattoos on his arms and his back, and he tells you he's in very severe pain. Where would you position opioid drugs in relation to other therapies for that pain syndrome?

In contrast, if you have a seventy-five-year-old woman with bad osteoarthritis of several joints who has had a bleeding ulcer and comes in reporting pain, and your history demonstrates that the patient has been a teetotaler for sixty years, has no family history of addiction, and tells you that she would rather do anything but take a pain medicine, where would you position the trial of opioid therapy for that person?

You'd have to be a pretty stupid clinician to say, *Oh, yes, they both get them first or they both get them last*. It makes no sense.

This was Portenoy's overstory. The old overstory, he argued, missed the point. People like Madden were far too concerned about the possible damage that could be done by a small group of wayward physicians — the Nathan Housmans of the world — with the result that they had imposed restrictions that made it all but impossible for the rest of the profession to deal with the very real problem of pain. "What we're trying to say," he argued, "is that physicians have to feel completely empowered and comfortable that they can use these drugs for legitimate medical purposes." Madden had worried about the dangerous few. Portenoy focused on the virtuous many.

Portenoy became a superstar. To recruit him, Beth Israel Medical Center in Manhattan created a special pain center. The waiting list to see him was four months long. He was constantly in the news or giving speeches. He was called the King of Pain. Meanwhile, the Maddenites looked on with horror. What was Portenoy thinking? The debate raged at meetings of pharmacists, medical society conferences, and in seminars at think tanks. Policymakers in Washington, DC, wrote position papers. Legislatures took sides.

In the spring of 1991, the National Institute on Drug Abuse (NIDA) held a small meeting in suburban Maryland. Someone in the White House had wondered if triplicate prescription should become a national requirement, and NIDA had been asked to investigate. The institute rounded up everyone who might know something about the issue and invited them to a hotel near NIDA's headquarters. Russell Portenoy was there, of course. (There was no way to have a conference on painkillers in those years without him in attendance.) He spoke at length. He was worried, he said, about the risk of *under*prescribing painkillers. Also in attendance were representatives of the pharmaceutical industry, state medical boards, public-health groups. Papers were presented, panelists bickered. Finally a man named Gerald Deas, an African American doctor who worked in a tough neighborhood in New York City, stood up and shook his fist at the Portenoy people. "I wish that anyone who opposes triplicate prescription could walk with me into the real world where these regulations are saving lives," he said. The discussion got *heated*.

In the end, the triplicate-expansion plan went nowhere. Portenoy's ideas gained new followers. By the middle of the 1990s the number of triplicate states was down to five, representing barely a third of the American population: Texas, California, New York, Illinois, and Idaho. Everyone else went with Portenoy.

And there the matter rested — another obscure policy difference between the states, among a sea of obscure policy differences. Had you asked the average American in those years which side their state was on, they probably couldn't tell you. That's the nature of an overstory: Most of us don't bother to look up at the ideas circulating above in the forest canopy.

Except, that is, for an obscure drug company in Connecticut named Purdue Pharma.

5.

Purdue had been in the painkiller business for years, with a slow-release morphine tablet it called MS Contin. MS Contin was used primarily by late-stage cancer patients, in hospices and back at home. It was a good business, but a small one.

The Sackler family, which ran Purdue, had grander ambitions. They switched their focus to oxycodone. Typically, oxycodone had been combined with acetaminophen or aspirin. That's what Percocet and Percodan are, respectively, and that combination made oxycodone harder to abuse, because if you consume too much acetaminophen, you will do serious damage to your liver. Some researchers call this a "governor's switch." (It's why the opioid diphenoxylate — which is commonly used to treat diarrhea — is always combined with atropine, which is poisonous in high doses: Try to get high on diphenoxylate and you'll pay the price.) Purdue's first innovation was to remove the acetaminophen governor's switch from oxycodone.

Purdue then raised the drug's dosage. Percocet and Percodan each have 5 milligrams of oxycodone. Purdue decided that its lowest dose pill would have *twice* that amount. Then Purdue created a special extended-release tablet, which meant that instead of having to swallow a pill every few hours and ride the ups and downs that come with taking an opioid, a patient could be soothed with an even, steady dose over an entire day. They called this new, repackaged painkiller OxyContin, then set out immediately to break the longstanding medical norm that reserved powerful painkillers for cancer patients. Purdue wanted to market it to *everyone*. Your back hurts? OxyContin. You just got your wisdom teeth out? OxyContin.

At Purdue headquarters, the new drug was the focus of much excitement. "OxyContin," said one of the original Sackler brothers, "is our ticket to the moon."

In the spring of 1995, Purdue hired a market-research firm called Groups Plus. OxyContin was still a few months away from final FDA approval, and Purdue wanted to plan its marketing strategy. Groups Plus set up five rounds of sessions with doctors in Fort Lee, New Jersey; Houston, Texas; and Westport, Connecticut. The doctors were a combination of primary-care physicians, surgeons, and rheumatologists, and they all regularly prescribed painkillers. Purdue wanted to know what the doctors thought of their idea for a high-dose, extended-release opioid.

First came the good news. Non-cancer pain — this giant untested market that Purdue wanted to crack open — turned out to be a big part of the physicians' practices. The doctors wanted more treatment options. "When discussing the concept of the 'ideal' pain killing medication," the Groups Plus report stated, "there was universal agreement that [the doctors in the focus group] would like to have the efficacy of the narcotics without the concern regarding side effects or addiction." That bit about no side effects or addiction didn't bother Purdue: They would just have their sales reps lie and say that OxyContin wasn't that addictive. "In our judgment," the report went on, "there definitely is an opportunity for Purdue...to build a significant business for OxyContin."

Then came the bad news. The sessions with the doctors from Houston were a disaster. Why? Texas was a triplicate state. The Houston doctors were living under the Madden overstory.

The triplicate laws seem to have a dramatic effect on the product usage behavior of the physicians. Specifically, the groups in Texas revealed almost no use of the Class II narcotics for treatment of non-cancer pain.

Class 2 or *Schedule 2* is the technical term for drugs that are potentially problematic if they aren't used appropriately, such as Percocet, Percodan, or codeine. OxyContin was going to be Schedule 2 as well, and the Houston doctors prescribed those drugs "less than five times a year...if at all." The report went on:

> The [Houston] doctors did not want to provide the Government with any ammunition to question their medical protocols relative to pain management. The mere thought of the government questioning their judgment created a high level of anxiety in the focus group room among the doctors.
>
> Writing triplicate prescriptions was more trouble than others, due to the details of the forms and the various people that need to be copied on them. To the extent that they can avoid this extra effort, they will try to follow alternate protocols.

The focus-group report ran for seventy pages, and again and again it returned to this point. The triplicate and non-triplicate states were like night and day.

> The [primary care physicians] and surgeons in the non-triplicate state (New Jersey) indicated a very high likelihood of using OxyContin for selective treatment of non-cancer related pain, and the rheumatologists in Connecticut also felt it had a place in their practice. However, the doctors in the triplicate state were not enthusiastic about the product at all...

And then:

> Among the physicians in these triplicate states who do use Class II narcotics in the treatment of non-cancer pain, our

research suggests the absolute number of prescriptions they would write each year is very small, and probably would not be sufficient to justify any separate marketing effort.

Purdue's management team read the Groups Plus report and took it seriously. The launch of OxyContin — one of the most sophisticated and aggressive drug-marketing campaigns the world of medicine has ever seen — was targeted at states without triplicate laws. So, no big push in New York State. But yes to West Virginia. No to Illinois. But yes to Indiana. No to California. But yes to Nevada. No to Texas and Idaho. But yes to Oklahoma and Tennessee — with the result that the opioid epidemic did not hit the *entire* United States equally. It became, instead, a perfect example of small-area variation. Opioids rained heavily only on those states where there was no triplicate program or Madden overstory to keep them in check.

Let's look again at the top five opioid-consumers. These are all "Portenoy states," without a triplicate program.

Nevada 1,019.9
West Virginia 1,011.6
Tennessee 938.3
Oklahoma 884.9
Delaware 881.5

Here is the per-capita opioid consumption for the same year in the Madden states.

Illinois 366
New York 441.6

California 450.2
Texas 453.1
Idaho 561.1

Illinois had *one-third* the opioid use of Nevada and West Virginia. New York had *half* the problem Tennessee did. Of the triplicate states, only Idaho came anywhere close to the national average.

If you burrow a bit further into the numbers, the differences grow even more astonishing. Here is the breakdown of how willing orthopedic surgeons were to prescribe opioids to their patients. The period is 2013 to 2016 — long after everyone was aware of how dangerous this class of drugs was. This is the geographic distribution of the top 10 percent of prescribers.

West 741 (8.7 percent)
Northeast 745 (8.8 percent)
Midwest 1,854 (21.8 percent)

The West is dominated by California — Paul E. Madden's state. Statistically, there were only a handful of high-prescribing orthopedists there. The Northeast is dominated by New York State. Same thing. But just look at the South — the triplicate-free zone, the land of the Portenoy overstory:

South 5,170 (60.8 percent)

Wow.

Think for a moment about how remarkable this is. In the years before the Second World War, a blustery, self-promoting drug warrior in San Francisco has the idea of making California's doctors use a special painkiller-prescription pad, with two carbon copies. That simple bureaucratic intervention evolves into an overstory — a narrative that says opioids are different, spurring the physician to pause and think before prescribing them. And that overstory is *so* compelling that when Purdue tests its new painkiller in a triplicate state half a century later, it runs into a brick wall.

Overstories *matter*. You can create them. They can spread. They are powerful. And they can endure for decades.

Today among economists, an entire cottage industry is devoted to the many ways that states with triplicate laws differ from all the others. So, take Massachusetts and New York. If New York had Massachusetts's opioid-overdose rate from 2000 to 2019, the economist Abby Alpert estimates that an additional 27,000 New Yorkers would have died of overdoses. *27,000.* Massachusetts is not poorer than New York. It doesn't have a higher unemployment rate. It doesn't have a bigger problem with gangs or organized crime or drug trafficking. The two states are like peas in a pod. The *only* relevant difference is that half a century ago New York forced doctors to make two additional carbon copies of every prescription they wrote — and Massachusetts did not. And those carbon copies saved thousands of lives.

Or take the current opioid crisis, which has long since moved on from OxyContin to fentanyl. Fentanyl can be created in a lab and is easily produced illegally. Triplicate laws don't apply to Chinese or Mexican drug lords and their American confederates. So you would think that the differences between triplicate and non-triplicate states would have faded away by now. Wrong! If Purdue sales reps put you on a certain path back in the late 1990s and early 2000s, you stayed on that path long after the reps had gone.

"We see a very quick increase in overdose deaths in the non-triplicate states," Alpert said, "and much slower growth in the triplicate states, and these trends continue, even twenty years after the launch."

Economic growth has been stronger in triplicate states during the opioid crisis. The health outcomes of babies were better there. Neglect of children was lower. Workforce participation was higher. Oh, and remember what Paul Madden said about the addict losing the "power to differentiate between right and wrong" — one of those overheated Maddenisms that makes us roll our eyes today? Here is the economist Yongbo Sim's conclusion, after comparing crime rates in triplicate and non-triplicate states:

> "I find that non-triplicate states at the time of OxyContin's introduction experienced a relative rise in both property (12%) and violent (25%) crimes compared to states with the triplicate prescription policy (triplicate states)."

In their analyses, economists are used to seeing differences of 1 or 2 percent. 25 percent is unheard of. "That's an absolutely huge impact," Sim continued. "Honestly, when I first got this result, I didn't really believe [it] myself."

Wherever he is now, Paul Madden is looking at us and saying, *I told you so.*

6.

Let us now turn to the second of the epidemic elements: superspreaders.

In 2002, the journal of the prestigious consulting firm McKinsey & Company published a long essay by one of its star consultants, Martin Elling. It was entitled: "Making More of Pharma's Sales Force," and its subject was the way pharmaceutical companies sold their products to doctors. For years, drugmakers simply divided the country into regions and had sales reps sell their products to doctors in their assigned territory. If you were a company with two heart drugs, you built a sales team that covered the cardiologists in every hospital in the country. At the time Elling wrote his piece, there were nearly 90,000 drug-company sales reps in the United States, and that number had doubled in the six years before then. The industry had built an army to influence physicians, and Elling said the strategy wasn't working.

"US pharmaceutical companies," he wrote, "have for decades relied on the 'pinball wizard' sales model: sales representatives bounce from one doctor's office to another in hopes of catching a few moments with physicians and influencing which drugs they prescribe."

Elling found this far too haphazard. Doctors were getting overwhelmed. Hospitals were making it harder and harder for sales reps to gain access to their physicians. The old tricks — wining and dining doctors, showering them with gifts and trips — were attracting criticism. Sales reps were getting burned out. The system, Elling wrote, is "costly, inefficient, and rife with dissatisfaction."

He went on:

...physicians feel besieged. Top-prescribing ones say that they now receive three to five times as many calls from sales reps as they did ten years ago.... One physician complained that the situation is 'becoming unbearable' and that reps 'are less knowledgeable, more pushy.' According to our survey, almost 40 percent of doctors' offices now limit the number of reps they admit each day.

What to do? Elling said the solution was for sales reps to understand that all doctors were not the same. Pharmaceutical companies had to learn how to "segment" physicians. Two orthopedic surgeons working in adjoining offices in the same hospital could have huge differences in the number and variety of the drugs they prescribed. Some doctors were simply worth more than others. A doctor who was thirty-five years old was of far greater value than a sixty-five-year-old doctor, even if the older doctor prescribed a lot of drugs. The sixty-five-year-old wasn't going to change his practice habits, and he was about to retire. Why bother with him? The thirty-five-year-old had room to grow.

Instead, Elling proposed, drug firms should use the prescribing habits of individual doctors to develop a sophisticated estimate of each doctor's "lifetime value." Even more importantly, Elling said, you had to "ascertain [a doctor's] attitudes about a number of issues..." He was vague about what he meant by "a number of issues," but anyone with any understanding of the world he was describing knew what he meant. Sales reps tended to be young and very attractive. Some doctors really responded to that kind of attention. A drug company that knew the identities of these "high responders" could go a long way. It was a radical argument —

one that broke with decades of practice in the pharmaceutical industry. And one company, above all others, took notice: Purdue Pharmaceutical.

Purdue called McKinsey in 2013.* A team of consultants drove up from New York to Purdue's headquarters in Connecticut. The Sacklers explained to McKinsey that the company was in crisis. Sales of OxyContin had soared from $49 million in the drug's first year on the market to over $1 billion in 2005. But the growth engine was stalled. The Department of Justice had just accused Purdue Pharma of misleading doctors about the addictiveness of OxyContin, and hit the company with one of the biggest fines in the history of the pharmaceutical business. OxyContin's reputation was suffering. Its patent was about to expire. Other manufacturers were plotting cheaper, generic versions of Purdue's painkiller. What should they do?

McKinsey got busy. They sent one of their brightest young associates to do a ride-along with an OxyContin sales rep in Worcester, Massachusetts. The consultant's findings were depressing:

> While he used to be able to host lunches at the hospitals, meet with the residents, and walk the floors, now hospitals say, "drop off your materials and we'll call you back."
>
> He has tried to take more creative approaches, such as creating a "face book" of prominent doctors from the hospital that he wants to meet and hanging out at nearby cafes, getting to know the hospital staff, etc. However, he has received a

---

* This was not their first time working together. Purdue first hired McKinsey in 2004.

number of negative responses from the hospital systems, including a letter from the largest hospital system in Worcester not to come back after he stood in the reception line to introduce himself to the office secretary.

It was everything Martin Elling had warned about. Purdue was playing pinball, and it wasn't working. So McKinsey came up with a new plan and called it, without irony, "Evolve to Excellence," or E2E, for short. When the company's cochairman, Richard Sackler, heard McKinsey's presentation, he emailed his cousin. "The discoveries of McKinsey are astonishing." Over the next decade, Purdue would pay McKinsey $86 million for its advice on "turbocharging" OxyContin's sales.

At the heart of the McKinsey OxyContin reboot was the following chart.

January – July 2013 Prescribers				
I Rx Decile	# Physicians	% Physicians	# Rx	Mean Rx Physicians Month
10	358	0.2%	617,887	246.6
9	778	0.5%	617,624	113.4
8	1,300	0.8%	617,149	67.8
7	2,182	1.4%	617,248	40.4
6	3,613	2.3%	617,056	24.4
5	5,668	3.5%	617,075	15.6
4	8,668	5.4%	617,056	10.2
3	13,636	8.5%	617,048	6.5
2	24,399	15.2%	617,331	3.6
1	99,825	62.2%	620,667	0.9

The story the chart tells is quite remarkable. It tracks the period from January through July of 2013, during which a total of 6.17 million OxyContin prescriptions were written. That number is then broken down into ten equal groups — *deciles* — and ranked from top to bottom. So, look at Decile 1, at the bottom of the chart. This is the largest group of prescribing doctors: 99,825. They wrote on average one OxyContin prescription in the six-month period. That's a trivial amount.

Decile 2 comprises 24,399 doctors. They wrote 3.6 prescriptions from January through July. Decile 3 is just over 13,500 doctors. They wrote on average 6.5 prescriptions in that time. The higher you go on the chart, the fewer physicians there are in each group, but the more prescriptions they write. Look at Decile 10. There are just 358 doctors in this group, but they wrote on average 247 prescriptions in that six-month window. OxyContin's success didn't ride on the backs of *most* American doctors, or even *some* American doctors. It was an epidemic driven by the tiny fraction of doctors in Deciles 8, 9, and 10 — roughly 2,500 doctors who among them wrote a staggering number of prescriptions. In the language of McKinsey's E2E, the physicians in those top three groups were the "Core" and "Super Core."

McKinsey's first bit of advice was blunt: "More than 50% of OxyContin primary calls are to low-decile (0-4) prescribers." It made no sense. That big group of doctors at the bottom of the chart, who could bring themselves to prescribe OxyContin only once or twice in the course of six months, were people from the Madden states. Or they were doctors who were intuitively wary of a high-dose opioid without a governor's switch. Or maybe they were grumpy old physicians, too set in their ways to start adopting a new drug. *Ignore them,* McKinsey said. *You want the superspreaders at the top.* Purdue listened.

"Purdue awarded points in a point system that allocated bonuses and rewarded sales representatives who had the highest percentage of total sales calls with 'super core' or 'core' prescribers." This is from one of the many criminal complaints filed against Purdue, when the company was finally called to task for its behavior. Purdue repeatedly emphasized to its sales staff: "focus solely on Core and Super Core selected prescribers."

Then McKinsey said: *You need to zoom in even further on those Core and Super Core, and figure out the ones who are most receptive to persuasion from sales reps.* They meant younger doctors trying to build a practice, or doctors too busy to bother with the more worrisome details of OxyContin's reputation, or simply doctors who — for one reason or another — liked spending time with sales reps.

Look at the next chart, which shows how Purdue changed tactics in the years after heeding McKinsey's advice. This is the total number of OxyContin sales calls in Tennessee, a non-triplicate state that had long been a fertile market for Purdue.

Between 2007 and 2016, the number of doctor visits by OxyContin sales reps goes up by nearly a factor of *five.* And that's not to every doctor in Tennessee; that fivefold increase was directed at the superspreaders.

In Chapter 6 we discussed the fact that superspreaders are profoundly different from the rest of us: There is something inherent in their physiology that makes them capable of producing orders of magnitude more virus than everyone else. The same was true of *their* superspreaders, Purdue

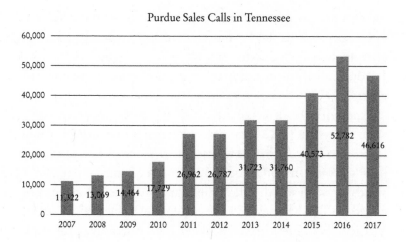

Purdue Sales Calls in Tennessee

discovered: They weren't wired like most doctors. When the Purdue sales representatives downplayed the risks of addiction — making the nonsensical claim that the long, slow, smooth pace with which the drug entered the bloodstream meant that it produced none of the euphoric highs that led to dependency — the superspreader believed them. When it became clear that OxyContin was being abused — that people were just grinding up OxyContin tablets and snorting the powder, getting twelve hours' worth of opioid in a single giddy rush — the superspreader was indifferent, or oblivious. The superspreader thought handing out drugs willy-nilly was what a doctor *did*.

One of Purdue's targets in Tennessee was a doctor named Michael Rhodes, who ran a pain clinic just north of Nashville. In 2007, he wrote 297 OxyContin prescriptions. That put him in the Core. So the local Purdue sales rep started calling on him, taking him out to dinner, showering him with gifts. Before Rhodes finally had his license revoked, he would meet in person with a Purdue rep 126 times — *that we know about,* because, as the Tennessee Attorney General's criminal complaint against Purdue states, "There are indications that Purdue called on him more often than reflected in the call notes."

And with that kind of attention, Rhodes blossomed like a rose. He wrote 1,082 OxyContin prescriptions in 2008. Now he was no longer Core. He was *Super* Core. He wrote 1,204 prescriptions in 2009 and 1,307 in 2010 — on and on, in a steady upward spiral. The complaint continues: "Purdue even called on Dr. Rhodes 31 times after the Tennessee Board of Medical Examiners placed his license on restrictive probation on May 22, 2013."

Most physicians would be annoyed by that kind of obsessive attention from a sales rep. They're busy. They have patients to see. They have families. Why would they want to spend all this time having lunch or dinner with someone who is trying to tell them how to do their job — *and who didn't even go to medical school?* Rhodes had the opposite reaction.

At one point Purdue did an analysis of how the Core and Super Core responded to sales calls. If you didn't visit them at all, Purdue found out, the number of OxyContin prescriptions they wrote would drop off a cliff. Unlike most doctors, the Super Core did not like to be ignored by salespeople. If you visited them one to four times a year, their prescriptions still declined. Even if you visited them eight times a year, twelve times a year, sixteen times a year, they still fell. The Super Core wanted love, and that frequency simply wasn't enough.

But if you visited them twice a month — month in, month out — what happened? *The number of prescriptions they wrote leaped.* Twenty-four visits a year was the tipping point. If you held the Super Core's hand and wined and dined them, they would be your best friend forever.

So the sales reps kept visiting Michael Rhodes. From the Purdue sales notes, it is clear that Rhodes's practice was in shambles. He was accused of insurance fraud. There were reports of overdose deaths among his patients. He was needy and helpless. "As I was sitting in his office, there were two patients in a knife fight outside the office's front door," one of the reps reported. "[Rhodes] said he has many patients saying that their doctors are referring patients to him because they can't write any narcotics but he can, he asked me why they cannot write it. Said his patient load that morning was 40 people…"

Forty patients in a single morning?

In May 2014, the sales rep and the Purdue district manager "called on Dr. Rhodes…and continued to encourage him to write more prescriptions, despite his objection." The district manager gave the sales rep a glowing report afterward:

Good delivery of Insight #16, developed constructive tension. Doctor gave the getting out of Pain Management objection. Good job refocusing him to appropriate patients for OxyContin because he still sees Pain Patients.

All told, from 2006 to 2015, Rhodes prescribed 319,560 tablets of OxyContin. Michael Rhodes was the Nathan Housman of Tennessee.

Purdue built its entire strategy around people like this. The highest-volume OxyContin prescriber in the country, a doctor in Connecticut, was having Purdue line up paid speaking engagements for him. If they stopped, he said, "the love may be lost." The *love*. Purdue's tie to its best customers was more than transactional; the sales rep and the physician had a relationship. In another case, a Purdue sales rep spoke to a pharmacist about one of their Super Core prescribers:

> The pharmacy manager says [the doctor] is known as the candyman…because she will immediately put every patient on the highest dose of narcotics she can.…He says when he goes to local pharmacist meetings, when her name comes up everyone in the room cringes and moans because of her practices. He says she is doing all kinds of wacky dosing and tablet strengths…

Between January 2010 and May 2018, someone from the Purdue team visited "the candyman" 300 times. In the past eight years, have you seen even your best friend 300 times?

Once the opioid epidemic was off and running, the epidemiologist Mathew Kiang calculated, the top 1 percent of doctors "accounted for 49 percent of all opioid doses." People like "the candyman" and Michael Rhodes prescribed 1,000 times more opioid doses than the average doctor. Purdue fueled an epidemic that would end up consuming the lives of hundreds of thousands of Americans based on the seduction of no more than a few thousand doctors concentrated in a handful of states.

The great lesson of COVID is that when it comes to an airborne virus, an epidemic doesn't need a lot of recruits. It just needs a single superspreader, armed with some rare physiological properties, to stand at the front of a room. The lesson of the opioid crisis is exactly the same. And do you see how vulnerable it made us? The majority of doctors — the *overwhelming* majority of doctors — treated opioid painkillers such as OxyContin with appropriate caution. The medical community as a whole behaved admirably. They were thoughtful. They looked at the evidence. They heeded the wisdom of the Hippocratic Oath: First do no harm. *But that was not enough to prevent us from the worst overdose crisis in history.* Why? Because a tiny fraction of doctors was not so thoughtful. And that tiny fraction was enough to kick-start the epidemic. Once again we are well beyond the Law of the Few here. This is the Law of the Very, Very, Very Few.

7.

The opioid crisis unfolded in three acts. The first was the decision by Purdue to avoid the states that subscribed to the Madden overstory. The second act began with McKinsey's diabolical reinterpretation of the Law of the Few. But the third act was perhaps the most catastrophic. It was when the group proportions of the crisis changed.

The final chapter in the opioid crisis began without fanfare. In the summer of 2010, Purdue made a terse announcement. The old OxyContin was to be retired. It would be replaced with what the company called *OxyContin OP*. OP looked the same. It had the same ingredients. But unlike the previous version, it couldn't be crushed into powder and snorted.* It had the consistency of a gummy bear. The days

---

* As was so often the case with Purdue, there was an ulterior motive. The original OxyContin was about to lose its patent protections, meaning that

when an addict could grind up one of Purdue's pills and get twelve hours' worth of opioid in one quick hit were over.

"I think everyone thought it was going to help," said David Powell, an economist at the RAND think tank. Some addicts might try switching to another drug, but many would simply stop — and surely the steady flow of new patients feeding the epidemic would slow down. Where else would they go? The people using OxyContin didn't think of themselves as traditional addicts. They were, in some cases, people with jobs and homes and status in their community who had been recklessly introduced to OxyContin. Sure, heroin could give them a high not dissimilar to OxyContin's, but these were not, by and large, the kinds of people who wanted to dabble with illicit drug markets.

"I think I know how to get OxyContin," Powell continued. "I would just go to a doctor and make something up. I have no idea how to get heroin. Right? That leap is huge. And so I think it was perceived that…it would not be a standard thing for people misusing OxyContin to say, 'I'm gonna go figure out how to get heroin.' That's a big leap."

It turns out that it wasn't a big leap at all.

Those who welcomed Purdue's reformulation assumed that people with drug problems had a reason for using whatever drug they did. The alcoholic who quietly got drunk on beer every afternoon at his neighborhood bar was not going to slide into injecting heroin in a parking lot. Even among the opioid class, there were distinctions: There were people who

---

cheaper generic versions would cannibalize its sales. The company needed a new version to differentiate itself from the competition.

snorted and people who injected and other people who just swallowed pills whole. The assumption was that the group proportions of the opioid crisis were relatively fixed, meaning that if you cracked down on one class of user then the overall size of the problem would shrink.

But that turned out to be terribly wrong. The group proportions weren't fixed at all. And what do we know from the Lawrence Tract and Harvard's long history and the work of scholars such as Rosabeth Kanter and Damon Centola? That epidemics are acutely sensitive to shifts in group proportions.

Take a look at the following chart. It shows the overdose-death rates for three classes of opioids. The first column is prescription opioids such as OxyContin. The second column is heroin. The third is synthetic opioids such as fentanyl.

Overdose Death Rates Involving Opioids, by Type, United States, 1999–2010
(Deaths per 100,000 people)

Year	Commonly Prescribed Opioids (Natural & Semi-Synthetic Opioids and Methadone)	Heroin	Synthetic Opioid Analgesics Excluding Methadone
1999	1.3	0.7	0.3
2000	1.4	0.7	0.3
2001	1.7	0.6	0.3
2002	2.3	0.7	0.4
2003	2.7	0.7	0.5
2004	3.1	0.6	0.6
2005	3.4	0.7	0.6

2006	4.1	0.7	0.9
2007	4.5	0.8	0.7
2008	4.6	1.0	0.8
2009	4.6	1.1	1.0
2010	5	1.0	1.0

These are the group proportions for the opioid crisis up until the point of OxyContin's reformulation. As you can see, more than five times as many people were dying from drugs like OxyContin than were dying from heroin and fentanyl. As strange as it is to say this, if you must have an opioid epidemic, these are the group proportions you want: You want the majority of users to be dependent on prescription drugs. A prescription-drug epidemic is powered by a company operating within the law, answerable to shareholders, and regulated by a government agency. The prescribers are medical professionals. Every transaction between company and physician, and every transaction between physician and patient, is recorded. Insurers — public and private — reimburse users. When things go wrong, we know they are going wrong. We have levers to push. We can find the superspreader doctors and try to stop them, track their patients and try to help them. In the end, the weight of lawsuits and criminal proceedings pushed Purdue Pharma into bankruptcy.

But what did reformulation do? It *shifted* those proportions. Against all expectations, prescription-drug users who couldn't crush up their OxyContin pills simply switched to heroin and fentanyl. Take a look at the same statistics for the years following reformulation.

Overdose Death Rates Involving Opioids, by Type,
United States, 2011–2020
(Deaths per 100,000 people)

Year	Commonly Prescribed Opioids (Natural & Semi-Synthetic Opioids and Methadone)	Heroin	Synthetic Opioid Analgesics Excluding Methadone
2011	5.1	1.4	0.8
2012	4.7	1.9	0.8
2013	4.6	2.7	1.0
2014	4.9	3.4	1.8
2015	4.9	4.1	3.1
2016	5.4	4.9	6.2
2017	5.4	4.9	9.0
2018	4.7	4.7	9.9
2019	4.4	4.4	11.4
2020	5.1	4.1	17.8

Prescription-drug deaths — the least of the three evils — go up slightly over the next decade. But the number of fatal overdoses from heroin go up 350 percent by 2017. And the number of people killed by fentanyl goes up *22-fold*, from what is basically a rounding error to a problem that dwarfs every previous opioid crisis in history.

Now the addicted had become the customers of criminals. Insurance was no longer paying for their drugs. Users had to find the money to fuel their addiction. They were buying a product made in some shady factory somewhere, laced with who-knows-what. They weren't snorting anymore. Now they were injecting, and injecting a drug is a hundred times more dangerous. Dirty needles are how you get HIV or hepatitis, abscesses and infections. Heroin use was cheaper for addicts — at first. But it ended up being more expensive, because addicts used so much more of the drug, and the quality was so uneven, and it took so much more time to find and buy. If you wanted to quit, withdrawal from heroin was an order of magnitude worse than going cold turkey from Oxy-Contin: explosive diarrhea, vomiting, overwhelming pain. And if you had small children, as many opioid addicts did, you were a much worse parent on heroin than you had been on OxyContin. Abuse and neglect of children soared. And in time heroin gave way to fentanyl, and fentanyl was even deadlier and more addictive.

Can you sue your local drug lord, or regulate them, or inspect the factory where they make their fentanyl? By the time the epidemic moved on to fentanyl, many users were simply ordering their fixes online and having them delivered through the mail. How do you stop that? The opioid problem is now so bad that the early days of the epidemic — when it was all just OxyContin — look positively bucolic by comparison. We would have been better off had we said no to Purdue's reformulation in 2010 and kept things the way they were.

But how on earth would we have done that? In the course of this book, we've talked about the hard choices epidemics present us with. The Lawrence Tract wanted to fight white flight. But that meant they had to deny a dwelling place to a black family. Superspreaders disproportionately drive the course of diseases like COVID. But acting on that fact requires that we single out a small minority of people. The opioid dilemma, however, was even harder. Someone would have had to stand up back in 2010 and say, *Look. We have two versions of a highly addictive drug. The original version is easily abused. The new and improved version is not. But we don't want the new and improved version. We want people to continue to crush their OxyContin and snort it, the way they have for the last fifteen years.* Can you imagine the reaction if health officials had taken this position? "It would be a really wild policy prescription, right?" Powell said. "It's the craziest idea. But I mean, given what we know now, I think it's the right one to have made. Yeah. You'd do it in a heartbeat."

Powell and a colleague, Rosalie Pacula, estimated what would have happened if Purdue had stuck with its original formulation of OxyContin. Here's their conclusion. The graph has two lines. The solid line is what actually happened in the United States. Look at how the overdose rate soars starting right after 2010, when reformulation occurs. The dotted "counterfactual" line is their estimate of what would have happened had things stayed exactly the same.

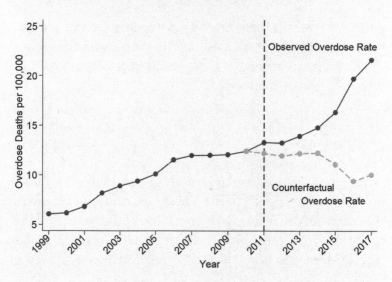

They write:

> By 2017, our estimates imply that reformulation increased overdose rates by over 11.6 overdoses per 100,000 people, more than a 100 percent increase relative to our counterfactual.

100 percent!

And notice that the line in Pacula and Powell's counterfactual analysis eventually goes *down*: That is, if the old Oxy-Contin had been left in place, the opioid crisis would have eased over time. As they write:

> The estimated decrease would be consistent with policy-driven improvements and changes in prescribing patterns beginning to reverse the course of the opioid crisis in the absence of growth in illicit opioid markets.

In other words, we were slowly winning the war on opioids. But we never really had an honest conversation about how epidemics work. So along came OxyContin OP, and everything went sideways.

8.

I promised you, at the beginning of this book, a forensic analysis of the opioid crisis. So here it is. A little company in Connecticut decided to reinvigorate one of the hoariest of the poppy's gifts to humanity. But enough states were still under the Madden overstory that the United States was spared a truly national epidemic. Instead, the army of OxyContin sales representatives descended on the non-triplicate states, and the US got small-area variation. Then McKinsey came in and refocused Purdue's marketing toward the superspreaders. The Purdue sales reps told the Core and the Super Core doctors that when it came to OxyContin, addiction was rare, and that patients could tolerate high doses for weeks on end. Of course that wasn't true. But the standards of evidence necessary for convincing Deciles 1 through 7 weren't nearly as rigorous with the Core and the Super Core physicians. The likes of Michael Rhodes weren't fact-checking the claims of their favorite sales rep with the *Journal of the American Medical Association*.

So OxyContin got an extra decade of life. Many more patients became addicted. On the street it was known as the "Rolls Royce" of opioids, because it produced such a smooth high. Purdue pushed harder. The Core and Super Core responded. OxyContin sales hit $3 billion a year. Then came reformulation, making the pill all but impossible to crush and snort, as users had been doing for a decade. So the people who had been addicted to OxyContin switched to heroin. Then they switched from heroin to fentanyl. And finally they shifted from fentanyl to some combination of all of the above, mixed in with tranquilizers and veterinary drugs and whatever else was at hand. By the early 2020s, the opioid epidemic that had begun back in 1996 with the introduction of Oxy-Contin was claiming the lives of almost 80,000 Americans a year.

Two decades into a pandemic, that line should be going down, not up.

"I have tried to figure out, was — is there anything that I

United States Opioid Overdose Deaths, 1999–2022

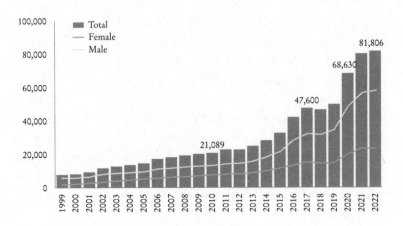

could have done differently, knowing what I knew then, not what I know now," Kathe Sackler said. Remember that quote from the very beginning of the book? She went on: "And I have to say, I can't."

That is very hard to accept. But so is the story that we tell ourselves that we bear no responsibility for the epidemics that surround us — that they come out of nowhere, that they should always surprise us.

Epidemics have rules. They have boundaries. They are subject to overstories — and *we* are the ones who create overstories. They change in size and shape when they reach a tipping point — and it is possible to know when and where those tipping points are. They are driven by a number of people, and those people can be identified. The tools necessary to control an epidemic are sitting on the table, right in front of us. We can let the unscrupulous take them. Or we can pick them up ourselves, and use them to build a better world.

Acknowledgments

The great economist Albert O. Hirschman once wrote:

> Creativity always comes as a surprise to us; therefore we
> can never count on it and we dare not believe in it until it
> has happened. In other words, we would not consciously
> engage upon tasks whose success clearly requires that cre-
> ativity be forthcoming. Hence, the only way in which we
> can bring our creative resources fully into play is by mis-
> judging the nature of the task, by presenting it to ourselves
> as more routine, simple, undemanding of genuine creativ-
> ity than it will turn out to be.

I thought about Hirschman's words a lot while writing
this book. I started with the idea of doing a quick and simple
refresh of *The Tipping Point*, on the occasion of its twenty-
fifth anniversary. I thought, *Oh, this will be easy*. But halfway in, I realized I wanted to write an entirely new book. I
brought my "creative resources fully into play" only because
I misjudged the nature of my task. So thank you, Albert O.,
for — as always — explaining how things really work.

My dear friend Jacob Weisberg was the person who suggested that I return to *The Tipping Point*. Thank you, Jacob.

I was helped along the way by a long list of generous and
insightful colleagues. Tali Emlen found a million things for
me. I have a shorthand I use in the subject line of all my
research requests: "Magic Powers." Tali has magic powers.

Nina Lawrence assisted on a hundred interviews. (When I could see Nina nodding happily on the other side of the studio glass, I knew I was on to something.) Adam Grant, Ben Naddaf-Hafrey, Eloise Lynton, Dave Wirtshafter, Mala Gaonkar, Meredith Kahn, and Charles Randolph all read early drafts and gave me incredibly helpful comments. The audiobook version of this book — which you should listen to because it's really amazing! — was the creation of Louis Mitchell, Alexandra Gareton, and Kerri Kolen.

Asya Muchnick, my editor at Little, Brown, read the manuscript so many times I began to fear for her sanity — and every time she did, the book got better. Thank you, Asya. Jael Goldfine fact-checked everything brilliantly. Then my manuscript fell into the capable hands of the wizards at Little, Brown: Ben Allen, Pat Jalbert-Levine, Melissa Mathlin, Allan Fallow, Katherine Isaacs, Deborah Jacobs, and Kay Banning.

I have the same agent today as I did when I wrote the original *Tipping Point:* Tina Bennett. You are the best, Tina. Thank you to all of my colleagues at Pushkin Industries, who endured my many absences while I was writing this book.

And most of all, thanks to my family — Kate, Edie, and Daisy. You are why I get up every morning, and why I feel the sun even on the darkest of days.

Notes

INTRODUCTION: THE PASSIVE VOICE

You can read the testimony of David Sackler, Kathe Sackler, and Purdue Pharma CEO Craig Landau before the House of Representatives' Committee on Oversight and Reform, during the hearing held on December 17, 2020, online. You can also view a full video recording on the YouTube page of the Oversight Committee Democrats.

For the written transcript, see https://www.govinfo.gov/content/pkg/CHRG-116hhrg43010/html/CHRG-116hhrg43010.htm; for the video, see https://www.youtube.com/watch?v=p3NgsWWzrH0

PART ONE: THREE PUZZLES

CHAPTER ONE: CASPER AND C-DOG

The Yankee Bandit's six-bank robbery spree is detailed in Chapter 2 ("Everybody Likes Eddie") of William Rehder and Gordon Dillow's *Where the Money Is: True Tales from the Bank Robbery Capital of the World* (W. W. Norton & Company, 2004); see especially pages 67–69. Rehder and Dillow likewise relate most other anecdotes about the Los Angeles bank-robbery surge of the 1970s, '80s, and '90s, including accounts of the West Hill Bandits (121–124); Casper and C-Dog (all of Chapter 3, but especially 113–121 and 124–157); the Eight Trey Gangster Crips (155); and the Nasty Boys (144–147). The quote from Casper about the economics of robbing banks is from page 115 of Rehder and Dillow's book.

I also learned about Casper and C-Dog in newspaper articles such as Jesse Katz's "Pair Sentenced for Bank Holdups Using Youngsters" (*Los Angeles Times,* November 2, 1993) and Robert Reinhold's "Los Angeles 'Fagins' Admit to Series of Bank Robberies" (*New York Times,* October 31, 1993). The number of takeovers executed by the Nasty Boys is noted in John Greenwald's "Nasty Boys, Nasty Time" (*Time* magazine, December 21, 1993): https://time.com/archive/6721956/nasty-boys-nasty-time/

The drop in bank robberies in Los Angeles following Casper and C-Dog's arrest was reported in Reinhold's "Los Angeles 'Fagins.'" There is also a helpful chart of bank robberies in L.A. from 1983 to 1995 in Brittny Mejia's "What happened to L.A. bank robbers who did heists in the 90s?" (*Los Angeles Times*, March 14, 2024): https://www.nytimes.com/1993/10/31/us/los-angeles-fagins-admit-to-series-of-bank-robberies.html and https://www.latimes.com/california/story/2024-03-14/los-angeles-bank-robbers-la-heists-out-of-prison

For national bank-robbery statistics from 1967 through 1980, see James Francis Haran's 1982 dissertation for Fordham University, "The Losers' Game: A Sociological Profile of 500 Armed Bank Robbers": https://research.library.fordham.edu/dissertations/AAI8219245/

"Nothing to Lose: A Study of Bank Robbery in America" is an unpublished Yale PhD dissertation by George M. Camp from 1968: https://ojp.gov/ncjrs/virtual-library/abstracts/nothing-lose-study-bank-robbery-america

The data for the number of bank branches in the United States can be found using the "BankFind Suite" tool of the Federal Deposit Insurance Corporation (FDIC). The number of branches across the country jumped from 21,839 in 1970 to 63,631 in 1999.

You can read about Willie Sutton's "visit" to the Manufacturers Trust Company branch in Queens, as well as other details about his life, in his 2004 memoir, cowritten with Edward Linn, *Where the Money Was: The Memoirs of a Bank Robber*, especially pages 1–11. The date of that robbery is specified in the *New York Daily News* story from the day of his 1952 arrest for the crime, archived on their website: https://www.nydailynews.com/2016/02/18/the-day-willie-the-actor-sutton-prolific-bank-robber-was-arrested-in-brooklyn-in-1952/

In his 1953 memoir, *I, Willie Sutton: The Personal Story of the Most Daring Bank Robber and Jail Breaker of Our Time* (written with Quentin Reynolds), Sutton claimed to have stolen $2 million from banks—around $20 million today.

There's an excellent overview of the Lyndon Johnson administration's Regional Medical Program, under which John Wennberg began his pioneering research on small-area variation, in the National Library of Medicine's "Profiles in Science" collection for the program: https://profiles.nlm.nih.gov/spotlight/rm

If you'd like to read Wennberg's original small-area variation research paper about medical care in Vermont, it was published in *Science* in 1973: "Small Area Publications in Health Care Delivery" (*Science* 182, December 14, 1973: 1102–08). The paper is available to read on the Dartmouth Digital Commons: https://digitalcommons.dartmouth.edu/cgi/viewcontent .cgi?article=3596&context=facoa. If you *don't* want to read the whole paper, the research (and Wennberg's career) are well summarized in two different articles in *Dartmouth Medicine*, one by Maggie Mahar in the winter 2007 issue and the second by Shannon Brownlee in the fall 2013 issue. Both are available online: https://dartmed.dartmouth.edu/winter07 /pdf/braveheart.pdf and https://dartmed.dartmouth.edu/fall13/pdf/from _pariah_to_pioneer.pdf

Wennberg's quotes about Stowe and Waterbury are taken from "Wrestling with Variation," a 2004 interview he gave the journal *Health Affairs,* available on Academia.edu: https://www.academia.edu /18579681/Wrestling_With_Variation_An_Interview_With_Jack _Wennberg

The data comparing Middlebury, Vermont, and Randolph, New Hampshire, was gathered for Wennberg's 1977 paper, "A Test of Consumer Contributions to Small Area Variations in Health Care Delivery" (*Journal of the Maine Medical Association* 68, no. 8: 275–79). It was later analyzed in Wennberg's 2010 book, *Tracking Medicine: A Researcher's Quest to Understand Health Care,* which is where the chart comparing the cities in Chapter 1 is from. You can view the paper here: https://core.ac.uk/download/pdf/231133032.pdf

Wennberg, along with other researchers, discovered that "patient demand is relatively unimportant in explaining variations" in health-care expenditures. Their 2019 study was published in the *American Economic Journal: Economic Policy* 11, no. 1: 192–221, available online at the National Library of Medicine: https://www.ncbi.nlm.nih.gov /pmc/articles/PMC7444804/

The rates of physician visits during the last two years of patients' lives are drawn from the Dartmouth Atlas's "Care for Chronically Ill" dataset. You can find these figures in the longitudinal spreadsheet of data from 2008 to 2019, calculated by HRR (hospital referral region). Specifically, I looked at Column J ("Physician Visits per Decedent During the Last Two Years of Life") in 2019 for the United States (HRR 999),

Los Angeles (HRR 56), and Minneapolis (HRR 251): https://data.dart mouthatlas.org/eol-chronic/#longitudinal

Vaccination rates for California middle schools are on the California Department of Public Health website. I looked at the 2012–2013 immunization data for seventh graders: https://eziz.org/assets/docs/shotsfor school/2012-13CA7thGradeData.pdf

Other years and grades are viewable here: https://www.cdph.ca.gov /Programs/CID/DCDC/Pages/Immunization/School/tk-12-reports .aspx

You can view the CDC's report on the Disneyland measles outbreak, as well as the prior California outbreak in 2014, on the agency's website: https://www.cdc.gov/mmwr/preview/mmwrhtml/mm6406a5.htm and https://www.cdc.gov/mmwr/preview/mmwrhtml/mm6316a6.htm

There's a good overview on Wikipedia of the 2015 "anti-Waldorf" law, which removed the personal-belief exemption from school vaccine requirements: https://en.wikipedia.org/wiki/California_Senate_Bill_277

CHAPTER TWO: THE TROUBLE WITH MIAMI

Unfortunately, the bulk of the transcripts from the Philip Esformes jury trial are not freely available. I bought them (they are expensive). And the file is far too massive to replicate here. But the *New York Times* published multiple excerpts, including the sentencing hearing from September 12, 2019, during which Esformes offered the tearful testimony that opens this chapter. Rabbi Lipskar and Esformes's lawyer Howard Srebnick offered their thoughts on Esformes during this hearing: https:// int.nyt.com/data/documenttools/2019-04-transcript-sentencing-show -temp/5f1878a90b593c85/full.pdf

Some other details — for instance, about Esformes's *Playboy*-model escort — were taken from another excerpt published by the *New York Times*, the transcript from the hearing held on March 29, 2019: https://int.nyt .com/data/documenttools/2019-03-29-transcript-discuss-closet-and -payment/ca95687269783a73/full.pdf

Many other passages — including details about Esformes, his business, and his trial — were taken from the trial transcript, largely from the testimony of Guillermo "Willy" Delgado, Gabriel "Gaby" Delgado, and Nelson Salazar.

You can watch videos of Philip Esformes's sons playing basketball and running drills: https://www.youtube.com/watch?v=pP-nPQTxVMo and https://www.youtube.com/watch?v=4JXFrWd1TCA

An account of Morris Esformes's unique automobile and his tense sit-down with the reporters in his Lakers uniform was reported in *Mother Jones*: https://www.motherjones.com/politics/2023/11/philip-esformes -trial-morris-medicare-fraud-prosecution-donald-trump-clemency/

For Elisa Sobo's study of Waldorf families, see "Social Cultivation of Vac-cine Refusal and Delay Among Waldorf (Steiner) School Parents," *Medical Anthropology Quarterly* 29, no. 3 (September 2015): 279–436.

The Waldorf promotional video quoted in this chapter was created by the Chicago Waldorf School: https://www.youtube.com/watch?v=wLPr HJ8Ve_I

The blog post of The Waldorf Mom, titled "Vaccines: My Journey," can be read here: https://waldorfmom.net/natural-health/vaccinations/

David Molitor elaborates on his research on small-area variation among heart-attack treatment in his paper "The Evolution of Physician Practice Styles: Evidence from Cardiologist Migration," published in the Febru-ary 2018 issue of *American Economic Journal: Economic Policy*, vol. 10, no. 1: 326–56. The figures for Buffalo's and Boulder's rates of heart cathe-terization are from the appendix in "Table C.2: HRR cath rank" on page 21: https://www.ncbi.nlm.nih.gov/pmc/articles/PMC5876705/#SD1

The proportion of US GDP spent on health care in 2022 comes from the website of the Centers for Medicare and Medicaid Services: https:// www.cms.gov/data-research/statistics-trends-and-reports/national -health-expenditure-data/historical

The respective figure for Canada is from the Canadian Institute for Health Information: https://www.cihi.ca/en/national-health-expenditure -trends-2022-snapshot

The figures for Medicare enrollment and spending are likewise from the web-site of the Centers for Medicare and Medicaid Services. For enrollment, see https://data.cms.gov/summary-statistics-on-beneficiary-enrollment /medicare-and-medicaid-reports/medicare-monthly-enrollment; for spending, see https://www.cms.gov/data-research/statistics-trends-and -reports/national-health-expenditure-data/nhe-fact-sheet

For estimates of the annual cost of Medicare fraud, see https://www
.cnbc.com/2023/03/09/how-medicare-and-medicaid-fraud-became-a
-100b-problem-for-the-us.html

The data on Medicare durable-equipment spending in Florida comes from
the Dartmouth Atlas. The 2003–2010 dataset on Medicare reim-
bursements, organized by HRR (hospital referral regions), includes
the listed Florida regions: https://data.dartmouthatlas.org/medicare
-reimbursements/#custom-state

The history of 1980s Miami — including the population and crime data, as
well as the account of Isaac Kattan Kassin — is drawn from *The Year
of Dangerous Days* by Nicholas Griffin (Simon & Schuster, 2021).
Additional details about Miami's underground economy come from
Rebecca Wakefield's 2005 article "Awash in a Sea of Money" in the
Miami New Times.

Miami mayor Maurice Ferre's quote on the influx of Cubans after the
Mariel boatlift can be found in Charles Whited's *Miami Herald* column, "Oval Office Finally Gets Message on Refugee Help" (May 8,
1980), which is also cited in Griffin, *The Year of Dangerous Days*:
https://www.newspapers.com/image/628982264/?match=1&terms
=Oval%20Office%20Finally%20Gets%20Message%20on%20Refugee
%20Help

Details about (and even the floor plan of) the Fontainebleau Park Office
Plaza can be found in a public-investment presentation: https://www
.thezylberglaitgroup.com/wp-content/uploads/2020/01/Fontainebleau
-Park-Office-Plaza-OM-1.pdf. (The floor plan used in the book, however — given that it's a photograph I took while visiting the building —
differs slightly.)

The list of Columbia/HCA executives ordered to appear before a grand jury
in 1997 was reported in the (Oklahoma City) *Journal Record*: https://
journalrecord.com/1997/08/allegations-lead-to-lessons-in-legal-lingo/.
You can read more about the fraud case against Columbia/HCA in the
Justice Department's 2003 press release detailing the company's settlement, which called it the "largest health care fraud case in U.S history":
https://www.justice.gov/archive/opa/pr/2003/June/03_civ_386.htm.
There's also a good primer on the case in PolitiFact's fact-check of a 2010
Democratic attack ad that accused Scott of health-care fraud during his
2010 gubernatorial run: https://www.politifact.com/article/2010/jun/11
/rick-scott-and-fraud-case-columbiahca/

You can read about Esformes's legal journey in "Behind Trump Clemency, a Case in Special Access" (Kenneth P. Vogel, Eric Lipton, and Jesse Drucker, *New York Times*, December 24, 2020): https://www.nytimes.com/2020/12/24/us/politics/trump-pardon-clemency-access.html

CNBC reported on the Supreme Court's rejection of Esformes's appeal to stop his retrial, as well as his eventual guilty plea preventing a second trial: https://www.cnbc.com/2023/12/15/trump-clemency-recipient-philip-esformes-loses-supreme-court-bid.html

CHAPTER THREE: POPLAR GROVE

I learned about Poplar Grove in Anna S. Mueller and Seth Abrutyn's *Life Under Pressure: The Social Roots of Youth Suicide and What to Do About Them* (Oxford University Press, 2024). Quotes from Poplar Grove residents (and indeed most of the information about the town's suicide crisis) come from that book, or from my separate conversations with Mueller and Abrutyn.

The history of zookeeping and captive-breeding programs, along with the stories of the cheetah- and Florida panther–breeding crises, is drawn from Stephen O'Brien's *Tears of the Cheetah: The Genetic Secrets of Our Animal Ancestors* (St. Martin's Griffin, 2005), especially chapter 2 ("Tears of the Cheetah") and chapter 4 ("A Run for Its Life — The Florida Panther").

For an overview of the term *monoculture*, see the *Oxford English Dictionary*'s fact sheet for the word: https://www.oed.com/dictionary/monoculture_n?tl=true#:~:text=The%20earliest%20known%20use%20of,Etymons%3A%20mono%2D%20comb

The survey in which teenagers described the social crowds (jocks, druggies, preps, and so on) at their Midwestern high school was taken from "Multiple Crowds and Multiple Life Styles: Adolescents' Perceptions of Peer-Group Stereotypes," a paper by B. Bradford Brown, Mary Jane Lohr, and Carla Trujillo that was published in the book *Adolescent Behavior and Society: A Book of Readings* (McGraw-Hill, 4th edition, 1990).

The graph of student perception of social distance among various social groups is from Brown's February 1996 paper, "Visibility, Vulnerability, Development, and Context: Ingredients for a Fuller Understanding of Peer Rejection in Adolescence" (*Journal of Early Adolescence* 16, no. 1).

The quote from the "apoplectic" private breeder is by Don Shaw, founder of the Panther Survival Project. It can be found on page 28 of the August 2, 1993, issue of the (Fort Myers) *News-Press*, available to view on Newspapers.com.

PART TWO: THE SOCIAL ENGINEERS

CHAPTER FOUR: THE MAGIC THIRD

A map of the Lawrence Tract can be viewed on Nanosh Lucas's website, which collects most of the public research and published writing on the project: https://www.lawrencetract.com/

The account of the white homeowner in Germantown, Philadelphia, in 1957 who sold her house to a black family, including the quotes from her neighbors, is from Chester Rapkin and William Grigsby's "The Demand for Housing in Racially Mixed Areas: A Study of the Nature of Neighborhood Change," a research report for the Commission on Race and Housing and the Philadelphia Redevelopment Authority (University of California Press, 1960), specifically pages 140–41.

The data on the racial demographics of the Russell Woods neighborhood in Detroit comes from a report by graduate students at the University of Pennsylvania School of Design titled "Russell Woods-Nardin Park: A Tactical Preservation Plan." It can be viewed online at https://www.design.upenn.edu/sites/default/files/uploads/Detroit_Book_June2019-compressed-min_compressed%20%281%29.pdf

I found the figures for the change in the white population of Atlanta in the 1960s and 1970s (as well as the nickname THE CITY TOO BUSY TO HATE) on page 5 of Kevin Kruse's *White Flight: Atlanta and the Making of Modern Conservatism* (Princeton University Press, 2005).

Saul Alinsky's May 5, 1959, testimony in Chicago before the US Civil Rights Commission on housing is quoted several times in this chapter. The quote by the community leader ("Let there be no mistake about it. No white Chicago community wants Negroes") was Alinsky and it's on page 771 of the publication titled "Hearings Before the United States Commission on Civil Rights: Housing" by the United States Government Printing Office.

You can find Morton Grodzins's comments on white flight and the "tip point" in his article "Metropolitan Segregation," published in *Scientific American* 197, no. 4 (October 1, 1957): https://www.scientificamerican.com/article/metropolitan-segregation/

Rosabeth Kanter's pioneering study of group proportions, "Some Effects of Proportions on Group Life: Skewed Sex Ratios and Responses to Token Women," was published in the *American Journal of Sociology* 82, no. 5 (March 1977): 965–90. Certain details about the research are taken from my interview with her. https://www.jstor.org/stable/2777808?seq=5

Most details about the life of Ursula Burns are from my conversation with her. Others are from her memoir, *Where You Are Is Not Who You Are* (Amistad/HarperCollins, 2021).

Indra Nooyi's memoir is *My Life in Full: Work, Family and Our Future* (Portfolio, 2021). The part about the reaction in the press to her becoming Pepsi's CEO is on page 192.

The count of Fortune 500 CEOs of Indian origin comes from the Indian business outlet CNBCTV-18. See https://www.cnbctv18.com/business/companies/what-makes-indian-origin-ceos-rise-to-the-top-of-fortune-500-companies-14446172.htm

Heather Haddon's *Wall Street Journal* profile of Starbucks CEO Laxman Narasimhan, in which his Indian heritage is *not* mentioned, appeared on September 27, 2023, and is entitled "With Howard Schultz Gone, New Starbucks CEO Looks to Reset": https://www.wsj.com/business/hospitality/starbucks-ceo-seeks-to-improve-servicefor-baristas-a4a0bf77

As quoted on Merriam-Webster's website, Homer Bigart wrote that "some white parents may reluctantly accept integration to the extent of 10 to 15 per cent" (*New York Times,* April 19, 1959): https://www.merriam-webster.com/wordplay/origin-of-the-phrase-tipping-point

The real-estate executive interviewed by the Civil Rights Commission in Chicago was Robert H. Pease, vice president of Draper and Kramer Inc. His quotes are on page 761 of the hearing transcript published by the United States Government Printing Office.

The quoted head of the DC school system is Carl F. Hansen, who was the region's superintendent of schools from 1958 to 1967. The relevant information is on pages 67–68 of his memoir, *Danger in Washington: The Story of My Twenty Years in the Public Schools in the Nation's Capital* (Parker Publishing Company, 1968).

Alvin Rose testified at the same 1959 US Civil Rights Commission hearing referenced above.

Vicki W. Kramer, Alison M. Konrad, and Samru Erkut's study of fifty female executives found that a critical mass of women on a corporate board resulted in a more "open and collaborative" dynamic and increased "the amount of listening." See "Critical Mass on Corporate Boards: Why Three or More Women Enhance Governance," a 2006 report by the Wellesley Centers for Women: https://www.wcwonline.org/pdf/CriticalMassExecSummary.pdf

A 2023 survey of male and female executives by *Harvard Business Review* found that women are "more willing to ask in-depth questions, and seek to get things on the table": https://hbr.org/2023/11/research-how-women-improve-decision-making-on-boards

You can read about Sukhinder Singh Cassidy's project theBoardlist here: https://www.theboardlist.com/about

There are two parts to Damon Centola's research on tipping points. He developed his name-guessing game (and figured out how long it took for a group to converge on a name) in his 2015 paper "The spontaneous emergence of conventions: An experimental study of cultural evolution" (*PNAS* 112, no. 7, February 2015). In a 2018 follow-up, Centola introduced dissidents into the game and discovered that it took roughly 25 percent adoption to tip the group to a new name ("Experimental evidence for tipping points in social convention," *Science* 360, no. 6393: 1116–19). For Centola's 2015 study, see https://www.pnas.org/doi/full/10.1073/pnas.1418838112#abstract; for his 2018 study, see https://www.researchgate.net/publication/325639714_Experimental_evidence_for_tipping_points_in_social_convention

For the analysis of how integration affects math achievement among black students, see "A critical race theory test of W.E.B. DuBois' hypothesis: Do Black students need separate schools?" by Tara J. Yosso, William A. Smith, Daniel G. Solórzano, and Man Hung, in *Race Ethnicity and Education* 25, no. 4 (October 2012): 1–19. https://www.tandfonline.com/doi/full/10.1080/13613324.2021.1984099

Their study drew on the Early Childhood Longitudinal Study data for the kindergarten class of 1998–99 (ECLS-K), which can be viewed here: https://nces.ed.gov/ecls/Kindergarten.asp

There's also a handy summary of it all in *Penn Today*: https://penntoday.upenn.edu/news/damon-centola-tipping-point-large-scale-social-change

You can read about the black neighborhood of Ramona Street (as well as housing segregation in Palo Alto) at PaloAltoHistory.org: https://www.paloaltohistory.org/discrimination-in-palo-alto.php

Many details about the Lawrence Tract's development is from an oral history done with Gerda Isenberg, one of the founders of the Palo Alto Fair Play Committee (sometimes referred to as the Fair Play Council), especially pages 66–71. Conducted in 1990 and 1991 by the California Horticulture Oral History Series, it was published in 1991 by the Regents of the University of California and is available online: https://digitalassets.lib.berkeley.edu/rohoia/ucb/text/nativeplantsnurse00isenrich.pdf

Many of the quotes from residents come from Loretta Green's story in the *Peninsula Times-Tribune*, "A lot has happened in thirty years" (March 31, 1980): https://static1.squarespace.com/static/6110410394c5a42a59b83b98/t/63040fcbe009a224275e9da1/1661210572767/loretta_green.pdf

The story of the sale that threw off the racial proportions is recounted in Richard Meister's "Laboratory for Equality: Palo Alto's Interracial Housing Experiment" (*Frontier* magazine, 1957) as well as in Dorothy Strowger's "The Lawrence Tract: Laboratory of Interracial Living," her November 1955 term paper for an undergraduate sociology class. (I don't know which college Strowger was attending.)

CHAPTER FIVE: THE MYSTERIOUS CASE OF THE HARVARD WOMEN'S RUGBY TEAM

The Princeton-versus-Harvard women's game I describe at the start of the chapter took place on October 14, 2023. The livestream with the narration that I quote can be viewed on YouTube: https://www.youtube.com/watch?v=EbIkDEn1eXE

You can see the 2023–2024 season record of the Harvard women's rugby team here: https://gocrimson.com/sports/womens-rugby/schedule/2023-24

For a list of colleges with the most sports teams in 2023, visit https://sportsbrief.com/other-sports/35102-which-college-sports-teams-united-states-america/

Figure 1 in the *UCLA Law Review* article "Race and Privilege Misunderstood: Athletics and Selective College Admissions in (and Beyond) the Supreme Court Affirmative Action Cases" (June 6, 2023) includes a bar chart of student athletes as a percentage of undergraduates at elite public and private universities. Here, you'll see Harvard dwarf Michigan.

In 2012, the *Harvard Crimson* ran an announcement by Samantha Lin and Justin C. Wong of the founding of the women's varsity rugby team, "Harvard Women's Rugby Named Varsity Sport." Another feature, this one in 2019, covered the recruiting process to build the team. See https://www.thecrimson.com/article/2012/11/8/harvard-womens-rugby-varsity-sport/ and https://www.thecrimson.com/article/2019/1/23/rugby-2018-feature/

The statistic that ALDCs make up 30 percent of Harvard's student body is repeated in various SFFA (Students for Fair Admissions) documents over the years. Justice Sonia Sotomayor mentions it in her dissent on page 44 of the Supreme Court decision in *SFFA v. President and Fellows of Harvard College.* See https://www.supremecourt.gov/opinions/22pdf/20-1199_hgdj.pdf

Both Adam Mortara and William Fitzsimmons testified in the bench trial in the 2018 version of the case that preceded the Supreme Court in a district court in Boston. Mortara gave his opening statement on Day 1, while Fitzsimmons defended Harvard's athletics program on Day 3. Although the transcripts are not public, the *Harvard Crimson* published a thorough summary of the entire trial. Day 1 is at https://www.thecrimson.com/article/2018/10/16/admissions-trial-day-one and here is Day 3: https://www.thecrimson.com/article/2018/10/18/day-three-harvard-admissions-trial/

The quote about Harvard recruiting a squash player in New Zealand appears in the *Harvard Crimson* feature on athlete admissions (Delano R. Franklin and Devin B. Srivastava, "The Athlete Advantage," May 2019). See https://www.thecrimson.com/article/2019/5/28/athlete-advantage-commencement-2019/

The history of Columbia's and Harvard's Jewish-admissions quotas and Abbott Lawrence Lowell comes from Jerome Karabel's *The Chosen: The Hidden History of Admission and Exclusion at Harvard, Yale, and Princeton* (Houghton Mifflin Company, 2005), especially chapter 3: "Harvard and the Battle over Restriction." The fraternity song is on page 87.

The lists of Asian Americans enrolled at Caltech and Harvard are taken from the SFFA complaint against Harvard (see Table B, page 54). The table of Harvard admissions broken down by race is also from the complaint (see Table C, page 67): https://studentsforfairadmissions .org/wp-content/uploads/2014/11/SFFA-v.-Harvard-Complaint.pdf

Sociological research about the extraordinary rate of postgraduate degrees among Nigerians was taken from Leslie Casimir's *Houston Chronicle* article, "Data show Nigerians the most educated in the US" (January 12, 2018): https://www.chron.com/default/article/Data-show-Nigerians -the-most-educated-in-the-U-S-1600808.php

Many quotes and details about the events of the *US v. Khoury* trial — including the testimony of "Jane," Meg Lysy, and Timothy Donovan — are taken from the transcript (which is not publicly available).

Marianne Werdel's breakdown of the costs of playing junior tennis appears in two blog posts, "Let's Break Down the Cost of Junior Tennis Part 1" and "Part 2." You can read them on Wayback Machine: https://web.archive.org/web/20190321205917/https://mariannewerdel .com/2018/03/20/1471/ and https://web.archive.org/web/20180814123310 /https://mariannewerdel.com/2018/03/21/lets-break-down-the-cost -of-junior-tennis-part-2/

You can visit Timothy Donovan's tennis-consulting website here: https:// donovantennis.com/consulting/

The biographies of Harvard's women's rugby players are available on their team-roster website. See https://gocrimson.com/sports/womens-rugby /roster

The Sacramento rugby club that lists the schools for which its alumni have played is the Land Park Harlequins: https://www.goharlequins.com /index.cfm/alumni-colleges-elite-tournaments/

The trial transcript of the Supreme Court case *Fisher v. University of Texas* is available online. Be aware that Abigail Fisher's case went to the Supreme Court twice, first in 2013 and then again in 2016. All quotes from the trial are from the 2013 proceedings: https://www .supremecourt.gov/oral_arguments/argument_transcripts/2012/11 -345.pdf

For the student-body demographics of the University of Texas at Austin around the time that Abigail Fisher brought suit against the institution, see https://news.utexas.edu/2008/09/18/fall-enrollment-at-the -university-of-texas-at-austin-reflects-continuing-trend-toward -more-diverse-student-population/

You can read Harvard's full statement on the Supreme Court's decision in the SFFA case here: https://www.harvard.edu/admissionscase/2023 /06/29/supreme-court-decision/

Chapter Six: Mr. Index and the Marriott Outbreak

The account of the Biogen conference is taken from the *Boston Globe* article by Mark Arsenault ("How the Biogen Leadership Conference in Boston Spread the Coronavirus," March 10) and the *New York Times* story by Farah Stockman and Kim Barker ("How a Premier U.S. Drug Company Became a Virus 'Super Spreader,'" April 12, 2020): https:// www.bostonglobe.com/2020/03/11/nation/how-biogen-leadership -conference-boston-spread-coronavirus/ and https://www.nytimes.com /2020/04/12/us/coronavirus-biogen-boston-superspreader.html

Additional details about the Research Triangle branch of the outbreak in North Carolina are from the *News & Observer*'s "Biogen sends RTP workers home after employees test positive for coronavirus" (Zachery Eanes, March 9, 2020) and the *Triangle Business Journal*'s "Emails show urgency as NC officials grappled with cases from Biogen super-spreader conference" (Lauren Ohnesorge, June 1, 2021): https://www .newsobserver.com/news/business/article241025271.html and https:// www.bizjournals.com/triangle/news/2021/06/01/nc-biogen-covid -cases-how-state-officials-reacted.html

The story of Boston's first COVID case is from "UMass Boston student has coronavirus; first case in Massachusetts" by Lisa Kashinsky (*Boston Herald*, February 1, 2020) and a press release on the official City of Boston website: https://www.nbcnews.com/news/us-news/coronavirus -case-boston-1st-massachusetts-8th-u-s-n1123096 and https://www

.boston.gov/news/first-case-2019-novel-coronavirus-confirmed
-boston

You can read about how the Broad Institute created its large-scale emergency diagnostic testing lab in an article on that outfit's website:
https://www.broadinstitute.org/news/how-broad-institute-converted
-clinical-processing-lab-large-scale-covid-19-testing-facility

Jacob Lemieux and his colleagues' research on the Biogen outbreak, the
C2416T strain, and the path of COVID-19 through Boston can be
found in their article "Phylogenetic analysis of SARS-CoV-2 in Boston highlights the impact of superspreading events" (*Science* 371, no.
6529, December 10, 2020): https://www.science.org/doi/10.1126/science
.abe3261

More details about my trip to Denver with Donald Stedman appear in my
story about it for *The New Yorker*, "Million-Dollar Murray" (February 5, 2006): https://www.newyorker.com/magazine/2006/02/13/million
-dollar-murray

"A well-tuned car made since 1983 emits 1 gram of carbon monoxide per
mile," Stedman told Andrew Bowser of United Press International in
1997, whereas "older cars emit about 10 to 20 grams per mile." And
"gross polluters"? They "emit around 100 grams per mile." See https://
www.upi.com/Archives/1996/03/27/Donald-H-Stedman-can-monitor
-how-much-exhaust-is/4961827902800/

The chart of vehicle emissions per decile of drivers in Los Angeles is
adapted from "Real-World Vehicle Emissions Measurement," a presentation by Donald Stedman and Gary A. Bishop at the ARPA-E
Powertrain Innovations in Connected and Autonomous Vehicles
Workshop: https://arpa-e.energy.gov/sites/default/files/06_Bishop.pdf

For the Italian research on how electrifying vehicles would impact emissions, see Matteo Böhm, Mirco Nanni, and Luca Pappalardo, "Gross
polluters and vehicle emissions reduction," *Nature Sustainability*
5 (June 9, 2022): 699–707. https://www.nature.com/articles/s41893
-022-00903-x

Denver had such terrible air quality in the 1970s and '80s that it became
infamous for the "brown cloud" hanging over the city. It cleaned up
its act by the 2000s but has been sliding since the mid-2010s (wild-
fires in the area haven't helped). In 2022, the Environmental Protection Agency officially downgraded the Denver area to a "severe"

air-quality violator. See "Air Quality Is Getting Worse in Denver" by Alayna Alvarez, Alex Fitzpatrick, and Kavya Beheraj (*Axios*, May 5, 2023): https://www.axios.com/local/denver/2023/05/05/denver-air-quality-ozone-pollution

For William Ristenpart's research on the airborne nature of COVID, see "The coronavirus pandemic and aerosols: Does COVID-19 transmit via expiratory particles?," a report he cowrote with Sima Asadi, Nicole Bouvier, and Anthony S. Wexler for *Aerosol Science and Technology* 54, no. 6 (April 2020): 635–38. https://www.ncbi.nlm.nih.gov/pmc/art icles/PMC7157964/

Some of the World Health Organization's social-media posts insisting that COVID-19 is not airborne appear at https://x.com/WHO/status /1243972193169616898?lang=en, https://www.facebook.com/WHO/posts /fact-covid-19-is-not-airborne-the-coronavirus-is-mainly-transmitted -through-drop/3019704278074935/, and https://www.instagram.com /p/B-UieTUD42A/?igshid=177u2acyfs7oy

For the study about the alpha variant's rapid leveling up in aerosol production, see the paper "Infectious Severe Acute Respiratory Syndrome Coronavirus 2 (SARS-CoV-2) in Exhaled Aerosols and Efficacy of Masks During Early Mild Infection," published in *Clinical Infectious Diseases* 75, no. 1 (July 2022): e241–e248. https://www.ncbi.nlm.nih .gov/pmc/articles/PMC8522431/#:~:text=The%20alpha%20variant %20was%20associated,swabs%2C%20and%20other%20potential %20confounders

The WHO eventually did concede that COVID-19 is airborne, as documented on its FAQ page, "Coronavirus disease (COVID-19): How is it transmitted?," which is marked as having last been updated on December 23, 2021: https://www.who.int/news-room/questions-and -answers/item/coronavirus-disease-covid-19-how-is-it-transmitted

The 1970s study of the highly infectious little girl with measles in Rochester is from E. C. Riley, G. Murphy, and R. L. Riley's "Airborne Spread of Measles in a Suburban Elementary School" in the *American Journal of Epidemiology* 107, no. 5. A helpful retrospective discussion of it also appears in Amir Teicher's superb survey of superspreader research, "Super-spreaders: a historical review" (*The Lancet*, June 2023). I drew from the latter for my history of the term: https://www.thelancet .com/journals/laninf/article/PIIS1473-3099(23)00183-4/fulltext

The study about aerosol emission and vocal volume from Ristenpart's lab that I discuss is titled "Aerosol emission and superemission during human speech increase with voice loudness" in *Scientific Reports* 9, article 2348 (February 2019). It was cowritten by Sima Asadi, Anthony S. Wexler, Christopher D. Cappa, Santiago Barreda, and Nicole M. Bouvier. See https://www.ncbi.nlm.nih.gov/pmc/articles/PMC6382806/

For David Edwards's particle-counting research about the factors that result in high aerosol emission, see "Exhaled aerosol increases with COVID-19 infection, age, and obesity" in *Biological Sciences* 118, no. 8 (February 2021). I found Figure 1 and its analysis especially relevant: https://www.pnas.org/doi/10.1073/pnas.2021830118

The British COVID-19 challenge study has yielded a number of publications and lots of media coverage. I first read about it in "Safety, tolerability and viral kinetics during SARS-CoV-2 human challenge in young adults" (*Nature Medicine* 28, March 2022: 1031–41) and "Viral emissions into the air and environment after SARS-CoV-2 human challenge: a phase 1, open label, first-in-human study" (*The Lancet Microbe* 4, no. 8, August 2023: E579–E590). See https://www.nature.com /articles/s41591-022-01780-9#data-availability and https://www.thelancet .com/journals/lanmic/article/PIIS2666-5247(23)00101-5/fulltext

For more on why it makes sense to drink water, see "Inadequate Hydration, BMI, and Obesity Among US Adults: NHANES 2009–2012" in *Annals of Family Medicine* 14, no. 4 (July 2016): 320–24. https://www .ncbi.nlm.nih.gov/pmc/articles/PMC4940461/#b24-0140320

The quote from Adam Kucharski's *The Rules of Contagion: Why Things Spread — And Why They Stop* (Basic Books, 2020) can be found on page 70. Incidentally, Kucharski takes issue in his book with my description of the role of superspreaders in the HIV epidemic and sexually transmitted diseases. I think he might be right. But Kucharski wrote his book before COVID. And I think the lesson from the pandemic is that superspreaders play an enormous role in the spread of respiratory viruses.

PART THREE: THE OVERSTORY

CHAPTER SEVEN: THE L.A. SURVIVORS' CLUB

Fred Diament's biography and quotes are from two different oral histories, one done in 1983 on behalf of the Holocaust Documentation

Archive at the University of California Los Angeles and another done by the Simon Wiesenthal Center in the same city. Both are in the United States Holocaust Memorial Museum's online archive: https://collections.ushmm.org/search/catalog/irn503585 and https://collections.ushmm.org/search/catalog/irn513291

His life is nicely summarized in the obituary by Elaine Woo in the *Los Angeles Times*, "Fred Diament, 81; Survivor of Holocaust Taught Many About It" (November 28, 2004), which also mentions him meeting Sig Halbreich in Sachsenhausen: https://www.latimes.com/archives/la-xpm-2004-nov-28-me-diament28-story.html

You can read more about Sig Halbreich in an oral history conducted in 1992 on behalf of the United States Holocaust Memorial Museum, as well as his obituary in the *Los Angeles Times*, "Siegfried Halbreich dies at 98; Holocaust survivor lectured on his experience" (Elaine Woo, September 21, 2008). For Halbreich's oral history, see https://collections.ushmm.org/search/catalog/irn505567; for his obituary, see https://www.latimes.com/local/obituaries/la-me-halbreich21-2008sep21-story.html?utm_source=pocket_reader

Quotes and information about Masha Loen are from her United States Holocaust Memorial Museum oral history, as well as from Rachel Lithgow's obituary of Loen in *Jewish Journal*, "Masha Loen, the last living founder of the Los Angeles Museum of the Holocaust, dies" (September 8, 2016). For the oral history, see https://collections.ushmm.org/search/catalog/irn504632; to read Loen's obituary, visit https://jewishjournal.com/los_angeles/189643/

This history of what I dubbed the Los Angeles survivor's club is largely from my conversation with Rachel Lithgow, executive director of the American Jewish Historical Society and past director of the Holocaust Museum LA.

The translation of Hersh Glick's "Partisan Song" ("Zog nit keyn mol") is taken from Wikipedia: https://en.wikipedia.org/wiki/Zog_nit_keyn_mol

Making a list of Holocaust museums and memorials is not straightforward. We used the following set of criteria: First, it needed to be an established brick-and-mortar museum. Second, it must be focused on the Holocaust. We did not include museums that are also Jewish museums, even if they have a Holocaust wing. It could not be part of a university or college, and it could not be part of a larger organization unrelated to the Holocaust.

Peter Novick's *The Holocaust in American Life* (Houghton Mifflin, 1991) is quoted several times throughout this chapter. Novick's remark about the "strange rhythm" of the history and memory of the Holocaust is from page 1 of that book. His quote about the *New Leader* personal essays, in which not one mentioned the Holocaust, appears on pages 105 and 106. Novick quotes the head of the AJC on pages 121–123. The observation by the German journalist can be found on page 213.

If you visit the index of the sixth edition of H. Stuart Hughes's *Contemporary Europe: A History* from 1965 (it was first printed in 1961 by Prentice-Hall Inc.), you can find these passages listed under "Jews," as well as the mentions of Arnold Schoenberg.

I reviewed volume two of Samuel E. Morison and Henry S. Commager's 1962 edition of *The Growth of the American Republic* (Oxford University Press). The quoted passage that gets Anne Frank's name wrong is on page 839.

Gerd Korman surveyed postwar history textbooks for mentions of the Holocaust in his 1970 article "Silence in America Textbooks." It's available online via Cornell University's ILR School's Digital Commons: https://core.ac.uk/download/pdf/5122084.pdf

Renée Firestone's quotes and biography are from clips of her oral history, which is available on USC's Shoah Foundation website: https://sfi.usc.edu/playlist/renee-firestones-playlist

Lidia Budgor's quotes are from her oral history with the USC's Shoah Foundation; unfortunately, it is not publicly available.

The chart showing the rising use of the uppercase *Holocaust* versus the lowercase *holocaust* is from a Steve Freiss article in *The New Republic*, "When 'Holocaust' Became 'The Holocaust': An etymological mystery" (May 17, 2015): https://newrepublic.com/article/121807/when-holocaust-became-holocaust. Freiss's chart was based on a word search of databases of publicly available print media.

The anecdote about Paul Klein and Irwin Segelstein being inspired to make *Holocaust* after walking past World War II books in a shop window is from an article by Kay Gardella in the *New York Daily News*

(April 30, 1978). It's available on Newspapers.com: https://www.news
papers.com/image/483140056/?match=1&terms=irwin%20segelstein
%2C%20paul%20klein%20holocaust

I learned about Segelstein in articles such as the *New York Times*'s "TV:
Silverman Starts by Hiring Irwin Segelstein" (June 10, 1978) and the
Boston Globe's "An Executive Who Survived" (June 19, 1978): https://
www.nytimes.com/1978/06/10/archives/tv-silverman-starts-by-hiring
-irwin-segelstein-mourning-becomes.html and https://www.newspapers
.com/image/436701993/?match=1&terms=paul%20klein%2C%20irwin
%20segelstein%20holocaust

I also read about Klein in articles such as the column by *Washington Post*
television critic Tom Shales, "Trial movie made quickly," which
appeared in the *Nevada State Journal* on May 6, 1981: https://www
.newspapers.com/image/1012369783/?match=1&terms=irwin%20
segelstein%20paul%20klein%20mercedes. The same *Boston Globe*
piece cited above, "An Executive Who Survived," recounts Klein's
"moron" comments.

You can read about the "least objectionable program" in the Seth Schiesel
obituary of Klein, "Paul L. Klein, 69, a Developer of Pay-Per-View
TV Channels" (*New York Times*, July 13, 1998). TV critic Tom Shales
also did a story on Klein, titled "A Programmer's Maxims" (*Washington Post*, December 6, 1977): https://www.nytimes.com/1998/07/13
/business/paul-l-klein-69-a-developer-of-pay-per-view-tv-channels
.html and https://www.washingtonpost.com/archive/lifestyle/1977/12
/07/a-programmers-maxims/fecbd2f7-7ca6-4d57-870f-416a3b6e8b8a/

Wikipedia devotes an entire page to Klein's "jiggle television" comments:
https://en.wikipedia.org/wiki/Jiggle_television

The anecdote about Lorne Michaels's speech to Segelstein after the latter
threatened to quit is on page 513 of Bill Carter's *The War for Late
Night: When Leno Went Early and Television Went Crazy* (Viking,
Penguin Random House, 2011).

I've quoted only a portion of Segelstein's rant. The opening part is just as good:

> "Let me just take you through what will happen when you
> leave," Segelstein began. "When you leave, the show will
> get worse. But not all of a sudden — gradually. And it will
> take the audience a while to figure that out. Maybe two,
> maybe three years. And when it gets to be, you know,

awful, and the audience has abandoned it, then we will can-
cel it. And the show will be gone, but we will still be here,
because we are the network and we are eternal."

Sadly, Irwin Segelstein is long dead. I would have loved to interview him.

The story about Klein picking Segelstein up for work is on page 196 of Sally
Bedell's biography of Fred Silverman, *Up the Tube: Prime-Time TV
and the Silverman Years* (Viking, Penguin Random House, 1981).

Meryl Streep's comments about shooting *Holocaust* are from page 182 of
Michael Schulman's biography of Streep, *Her Again* (HarperCollins,
2017).

Details about the cost and duration of creating *Holocaust* are taken from
the Frank Rich story for *Time* magazine, "Television: Reliving the
Nazi Nightmare" (April 17, 1978): https://content.time.com/time
/subscriber/article/0,33009,916079-3,00.html

Holocaust director Marvin Chomsky's quotes are from his oral history
with the Directors Guild of America: https://www.dga.org/Craft
/VisualHistory/Interviews/Marvin-Chomsky.aspx?Filter=Full
%20Interview

The scene of *Holocaust* described is the closing scene of the second episode in the series. It's available on YouTube, starting at roughly 1:22:
https://www.youtube.com/watch?v=7sBBtTXa4U8&t=1s

Elie Wiesel's comments on *Holocaust* were made in a piece for the *New York
Times* entitled "The Trivializing of the Holocaust" (April 16, 1978):
https://www.nytimes.com/1978/04/16/archives/tv-view-trivializing-the
-holocaust-semifact-and-semifiction-tv-view.html

Data about *The Big Bang Theory* and other TV-finale viewing numbers
are from the introduction to *The Rise and Fall of Mass Communication* by William L. Benoit and Andrew C. Billings, pages 1 and 2.
A copy is available online: https://api.pageplace.de/preview/DT0400
.9781433164231_A45242566/preview-9781433164231_A45242566.pdf

Larry Gross's research on how television viewership homogenizes political opinion, including the chart titled "Television viewing and attitudes
about blacks, by self-designation," is from his publication "Chart-
ing the Mainstream: Television's Contributions to Political Orienta-
tions," cowritten with George Gerbner, Michael Morgan, and Nancy

Signorielli. *Journal of Mass Communication* 32, no. 2 (June 1982): 100–27. https://web.asc.upenn.edu/gerbner/Asset.aspx?assetID=376

Information about the Bisingen concentration camp and the story of the dilemma over the signage on the cemetery is retold on Museum Bisingen's website: https://museum-bisingen.de/en/history/commemoratory-history/

The Jewish historian quoted about the Jackson-Vanik Amendment is Hadas Binyamini, writing in her *Jewish Currents* story "Henry 'Scoop' Jackson and the Jewish Cold Warriors" (May 24, 2022): https://jewishcurrents.org/henry-scoop-jackson-and-the-jewish-cold-warriors

Quotes and information about Zev Weiss are from his "In Memoriam" tribute video and obituary on the Holocaust Educational Foundation of Northwestern website: https://hef.northwestern.edu/about/news/in-memoriam-theodore-z.-weiss1.html and https://www.youtube.com/watch?v=jDbRTL9QRzA

Viewing numbers for *Holocaust* are from "NBC-TV Says 'Holocaust' Drew 120 Million" (*New York Times,* April 21, 1978): https://www.nytimes.com/1978/04/21/archives/nbctv-says-holocaust-drew-120-million.html

Details about the reception and impact of *Holocaust* in West Germany are from "'Holocaust' on West German Television: The (In)Ability to Mourn?" by Werner Sollors, published in *The Massachusetts Review* 20, no. 2 (Summer, 1979): 377–86. https://www.jstor.org/stable/25088965

NBC's Herbert Schlosser recounted suggesting a new name for *Holocaust* in his oral history with the Television Academy Foundation (part 7): https://interviews.televisionacademy.com/interviews/herbert-s-schlosser?clip=96441#interview-clips

CHAPTER EIGHT: DOING TIME ON MAPLE DRIVE

You can read Timur Kuran's "The Inevitability of Future Revolutionary Surprises," originally published in the *American Journal of Sociology* 100, no. 6 (May 1995: 1528–51), in full on JSTOR: https://www.jstor.org/stable/2782680

Vaclav Havel's 1978 essay "The Power of the Powerless" can be read in full online thanks to the International Center on Nonviolent Conflict. It was translated into English by John Keane and published as a book titled *The Power of the Powerless: Citizens Against the State in Central Eastern Europe* (Routledge, 1985): https://www.nonviolent-conflict.org/wp-content/uploads/1979/01/the-power-of-the-powerless.pdf

In his 1987 essay "Meeting Gorbachev," Havel scolded his countrymen for welcoming Soviet president Mikhail Gorbachev. See page 266 of *Without Force or Lies: Voices from the Revolution of Central Europe in 1989–90* by William M. Brinton and Alan Rinzler (Mercury House, 1990).

The original 1969 edition of David Reuben's *Everything You Always Wanted to Know About Sex* (*But Were Afraid to Ask)* was published by McKay Company Inc. Quotes are from Chapter 8, "Male Homosexuality" (129–51). A version is available to view on Internet Archive: https://archive.org/details/in.ernet.dli.2015.38746/page/n141/mode/1up

Reuben's accolades were recounted in two articles, one for the *Chicago Tribune* ("Everything You Always Wanted to Know About Dr. David Reuben*," February 23, 1999) and the other for the *Los Angeles Times* ("Singular Sensations: Richard Bach, Marabel Morgan and David R. Reuben each wrote one bestseller. Then, despite subsequent efforts, each slipped from the limelight," S. J. Diamond, February 1, 1993): https://www.chicagotribune.com/1999/02/23/everything-you-always-wanted-to-know-about-dr-david-reuben/ and https://www.latimes.com/archives/la-xpm-1993-02-01-vw-992-story.html?utm_source=pocket_shared

The February 2004 speech in which President George Bush announced his support for a constitutional amendment that would ban same-sex marriage can be read on CNN: https://www.cnn.com/2004/ALLPOLITICS/02/24/elec04.prez.bush.transcript/

The Wikipedia page is a good overview of the amendment, which never passed: https://en.wikipedia.org/wiki/Federal_Marriage_Amendment

Dianne Feinstein's "too much, too fast, too soon" can be found in Dean E. Murphy's story for the *New York Times*, "Some Democrats Blame One of Their Own" (November 5, 2004): https://www.nytimes.com/2004/11/05/politics/campaign/some-democrats-blame-one-of-their-own.html

Bonnie Dow's analysis of the representation of women and feminism on TV programs such as *The Mary Tyler Moore Show, Phyllis, Maude, Rhoda*, and others comes from her book *Prime-Time Feminism: Television, Media Culture, and the Women's Movement Since 1970* (University of Pennsylvania Press, 1996). Her rules for gay characters on television can be found in her 2010 paper, *"Ellen*, Television, and the Politics of Gay and Lesbian Visibility" (*Critical Studies in Media Communication* 18, no. 2: 123–40): http://ereserve.library.utah.edu/Annual/COMM/7460/Shugart/ellen.pdf

Vito Russo's death tally for queer characters is from his lavishly illustrated book *The Celluloid Closet* (Harper & Row, 1981); you'll find it in the "Necrology" section on pages 347–49. A free version is available online: https://backend.ecstaticstatic.com/wp-content/uploads/2021/05/The-Celluloid-Closet.pdf

Jimmy Burrows spoke about his plan to keep America guessing whether Will and Grace will ever get together in an interview with the Television Academy Foundation. The quote starts at approximately 27:30: https://interviews.televisionacademy.com/interviews/james-burrows?clip=82224#interview-clips

Rick Santorum credited *Will & Grace* for moving the needle on gay marriage in a speech at the Midwest Republican Leadership Conference in 2013: https://www.youtube.com/watch?v=yGT4ZMv_OMc

Sasha Issenberg's book on the movement for same-sex marriage is *The Engagement: America's Quarter-Century Struggle Over Same-Sex Marriage* (Pantheon, 2021).

PART FOUR: CONCLUSION

CHAPTER NINE: OVERSTORIES, SUPERSPREADERS, AND GROUP PROPORTIONS

Martin Booth's history of the opium poppy is called *Opium: A History* (St. Martin's Griffin, 1999). His quote about the flower's contents can be found on page 3. His book is also the best source for the history of the various compounds extracted from the poppy over the years.

The Drug Enforcement Administration Museum has a good overview of opium poppies' history and chemistry: https://museum.dea.gov/exhibits

/online-exhibits/cannabis-coca-and-poppy-natures-addictive-plants
/opium-poppy

You can read Jessica Y. Ho's "The Contemporary American Drug Overdose Epidemic in International Perspective" in *Population and Development Review* 45, no. 1 (March 2019): 1–268. The chart of drug-overdose deaths by country is on page 13.

For Lyna Z. Schieber's research on state-by-state opioid-prescription practices, see "Trends and Patterns of Geographic Variation in Opioid Prescribing Practices by State, United States, 2006–2017" in *JAMA Network* 2, no. 3 (March 2019): e190665. The figures of doses prescribed per capita per state is "eTable 1" in the "Supplemental Content" document. See https://pubmed.ncbi.nlm.nih.gov/30874783/

No one has ever written a comprehensive biography of Paul E. Madden, to my knowledge. My account of him is pieced together from newspaper articles and my conversation with the historian David Courtwright. Madden's quotes about the perils of marijuana and other narcotics are from a pamphlet he published in 1940 titled "Marihuana: Our Newest Narcotic Menace"; it can be viewed on a website dubbed "the Reefer Madness Museum," which documents antimarijuana propaganda. The site dedicates an entire page to Madden, including an audio clip from his 1939 appearance on the radio program "Calling All Cars." See http://www.reefermadnessmuseum.org/otr/Madden.htm

You can see Madden displaying bags of confiscated cocaine (and read about him busting Japanese narcotics smugglers) in Santa Rosa's *Press Democrat,* "U.S. Agents Seize $300,000 in Smuggled Narcotics as Jap Vessel Raided at S.F." (July 21, 1940). See https://www.newspapers .com/image/276629364/?match=1&terms=paul%20e.%20madden %2C%20cocaine%2C%20associated%20press

The story about Madden babysitting the poppy-seed crop is in the *Fresno Bee* ("Narcotic Men Nip Start of Opium Growing in State," August 27, 1941): https://www.newspapers.com/image/701482802/?match=1&terms =paul%20e.%20madden%2C%20japan

For the illegal sales of morphine cough syrup for horses, see the *Los Angeles Times,* "Narcotics Head Steps In" (June 17, 1941): https://www .newspapers.com/image/380700019/?match=1&terms=paul%20 madden%20horse%20pharmacies

The triplicate-prescription law — that is, California's Assembly Bill No. 2606, which amended the state's Health and Safety Code to include the key language in section 11166.06 — is contained in the official record of the 1939 legislative session, *Assembly Bills, Original and Amended, Volume 15.*

Archival newspaper articles abound on Nathan Housman's trial (as well as the case of Frank Egan's murder of Jessie Scott Hughes, in which Housman was implicated). I've quoted from two of them, both of which ran in the *San Francisco Examiner*, "Medical Examiners Also Take Hand in Probe of Doctor" (September 1, 1939) and "Defense Censured at Housman's Trial" (January 16, 1940). See https://www.newspapers.com /image/959916290/?match=1&terms=nathan%20housman%2C%20 paul%20madden and https://www.newspapers.com/image/457420381 /?match=1&terms=I%20asked%20Doctor%20Housman%20several %20times%20for%20the%20records%2C%20and%20each%20time %20Doctor%20Housman%20said%20he%20had%20none

Madden's letter about triplicate prescription was published in the April 1939 issue of the California Medical Soceity's journal (vol. 50, no. 4: 313). It can be viewed online at the National Library of Medicine. The page is titled: "Subject: Proposed legislation on narcotic enforcement." See https://www.ncbi.nlm.nih.gov/pmc/issues/137313/

For a history of the first states to follow suit behind California, I relied on a March 2018 report called "History of Prescription Drug Monitoring Programs" by Brandeis University's Prescription Drug Monitoring Program Center. See https://www.ojp.gov/ncjrs/virtual-library/abstracts /history-prescription-drug-monitoring-programs

My history of Russell Portenoy is taken from his fascinating oral history, which can be downloaded from the International Association for the Study of Pain's "History of Pain Transcripts" website. I quote from pages 7, 19, and 29. See https://www.iasp-pain.org/50th-anniversary /history-of-pain-transcripts/

Portenoy's quote about pain treatment being "a little science, a lot of intuition, and a lot of art" is on page 22 of Barry Meier's *Pain Killer: An Empire of Deceit and the Origin of America's Opioid Epidemic* (Random House, 2018). His "gift from nature" quote appears in Patrick Radden Keefe's *New Yorker* article, "The Family That Built an Empire of Pain" (October 23, 2017). Portenoy weighed in on the supposedly "few side effects" of opioids in a story by Elisabeth Rosenthal for the *New York Times,* "Patients in Pain Find Relief, Not Addiction, in Narcotics" (March 28, 1993). See https://www.newyorker.com/magazine

/2017/10/30/the-family-that-built-an-empire-of-pain and https://www
.nytimes.com/1993/03/28/us/patients-in-pain-find-relief-not-addiction
-in-narcotics.html

NIDA published a monograph about the 1991 Maryland summit meeting on triplicate-prescription programs, titled "Impact of Prescription Drug Diversion Control Systems on Medical Practice and Patient Care." It includes contributions from both Portenoy and Gerald Deas: https://archives.nida.nih.gov/sites/default/files/monograph131.pdf

For "the number of triplicate states was down to five," see "Origins of the Opioid Crisis and Its Enduring Impacts" by Abby Alpert, William N. Evans, Ethan M. J. Lieber, and David Powell in *The Quarterly Journal of Economics* 137, no. 2 (May 2022): 1139–79. See https://www.ncbi .nlm.nih.gov/pmc/articles/PMC9272388/#FN14

Much of my history of Purdue Pharma is from Barry Meier's *Pain Killer*, including the account of the new formula and Groups Plus. The "ticket to the moon" quote is on page 41.

The explanation of the "governor's switch" is drawn from "The Hazards of Unwinding the Opioid Epidemic: Implications for Child Abuse and Neglect" by Mary F. Evans, Matthew C. Harris, and Lawrence M. Kessler in *American Economic Policy Journal: Economic Policy* 14, no. 4 (November 2022): 192–231. https://www.aeaweb.org/articles?id =10.1257/pol.20200301#:~:text=Our%20results%20suggest%20counties %20with,to%20must%2Daccess%20PDMP%20implementation

The 1995 focus-group study commissioned by Purdue Pharma and conducted by Groups Plus was made public in a 2001 civil action case, *McCaulley v. Purdue Pharma*. It can be viewed on Scribd: https://www.scribd.com /document/440306799/Purdue-focus-group-documents?secret _password=0jVgiWk1VXSR2dnIVqb4#

The geographic distribution of top opioid prescribers is from "Opioid Prescriptions by Orthopaedic Surgeons in a Medicare Population: Recent Trends, Potential Complications, and Characteristics of High Prescribers" in the *Journal of the American Academy of Orthopaedic Surgeons* (Venkat Boddapati et al., August 2020): https://www.researchgate.net /publication/343651712_Opioid_Prescriptions_by_Orthopaedic _Surgeons_in_a_Medicare_Population_Recent_Trends_Potential _Complications_and_Characteristics_of_High_Prescribers

Yongbo Sim's breakdown of crime rates in triplicate and non-triplicate states appears in "The effect of opioids on crime: Evidence from the introduction of OxyContin," *International Review of Law and Economics* 7 (June 2023): https://www.sciencedirect.com/science/article/abs/pii/S0144818823000145

Engy Ziedan and Robert Kaestner addressed the impact of opioids on infant health in their working paper for the National Bureau of Economic Research, "Effect of Prescription Opioids and Prescription Opioid Control Policies on Infant Health": https://www.nber.org/papers/w26749

For neglect of children, see "Longitudinal Changes in the County-Level Relationship Between Opioid Prescriptions and Child Maltreatment Reports, United States, 2009–2018" by Hyunil Kim, Eun-Jee Song, and Liliane Windsor in the *American Journal of Orthopsychiatry* 93, no. 5 (May 2023): 375–88. https://www.ncbi.nlm.nih.gov/pmc/articles/PMC10527856/

Martin Elling's 2002 article in the *McKinsey Quarterly* was titled "Making more of pharma's sales force: pharmaceutical companies have lost their focus on doctors. The key to higher sales is regaining it." You can read a preview of it on the periodical database Gale Academic OneFile: https://go.gale.com/ps/i.do?id=GALE%7CA90192565&sid=googleScholar&v=2.1&it=r&linkaccess=abs&issn=00475394&p=AONE&sw=w&userGroupName=anon%7E988676df&aty=open-web-entry

Purdue Pharma's sales revenue from 2008 to 2014 was recounted in a hearing before the House of Representatives' Committee on Oversight and Reform on December 17, 2020: https://www.govinfo.gov/content/pkg/CHRG-116hhrg43010/html/CHRG-116hhrg43010.htm

For information on the timeline of McKinsey's work for Purdue Pharma, including the total amount McKinsey charged for its consulting, see the April 27, 2022, hearing before the House of Representatives' Committee on Oversight and Reform, titled "McKinsey & Company's Conduct and Conflicts at the Heart of the Opioid Epidemic": https://www.congress.gov/117/meeting/house/114669/documents/HHRG-117-GO00-Transcript-20220427.pdf

Emails from McKinsey employee Jeanette Park, who accompanied an OxyContin sales rep on a call to physicians and pharmacies in Worcester, Massachusetts, can be viewed in the Opioid Industry Documents Archive maintained by the University of California San Francisco and

Johns Hopkins University: https://www.industrydocuments.ucsf.edu
/opioids/docs/#id=htvn0255

Richard Sackler's email calling McKinsey's discoveries "astonishing" appears
on page 12 of the transcript of a lawsuit brought by New York City
and twenty-one New York counties against McKinsey: https://www
.nyc.gov/assets/law/downloads/pdf/McKinsey%20Complaint.pdf

The chart of average OxyContin prescriptions per doctor divided into
deciles is from Purdue's 2013 annual marketing plan, which was
included in Purdue's settlement agreement announced on October 21,
2020. It can be downloaded from the Justice Department's press
release; the chart is on page 9 of Addendum A: https://www.justice
.gov/opa/pr/justice-department-announces-global-resolution-criminal
-and-civil-investigations-opioid

The quote about "OxyContin primary calls...to low-decile (0-4) prescribers" is on page 45 of a September 2013 presentation that McKinsey made
for Purdue. It can be viewed in the Opioid Industry Documents Archive:
https://www.industrydocuments.ucsf.edu/opioids/docs/#id=tfhf0257

The quote about the point system that Purdue used to award bonuses to
representatives who made the most sales calls with Core and Super Core
prescribers can be found in the 2018 complaint by the Common-
wealth of Virginia against Purdue Pharma: https://www.oag.state.va.us
/consumer-protection/files/Lawsuits/Purdue-Complaint-Unredacted
-2018-08-13.pdf

You can find the bar chart of Purdue sales calls per year in Tennessee on
page 17 of Tennessee's 2018 lawsuit against Purdue. The discussion
of Super Core prescriber Michael Rhodes is from the same suit, starting on page 139: https://www.tn.gov/content/dam/tn/attorneygeneral
/documents/foi/purdue/purduecomplaint-5-15-2018.pdf

The account of the Connecticut doctor who prescribed more OxyContin
than any other US practitioner is on page 36 of Addendum A in Purdue's settlement agreement with the Department of Justice. The
account of "the candyman" is on page 28: https://www.justice.gov
/opa/pr/justice-department-announces-global-resolution-criminal-and
-civil-investigations-opioid

For Mathew Kiang's calculation that 1 percent of doctors wrote 49 percent of prescriptions, see "Opioid prescribing patterns among medical

providers in the United States, 2003–17: retrospective, observational study" in *BMJ* 2020: 368 (January 29, 2020): https://www.bmj.com /content/368/bmj.l6968

These details are also discussed in a piece for the *New York Times* by Walt Bogdanovich and Michael Forsythe, entitled "McKinsey Proposed Paying Pharmacy Companies Rebates for OxyContin Overdoses" (November 27, 2020).

The chart of US death rates involving opioids by type from 1999 to 2020 is adapted from data provided by the National Center for Health Statistics. It can be found in NCHS Data Brief No. 428, "Drug Overdose Deaths in the United States, 1999–2020," by Holly Hedegaard, Arialdi M. Miniño, Merianne Rose Spencer, and Margaret Warner (December 2021). It corresponds to Figure 4, and the data table can be found in the "NOTES" section directly beneath the chart: https://www .cdc.gov/nchs/data/databriefs/db428.pdf

For David Powell's research about the impact of OxyContin's reformulation — as well as the counterfactual overdose rate had the drug not been reformulated — see Figure 6 of his paper with Rosalie Pacula, "The Evolving Consequences of OxyContin Reformulation on Drug Overdoses" in *American Journal of Health Economics* 7, no. 1 (Winter 2021): 41–67. https://www.ncbi.nlm.nih.gov/pmc/articles/PMC8460090/

A chart of US overdose deaths involving opioids (by year from 1999 to 2022) appears on the National Institute on Drug Abuse's web page titled "Drug Overdose Death Rates": https://nida.nih.gov/research -topics/trends-statistics/overdose-death-rates

Index

Note: *Italic* page numbers refer to illustrations.

Abrutyn, Seth
  on Annesdale, 77
  Life Under Pressure, 77–78, 84n,
    87–88, 90, 95, 96, 101–2, 103
  on Poplar Grove, 75–78, 83–84, 86,
    87–88, 95–96, 97, 180, 315n
acetaminophen, 278
aerosols
  COVID pandemic and, 185, 187,
    188–90, 189n, 324n
  study of, 185–87, 192n, 193–94
  tuberculosis and, 192n
affirmative action, 165, 170–71
African Americans
  college admissions policies and,
    150, 167–68
  moving out of the South, 108–9
  students' test scores, 128, 128n,
    129–30
  white flight and, 108–10, 119, 120
  whites' rejection of integration, 132
age, and aerosol production, 196
AIDS, 248, 253
Alinsky, Saul, 119–20, 136n, 316n
Allen, Woody, 238
Alpert, Abby, 283–84
American International College, 138
American Jewish Committee
  (AJC), 226
American Jewish Congress, 226
Annesdale, Poplar Grove compared
  to, 77, 89, 101
Anti-Defamation League, 226

antisemitism, 150, 212, 214, 226
Apocalypse Now (film), 210
apologies
  for corporate irresponsibility, 3–5
  for epidemics, 3–6, 8–9
  passive voice and, 6, 9
APS (aerodynamic particle sizer)
  machine, 192–93
Atlanta, white flight in, 109, 133
Auschwitz concentration camp,
  203–4, 212, 214, 218, 230
Australia, 265
Austria, 265

Bach, Richard, 331n
Baltimore, Ashburton neighborhood
  of, 109
bank branches, number of, 23, 310n
bank robberies
  crime wave of 1970s, 1980s, and
    1990s, 15–16, 20–21, 23, 309n
  exalted position of bank robber,
    14–15
  FBI investigations of, 13–16, 20,
    21, 23
  G-ride and, 17, 18, 19
  in Los Angeles, 13–21, 22, 23, 27,
    309n, 310n
  in New York City, 23–27
  nicknames for robbers, 13–16
  notepassers and, 16, 22
  puzzle of, 23, 26, 27, 36
beads-on-a-string instability, 195n

About the Author

Malcolm Gladwell is the author of seven *New York Times* bestsellers: *The Tipping Point, Blink, Outliers, What the Dog Saw, David and Goliath, Talking to Strangers,* and *The Bomber Mafia.* He is also the cofounder of Pushkin Industries, an audio-content company that produces *Revisionist History,* among other podcasts and audiobooks. He was born in England and raised in Canada, and lives outside New York with his family and a cat named Biggie Smalls.